How to Start and Build a Law Practice

Third Edition

Jay G. Foonberg

American Bar Association
Law Student Division
Section of Law Practice Management

The Section of Law Practice Management, American Bar Association, offers an educational program for lawyers in practice. Books and other materials are published in furtherance of that program. Authors and editors of publications have full opportunity to express legal interpretations and opinions. The material contained herein represents the opinions of the authors and editors and should not be construed to be the action of either the American Bar Association or the Section of Law Practice Management unless adopted pursuant to the By-laws of the Association. The opinions expressed do not reflect in any way a position of the Section or the American Bar Association.

The products and services mentioned in this publication are under trademark or service-mark protection. Product and service names and terms are used throughout only in an editorial fashion, to the benefit of the product manufacturer or service provider, with no intention of infringement. Use of a product or service name or term in this publication should not be regarded as affecting the validity of any trademark or service mark.

Ethical Considerations 2-16 and 2-26 excerpted from the Model Code of Professional Responsibility, copyrighted by the American Bar Association. All rights reserved. Reprinted with permission.

Library of Congress Catalog Card Number 91-72112
ISBN 0-89707-685-0 (paperbound)
ISBN 0-89707-684-2 (hardbound)

94 95   10 9 8 7 6 5

Discounts are available for books ordered in bulk. Special consideration is given to state bars, CLE programs, and other bar-related organizations. Inquire at Publications Planning and Marketing, American Bar Association, 750 N. Lake Shore Drive, Chicago, Illinois 60611.

Contents

Part III: Getting Equipped

Part IV: Getting Clients

Part V: Setting Fees

Preface to the First and Second Editions

This book, by its nature, is money-oriented. Its purpose is to assist the new lawyer in starting and building a law practice on a firm economic basis. Do not quote the book or sections out of context.

To succeed in the practice of law over a period of years requires a deep and sincere desire to help people. If you are looking upon your license to practice law simply as a ticket to making money, or as a one-way ticket out of the ghetto or barrio, then you are making a serious mistake. I would advise you not to proceed as a lawyer. You will do better as an insurance salesman or a teacher or an engineer. If you are entering the legal profession solely to make money, you are making a serious mistake. You might get lucky and make money in a given year, but over a period of years, you won't make it.

I repeat: to succeed in the long run, the practice of law requires a deep and sincere dedication to helping people. With proper management, the economic rewards will follow the rendering of high-quality legal services.

You are about to enter into a 30- or 40-year career as a lawyer. Don't do it unless you really and sincerely want to help people.

Preface to the Third Edition

In this third edition of *How to Start and Build a Law Practice*, I have tried to carry forward the fundamental purpose of this book, which is to teach a lawyer in a single book the basics of how to start and build a law practice. The book provides real-life, practical answers to the most commonly asked questions about starting and building a practice. I hope that when you open your practice you will use my suggestions, and that as your practice grows you will modify these suggestions by providing your own solutions based on the specific needs of your practice and your own personal preferences. You do not have to use my suggestions; you can use your own, but you do have to have solutions to your problems, whether they are these solutions or your solutions. These solutions do work, and this book is continually recommended by lawyers who have achieved success in their practices using this book.

Since the second edition was published in 1984, there have been three major factors that radically affect your starting a law practice. These are:

1. Technology;
2. Disciplinary activities;
3. The number of lawyers.

Much space is devoted in this third edition to personal computers, word processors, and office technology. A lawyer must be familiar with and able to use modern technology, not only to be cost- and time-efficient but, more importantly, to be able to represent a client properly when the lawyer representing the adverse party uses the latest technology. The new chapter will, at a minimum, alert you to what other lawyers in established firms are doing for their clients.

The sum of money required for technology and equipment can be substantial, so chapters have been added on doing a cash-flow budget, earning a living until you open your practice, financing your practice with bank credit cards, and practicing from your home.

Disciplinary efforts have increased against lawyers at every level. There is a 10 percent likelihood that someone will file a disciplinary complaint against you. The adoption by many states of the ABA's Model Rules of Professional Conduct has given disciplinary staffs specific guidelines for deciding when to investigate and prosecute a lawyer. The disciplinary staffs sometimes have a consumer-protection, anti-lawyer, prosecutorial mentality. They often are under pressure from their legislatures to investigate and discipline lawyers.

Four new chapters dealing with professional conduct and the Model Rules have been added. I hope these chapters, which include "Ten Rules for Avoiding Disciplinary Complaints" and "Fifty Ways to Win or Avoid the Ethics War," will cause you to examine your professional responsibility, both on a macro (profession-wide) and on a micro (personal) level. It was my intention to include the ABA Model Rules of Professional Conduct as an appendix to this book, but it proved impossible to do so. In fact, reliance on the ABA Model Rules can lead to problems for you, as many jurisdictions have rejected or modified sections of the Model Rules. I recommend that you contact your local licensing jurisdiction for a copy of the rules that will apply where you practice. The expansion of the section dealing with professional responsibility recognizes that an increasing number of law schools use this book as a supplementary source in the course on professional responsibility.

Lastly, the explosion in the number of lawyers has greatly affected how a practice is started and built. Lawyers and law firms aggressively market to get and keep clients. Many firms now hire in-house marketing people to try to take clients from other firms. Large sums of money are spent on public relations firms and media advertising in marketing efforts. I personally have helped firms by teaching their lawyers and even their nonlawyers the fundamentals of marketing. The lawyer who wants to start a law practice in today's competitive market must know marketing, a subject never taught in law school. I have included more tips for a new lawyer in this third edition.

In summary, this third edition includes the most current information you need to start and build a law practice.

Jay G. Foonberg
Beverly Hills, California
April 1991

Acknowledgments

The wheel was invented long ago. Since that time, many civilizations have independently reinvented the wheel, wasting many centuries. Some civilizations never discovered the wheel. Much time and effort could have been saved, had one civilization been able to copy others.

Many of the lessons in this book were taught to me by others. In some instances, I foolishly reinvented the wheel.

The California Association of Attorney-CPAs, assisted by the American Association of Attorney-CPAs, has sponsored the program "How to Start and Build a Law Practice" for many years. The questions of the new admittees highlighted the lack of knowledge. Several individual members of the associations, including Arnold Magasinn, David Slavitt, Irving Kellog, Richard Berger, Burton Rosky, and Jerrold Kaplan, have given unselfishly of themselves over the years to put on the program. It will never be possible to adequately acknowledge their participation.

Robert P. Wilkins of Columbia, South Carolina, suggested modifications to make the book understandable in view of regional differences, for which I am grateful. Monica Bay of California, Victoria Herring of Des Moines, Iowa, and Kathy Braeman of Cleveland, Ohio (now of Washington, D.C.), were very helpful in reviewing the first edition of this book to modify phraseology that could be perceived as sexist.

In the chapter on technology and computers, I've drawn heavily on the work of six people, whom I've listed alphabetically.

They are James W. Martin of Clearwater, Florida; J. Harris Morgan, Esq., of Greenville (Dallas), Texas; Robert P. Moses of Columbia, South Carolina; Rick Rodgers, Professor of Law and Computer

Consultant, Campbell University School of Law, Buies Creek, North Carolina; Richard Robbins, Esq., formerly Director, American Bar Association, Legal Advisory and Technology Advisory Council, Chicago, Illinois; Kline Strong of Salt Lake City, Utah; and Robert P. Wilkins, Esq., Director of RPW Learning Center, Lexington, South Carolina (which offers courses in Law Office Technology and Management).

Donna Killoughey of Arizona and Debra Bowen of California were helpful with their suggestions on practicing from a home. Donna Killoughey also assisted greatly in reviewing the new materials for the third edition.

It is impossible to give adequate credit and acknowledgment to Del Roberts of South Carolina. Del was the copy editor for the first edition, the second edition, and the third edition of this book. Del is the person who makes the material easier to understand and who eliminates the confusion of words or ideas not clearly expressed. We have worked together for more than a decade on this book and other books and articles. My respect and admiration for Del as a person and as a professional is complete. Very few people understand the contribution of the copy editor in producing a book. The copy editor is often the difference between a book being good and being excellent. Del has been a most important part of the continued success of this book over these many years.

Special acknowledgments are reserved for two people. One is J. Harris Morgan of Greenville, Texas, who first inspired me to teach these materials and who himself has given consistently of himself to the profession. The second person is my wife, Lois, who lovingly and patiently has suffered my being away from home over the years presenting this program in every state in the Union and several foreign countries, and who has commented critically on this publication.

Part I
Getting Started

Why Has This Book Been Written?

Why has this book been written? It has been written because there is a need for it. I have spoken to and worked with tens of thousands of new admittees throughout the United States over the last two decades. I know that the new lawyer needs and wants this information, and the information in this book cannot be found in any other single book. To get the information in this book, one would have to comb hundreds of periodicals and publications to get the raw information that would then have to be distilled; and unfortunately, the new lawyer doesn't know which raw information is needed, nor how to distill it.

Law schools are turning out about twice as many lawyers as the nation needs. We will have more than one million lawyers in the United States in 1995. Simultaneously, nonlawyers working under the general supervision of lawyers are doing work formerly done by lawyers. "Do-it-yourself" divorce, bankruptcy, and immigration enterprises are flourishing. No-fault liability insurance will have a significant effect on law practices. One-third of all small businesses fail within one year. Law firms of all sizes from two-lawyer partnerships to megafirms merge, break up, and go out of business.

The lawyer who enters the economic arena of private practice in an entrepreneurial capacity must know and master the principles of this book or else be independently wealthy to survive initially, and to flourish ultimately. The lawyer who heeds the lessons of the book will probably succeed. The lawyer who ignores them will float along from year to year, rolling up and down from an occasional "good year" to the more common struggling years, until he learns the lessons of this book or fails completely.

With due apologies to the world of academics, I have used a "nuts-and-bolts" approach in this book. Until recently, the law schools have not taught the materials in this book. Whether the reason is lack of qualified instructors or some other reason is immaterial. The end result is that at the present time, most law schools don't teach these materials, and this book is necessary.

For example, I have entitled one part of the book "Setting Fees" and have drawn upon empiric observations of my practice. In an academic setting, I might have done two or three years of research with surveys and two or three grants to end up with a chapter entitled "Socio-Economic Factors Considered by Providers of Professional Legal Services in Relation to the Socio-Economic Resources of Recipients of Professional Legal Services as Correlated to the Intricacies and Time Demand Factors Inherent in the Services Provided." I trust that the reader will appreciate this alternative "nuts-and-bolts" approach.

One of the beneficial offshoots of Watergate was the response of the law schools with respect to legal ethics. In 1970, when I first started participating in teaching new admittees *How to Start and Build a Law Practice,* about 10 percent of the new admittees knew what a trust account was. In January of 1975, at the height of the Watergate disciplinary publicity, almost one-half of the new admittees knew what a trust account was. In 1983, when the State Bar of California implemented mandatory trust account procedures, less than one-third of the lawyers had complied. By 1991, many states required courses in ethics or professional responsibility as a prior condition to admission. Among new admittees, however, about 80 percent know what a trust account is. I personally would expect 100 percent of new admittees to know and understand trust accounts, but accept that 80 percent is better than 10 percent. I believe the 1976 disclosure of these statistics has prompted law schools to spend 40 minutes out of a three-year curriculum on this important subject, and to include trust accounts in the bar exams.

The individual chapters of this book appear to be unconnected or not in sequence. This is intentional. In most cases, each chapter is intended to stand on its own without reference to other chapters. I have done this so that the new admittee can most easily find the general information needed. This results in some blank spaces, which may be aesthetically unsettling but which simplify use of the book.

A number of times in this book I refer to the Model Code of Professional Responsibility and its successor, the Model Rules of Professional Conduct. Every law student and lawyer should have copies of these important documents.

Should You Start
Your Own Practice?
(You Can Do It)

Lawyers who start their own law practices usually fall into one or both of two categories:

A. They have to.

B. They want to.

Lawyers Who Have to Start Their Own Practices

Frankly, I expect that many, if not most, of the new lawyers who start their own practices today have no choice. They would prefer to get jobs, but can't for various reasons, including:

1. They are in the 95% of a law school class who are not in the top 5% of the class.

2. They don't have a rich relative who can pressure a law firm to put a son or daughter on the payroll or risk losing the family's company as a client to the law firm that hires the son or daughter.

3. Neither they nor their parents belong to the "right" clubs or churches.

4. They didn't attend the "right" colleges or law schools.

5. They buy their clothes "off the rack" rather than having them custom-tailor-made and therefore wouldn't have the proper appearance with clients.

6. They lead a lifestyle that doesn't fit in with firm images.

7. Their wives or husbands just aren't the "type" to be social with partners' spouses.

8. They are the "wrong" (or right) color or were born to the wrong (or right) parents.

All of the above may or may not be valid reasons for being denied employment. I submit that *none* of the above reasons has the slightest correlation to success or failure as a practicing lawyer. (I expect those persons who satisfy all or part of the above list of requirements to disagree.)

Many of the people reading this book simply can't get jobs as lawyers to use their legal training so they must either start their own practice or leave the field of law. *This is a perfectly valid reason to start your own law practice.*

Lawyers Who Want to Start Their Own Practices

I opened my own doors right out of law school. To satisfy your curiosity I will tell you that I turned down several unsolicited job offers and walked away from a successful CPA practice to open my doors.

A classmate of mine went to work for a firm. My classmate told me, "Jay, you're crazy. You'll be worrying about getting clients and overhead and collecting fees, while I'm getting my paycheck. It will take you years to make up the difference between your earnings and my paycheck. At the end of five to seven years, with luck, you'll be a partner in a good firm and so will I. You're doing it the hard way."

To some extent he was right and to a great extent he was wrong. Let me list some of the factors with pros and cons:

1. *Personality.* I could take three months to two years in law libraries doing the scutwork of other lawyers, while I was being looked at with a magnifying glass for fear I might say or do something to embarrass the firm. When I believe another lawyer is wrong on the law I tell that person so (*after* documenting my position). I didn't want candid criticism of a legal position to cost me my job.

2. *Client Contact.* Three years of law school was enough. I wanted contact with clients and the responsibility of making decisions immediately. Another year of apprenticeship held no appeal for me. I had been an "apprentice" in two different unions and an "apprentice" with a CPA firm. To me an apprenticeship seemed more a matter of getting cheap profitable labor than of improving the quality of the work done by the apprentice.

3. *Practical Training.* Law firms hire associates because there is work to be done, not because the firm is interested in teaching new lawyers. In some firms there is no formal training program and in some others the training program is not functioning because the partners have little or no time to teach you anything. If they had that

time they wouldn't need the associates. Therefore, in many, if not most, instances you'll get just as much training in the law on your own as with a firm.

4. *Money.* My friend was simultaneously right and wrong. It took me five years until my cumulative earnings as a self-employed lawyer equalled what my cumulative earnings as an employee would have been. In my fourth year of private practice I was earning more than my classmates, but I had yet to make up for the difference of the first three years.

After the fifth year I was ahead of my friends, my employed classmates, etc. I've never fallen behind either on a year-by-year basis or on a cumulative basis.

After ten years some of my classmates had weathered the selection process and become junior partners in the large prestige law firms. They still earned less than I did.

I suppose that at some point I will fall behind my classmates with the large firms when they attain senior partnership. On the other hand, I believe that those of my classmates who initially or ultimately started their own practices are earning about as much as I am.

5. *Type of Legal Work.* As a CPA I had to work on matters where I frankly didn't care for the client or type of work or what the firm was doing for the client. I didn't want the problem as a lawyer of doing work on matters or for clients for whom I had no respect simply because they had money to hire lawyers and I was a lawyer. As my own boss I have greater freedom (not absolute freedom) to turn down cases and clients when I disagree morally with the legal principle espoused by the client.

6. *Security.* Except for some civil service situations, there is no such thing as job security in legal practice. If anything, I feel more secure standing on my own two feet than being dependent on the success or failure of an organization which I cannot control.

I've seen banks fire their entire legal division to "experiment on cost savings using outside counsel." If the experiment is a failure, some vice-president will shrug it off and the careers of some good lawyers who thought they had security will have been destroyed.

I've seen private law firms fire associates on a mass basis when a large client leaves.

I've seen law firms and corporations where there are two lawyers in line for every promotion. The better lawyer (better-liked lawyer may be more accurate) gets promoted and the other gets fired, and the competition starts again.

In the 1990s, law firms split up and merge and split up again like amoebae. Whole departments and individual lawyers suddenly find themselves unemployed and forced to start a law practice.

No, Virginia, except for some civil service positions, there is no security as a lawyer, other than what you carry under your hat. Security is both relative and illusory. Slaves on plantations had pretty good job security.

7. *Fringe Benefits.* Obviously there are many other fringe benefits to being your own boss:

    a. *Vacations.* Go when *you* want to go.

    b. *Tax Benefits.* There are huge tax benefits in being self-employed, compared to being on a job (including loss carry-forwards). These benefits, however, in the main are more significant to you after a few years in practice. At the beginning you need more income, not deductions.

    c. *Prestige.* A firm name with your name carries more prestige than working for another name firm. Being "self-employed" sounds better than being "unemployed."

8. *Avoiding Burnout and Career Dissatisfaction.* Many young lawyers accept high-paying jobs with megafirms and then are forced to work long hours to justify the high salaries. After two or three years, the lawyer is burned out or feels "used up" and quits the practice of law.

You'll have to work long hours in your own firm, but you'll feel good about it because you're doing it for yourself. You'll grow to love, not hate, the practice of law.

Risks of Failure

Nothing in life is guaranteed except death, and some religions claim they can guarantee against even death. There is a substantial risk of failure in opening up your own law practice. There is also risk if you accept a job with a law firm. Law firms merge, are absorbed, and go out of business. Megafirms open and close branches, leaving lawyers unemployed. There is also an element of luck involved. This is no more or less true with a law practice than with any other activity. Marriages fail, children and parents divide, even the Penn Central went bankrupt. I would not be candid if I didn't make clear the possibility of failure.

Should You Start Your Own Practice?

Are the risks justified by the rewards? In my opinion, YES. If you will follow the lessons of this book, you'll increase the rewards and decrease the risks. Go ahead. Whether you make it or not, you'll never regret having tried. The lessons of failure are more bitter than the lessons of victory, but they are valuable lessons, nonetheless. Even if you don't make it, you'll be a better lawyer and a better person for having tried. You may even find yourself able to get a job with a law firm since some law firms now look for lateral hires of experienced lawyers. Considering all the pros and cons, if you care enough about opening your own practice to be reading this book, you probably have what it takes to make it and successfully "start and build your own law practice."

How Soon Should You "Open Your Doors"?

As soon as possible. You will quickly develop a liking for the "finer things in life" such as fine cars, skiing, recreational travel, clothing, nice restaurants, spectator events such as theatre, football, basketball, etc., not to mention a good apartment or home. These fine things slowly but surely creep into your standard of living, imperceptibly raising your cost of living. It is easier to "bite the bullet" *before* developing a taste for these things than *after* you have all these personal expenses.

Should You Work on
a Job "for Experience"
Before Starting Your Practice?

Notwithstanding that you have a license to practice law and have been declared competent to practice law by your Supreme Court, you probably have some doubts about your ability to competently represent clients in court and give advice.

Working in Private Practice

I don't think that the "crutch" of six months' or a year's experience will assist you that much. Your "experience" may consist of doing research or making minor court appearances or preparing lesser documents. You will have relatively little client contact in most firms. The associates or partners to whom you are assigned will have relatively little time to spend with you discussing the case or "grading" what you turn in. Lack of supervision and review is a common complaint of new associates. If the firm had a lot of free time available to supervise and teach, it wouldn't need associates.

Except in very few firms, there is relatively little formal training.

The "experience" you are seeking usually consists of access to the firm's form files, a few minutes of advice now and then from a slightly senior associate, and even less advice from a partner.

It is my opinion that there is no great detriment in developing your own forms using form books available from the law library (see chapter on "How to Build a Good Form File"). In litigation matters, the clerks of court and other attorneys from whom you get work give you at least as much counseling as you would have gotten in a firm.

The limited amount of supervision you would receive in six

months to a year on a job does not in most cases justify delaying starting your practice.

Obviously the attorney who makes a commitment of one to five years in accepting a first job is taking a great risk and should be sure such a step will really be beneficial.

Working in Civil Service

At the time of the writing of this book, attorneys in civil service were receiving pay and fringe benefits equal to or in excess of those attorneys in private practice for the first few years.

My objections to civil service as a career are twofold:

1. *Limited Range of Professional Challenge.* In some jobs one can get five years of experience in five years. In other jobs one gets the same six months' experience ten times over. Some, if not many, civil service positions fall into this second category.

2. *The Pay Trap.* At the end of one, two, or five years, a lawyer in civil service has earned and is usually earning more than a counterpart in private practice. One often is limited in subsequent pay increases (but not limited in title promotion) because of rules not to earn more than a supervisor, etc. This results in a triangle with a small apex and a broad base. There is nowhere to go. The lawyer in private practice, however, can increase earnings without limitation. Even though a civil service lawyer can't go much farther in compensation, there are substantial pay and fringe benefits that would be reduced in private practice. Also, having proved ability in civil service, the lawyer must now prove ability in private practice.

There are some people who definitely are well suited for some civil service careers, but I doubt that many of them would be reading this book. The job security of civil service, lack of client pressures, little or no night or weekend work, generous retirement and medical plans, all combine to make it appealing to some lawyers.

Earning a Living Between Graduation and Opening Your Practice

Some lawyers have no choice but to start a law practice on a part-time basis while working at a full- or part-time job. This is totally contrary to my best advice, yet I recognize the facts of life are that some lawyers have no choice due to financial obligations or personal obligations—they will, in fact, start a law practice while working on another job.

Some of the more common reasons expressed to me for deferring the opening of a law practice include:

1. They wait for a spouse to finish school, job training or military training to then be assigned to a city. Only then will the lawyer know where he or she will be opening a practice.

2. They know where they want to practice, but for some reason have to wait a year or two before they can get there to open a practice.

3. They graduated law school heavily in debt and need money to repay student loans.

4. They want to accumulate as much cash as possible before starting a practice in order to have a year's living expenses on hand.

5. They want to earn money to enable them to purchase high-tech computers, word processors, printers, fax machines, software packages, etc.

6. They have personal problems or commitments due to timing in taking the bar exam, getting the results, or getting sworn in, any of which will necessarily delay the start of a law practice.

Lawyers often ask me for information on the kinds of work they can get with a law degree, other than traditional clerking jobs. This is not a book on how to get a job. Many such books written by job experts are available; and there are many consultants who will tell you everything you have to do to get a job, from what color paper to use for a resume, to how to sprinkle the salt and pepper on your entree. This also is not a book on what kind of law you should seek a career in. There are myriad articles and books on that subject.

My purpose in adding this chapter to the third edition is to give you some additional ideas on how to earn a living between law school and opening a practice. I've tried to point out whether or not the experience you would get in a particular nontraditional job will be of value to you when you open your own practice.

This chapter is based in part on an article I wrote for the *National Law Journal* and has been reprinted many times by state and local bar journals. It is not intended to include every job possibility; it is intended to get you thinking about ways to earn a living with your law degree until you can open your own practice. If you want to refer to the original article, it is titled "Nontraditional Jobs Where You Can Use a Law Degree."

1. *House Counsel.* This area of law is frequently referred to as corporate counsel, law division, or a similar title. Traditional law firms often price themselves out of the corporate legal market through over-pricing of services. A law division or house counsel generally can provide many, if not all, of the same services as the traditional law firm at much less cost. The higher cost of traditional law firms is due to many factors, including the refusal or inability of the traditional firm to adopt modern techniques and personnel management. Mismanagement of resources, which I feel is prevalent in traditional law firms, would not be tolerated in a corporate operation. Business consumers of legal services are now forming and enlarging their in-house legal staff. It has been said that a traditional law firm has a variety of clients with a variety of problems. House counsel has a single client with a variety of problems. This is definitely a growth area. Depending upon the particular job you secure, the experience may or may not be of value when you open your own firm.

2. *Legal Assistants and Paralegals.* (I have lumped these two together because I am tired of arguing about the differences, if any, between the two.)

If you can get a job as a legal assistant, the experience will be of great help to you in understanding the proper (and improper) utilization of legal assistants in a law firm. In law school you learned *why* law is practiced. As a legal assistant you can learn *how* law is practiced. A legal assistant can and should do anything a lawyer does except make court appearances and make decisions concerning legal rights and responsibilities. Accordingly, as a legal assistant you may get training and supervision that new associates in a firm do not get.

For various reasons, many law firms absolutely refuse to hire lawyers as legal assistants. One of the reasons for their refusal is that the firm feels the attorney is not looking for serious permanent employment as a legal assistant. When you meet this resistance you can honestly reply that you intend to work as a legal assistant for only six months, one year, or for whatever your schedule is. You should ask if they have any substantial client matter in the office or coming up which would make it in the firm's best interests to hire you for the duration of that matter. The firm then could consider you for temporary employment, or for employment for only that one case.

3. *"Rent-A-Lawyer" Temporary Agencies.* There are agencies that serve as a clearinghouse between lawyers seeking part-time or additional work and firms that need a lawyer for a particular case or for a limited period of time. Often a firm wants to take on a case for a particular client rather than refer it to another law firm, even though it cannot handle it without increasing its permanent staffing. These firms (and lawyers seeking work) go to an agency to match needs and availability. Some bar associations run these agencies. Typically, the lawyer is paid between $30 and $60 per hour and the agency gets an additional 10 percent as its fee. It may be worthwhile to familiarize yourself with as many of these agencies as you can. Be sure there is a written definition of responsibility for malpractice coverage. There is a sort of "grab bag" element of luck in terms of the work being of value to you in opening your own practice.

4. *Government.* Government, both state and local, has been in the past and will be in the future a major consumer of legal talent. It has been estimated that government at levels from local to federal employs between 10 and 15 percent of all lawyers. There are as many different jobs as there are government agencies. Some of these agencies hire lawyers in areas where one might not ordinarily consider an attorney.

With government jobs generally, as with house counsel, whether or not the experience can be of value to you when you open your own practice will depend on the job you get and the practice you start.

a. *Law Enforcement.* FBI and Treasury Agents and IRS Criminal Investigators are examples.

b. *Military.* The military services hire civilian lawyers to do work similar to the work done by career military officer lawyers. Contracts and litigation are common areas where military and civilian lawyers work side by side.

    c. *Other.* Get a Washington, D.C., telephone directory, a telephone directory from your state capital, and a local telephone directory, and simply send a form letter to the personnel section of each agency or department listing, asking if it hires lawyers. It may take some time to coordinate timing of applications, interviews, and the ultimate hiring. Many jobs that require lawyers are not civil service and, accordingly, may not be subject to the usual procedures. This is why it is necessary to write to each agency and department separately.

    Government is definitely a growth area for lawyers. People want increased regulation and layers of new laws on top of old laws, which require an increased number of lawyers to draft and administer these laws. Notwithstanding a Proposition 13, anti-growth sentiment on the part of the public, government will find a way to grow, making government law definitely a growth area.

    5. *CPA Firms.* The practice of accounting is very similar to the practice of law in many aspects. After traditional law firms and house counsel, CPA firms may be one of the largest employers of lawyers. The international CPA firms tend to be the main employers, although local CPA firms also hire lawyers. Some of the uses of lawyers in CPA firms are:

    a. *Tax Departments.* Even small local CPA firms often hire lawyers to work in their tax departments. Typical work would include research and tax opinions given to a client or given internally to a department, such as the audit department. The extent of active use of lawyers in a CPA firm varies from firm to firm. In some firms the attorney may go to Tax Court or to an administrative or local tax hearing, but not to a U.S. District Court. In some firms the attorney may review documents prepared by the client's counsel for tax effects. In some firms the attorney may draft legal documents.

    b. *Litigation Support or Litigation Services.* Many CPA firms work closely with law firms to lend support in such areas as document analysis, or to assist a law firm in handling major litigation.

    c. *International.* International CPA firms often use attorneys in the international department's offices to assist in a variety of ways.

    d. *Management Services.* CPA firms offer management advice to law firm clients, such as assistance in data processing and word processing.

6. *Law Firm Management.* Many law firms have professional administrative staffs. This is a phenomenon of the late 1980s. Law firms need management personnel to the same extent that any going business needs management. If you have had courses or experience in areas such as sales, marketing, advertising, public relations, printing, finance, personnel administration, training, accounting, budgeting, etc., you may be able to get a position in a law firm where, although you won't be practicing law, *per se,* your experience will stand you in good stead when you open your own practice. Many law firms prefer to hire a person who has a law school education to work better with lawyers and lend credibility. In some cases, however, law firms deliberately avoid using someone with a law degree.

7. *Computer and Hi-Tech Experience.* If you can spell PC, as in personal computer, there is a job in a law firm for you, either as an employee or as a consultant. Many law firms now know *what* they can do with a computer, but don't know *how* to do it. Frankly, it doesn't require much technical ability to put computer applications into law firms. Unfortunately (possibly fortunately for you), most lawyers over 40 can't figure out how to turn off a PC, much less program simple applications. Having a law degree will be helpful in understanding what the lawyers and support staff are doing. The experience also will help you when you open your own practice.

8. *Law Firm Consulting.* This is similar to law firm management except that it is done by outside consultants. This again is a new area which is opening up widely in the 1990s. I believe that the large international CPA firms may share, if not take, the lead in this area.

9. *Law Firm Marketing Administration and Consulting.* Professional law firm marketing has been given candid recognition by the profession during only the last two or three years. The National Association of Law Firm Marketing Administrators (NALFMA) came into being around 1985. The criteria or qualifications for becoming a law firm marketing administrator are varied and in a state of flux. As a lawyer, if you are admitted to practice, you legally and ethically can share fees with the firm you work for. You may be able to convince a law firm that it needs a marketing administrator. If you are the firm's first administrator and do not understand the function of a marketing administrator, buy a copy of my book *How to Get and Keep Good Clients,* Second Edition, available from Lawyers Alert Press, 30 Court Square, Boston, Massachusetts 02018, (800) 444-LAWS. Read the book. It'll probably take you about a year to install in the firm the various techniques described in the book. The expe-

rience will stand you in good stead when you open your own practice.

10. *Newsletter Writing and Publishing.* Writing and selling newsletters for lawyers and for their clients seems to be an exploding industry. I frequently get invited to be on the editorial board or to write for some new newsletter. Many law firms write their own newsletters, which they use as a form of advertising to get new clients and/or to communicate with existing clients. Some law firms buy "canned" or pre-written newsletters and send them to clients, passing them off as material developed by the firm. If you have any ability or interest in writing newsletter-style publications, you may be able to earn income writing or ghost writing for these publications. The experience may not do much for you in terms of your own practice, unless you intend to put out your own newsletter when you begin a practice. These newsletters typically are devoted to "recent developments in the law" or "how our law firm can help you," and require a hard-hitting writing style that is not consistent with the way most lawyers write.

11. *Government Regulation.* I am describing a career that does not yet exist in the United States. In Brazil, there is a profession known as *economista*. The profession is not equivalent to the American profession of economist. The *economista* has the responsibility of determining all government laws, regulations, etc., of the various administrative agencies that apply to the business. The *economista* also is responsible for advising the company on how to comply with these regulations. Normally, the *economista* is responsible directly to the president and occupies an important position within the enterprise. In some companies, the *economista* takes the place of house counsel, while in others, the *economista* assists the regular house counsel staff. Since this profession does not yet exist in the United States, it is difficult to create a name for the position. Perhaps the title should be "Corporate Vice-President, Governmental Regulations" or "Governmental Affairs," or some similar title.

12. *Banks and Insurance Companies.* Banks and insurance companies require large numbers of house counsel due to the scope and size of operations, and as government regulation of their activities increases. Many of the observations applicable to banks and insurance companies also will apply to house counsel in other industries.

a. *Litigation.* Many banks and insurance companies maintain a litigation firm that ostensibly is outside counsel. These firms typically defend cases where the institution feels the exposure is low compared to the costs of a defense, which could be high (relative to the exposure) if outside counsel were used. Often the lawyers employed in these firms are allowed to work on their own cases as long as it does not interfere with their regular workload. Insurance companies also use this type of firm for subrogation, and banks often use the firms for routine collection-type work.

b. *Forms*. Banks and insurance companies must generate myriad forms that have to comply with myriad regulatory rules and laws. These forms are more cheaply produced by house counsel than by outside counsel for a variety of reasons.

c. *Corporate*. Banks and insurance companies frequently have multiple corporate subsidiaries or affiliates, all of which require the typical corporate minutes, resolutions, etc.

d. *Administrative Regulation Compliance*. See "Government Regulation," above.

e. *Securities Law, Bankruptcy*. Secured creditor work, or "workouts" (agreements between a debtor and a creditor when the debtor is in default), are common for banks and insurance companies because of the large number of investments they make. The complexity of creditor rights laws often requires an attorney to do the workout.

The experience gained as house counsel generally is helpful to a point for a lawyer starting a practice. Often a house counsel position becomes repetitive and boring after six months to a year. Since you will be staying only long enough to open your own practice, the experience probably will be of value. If you are fortunate, you may be able to make some good contacts and get some office procedure experience that could be of help to you.

13. *Investment Banking*. For reasons that I truly do not understand, a large number of lawyers are being hired to do nonlegal work in investment banking (possibly in a capacity similar to a retail stockbroker). I do not see any relationship between working for a brokerage firm and opening your own law office, but I pass on to you that this may be a way of earning a living until you are ready to open your own firm.

14. *Labor Law*.

a. *Classic Labor Law*. Both unions and management hire large numbers of lawyers to advise the union or the employer of the limits of permissible conduct. Union lawyers also may provide various forms of workers' compensation law or FELA law for their members when they claim work-related injuries. Often the union lawyer represents both the union and the worker.

b. *Employer-Group Prepaid Insurance Plans.* I include this category because this area of law often is controlled or sponsored by unions, although certainly many nonunion groups also have these plans. This is an area of law where a group member pays, or has the employer pay, a certain amount of money per year or month or hour. The "legal group" of lawyers agrees to provide a certain quantity of legal services in specified areas for some part of the prepaid fee. The theory is that the legal group will lose money on many prepaid members but make up the losses on volume or on the occasional contingency fee. I seriously question the long-term economic viability of these plans as presently constituted. Certainly this may represent an area where an attorney can get experience in "preventative law." In any event, you can gain experience in a rather limited area while waiting to open your own practice.

15. *Legal Aid, Poverty Lawyers, Legal Defense Clinics, Store-Front Lawyers, and Other* Pro Bono Publico *Work.* It takes a special kind of person to do this kind of work. One must be highly motivated to provide legal services to people who otherwise might not be able to afford them. I've heard lawyers who work for these organizations compare the experience to that of being an intern in the emergency room of a county hospital: grueling hours of under-compensated work, but a wealth of hands-on experience. These law firms sometimes take on a case load far beyond their financial ability. The results can be a legal job of questionable quality for a client with little or no ability to pay for the amount of work and resources required. Many of my books, forms articles, etc., are used by these groups, and I willingly help them.

Although *pro bono* cases offer you exposure to a wide variety of work, you may not be able to give any one client or case the highest level of professional quality of law required. Your compensation probably will be more psychological than financial. In most cases, you must have passed the bar to secure this type of employment, but in some situations a law degree without a license is sufficient.

16. *Mediators, Arbitrators, Conciliation Counselors, etc.* Many people and companies are now turning to mediation, arbitration, or conciliation as an alternative to litigation. Many large corporations submit to arbitration and mediation of consumer complaints.

If you have some special skill outside of legal training, you may be able to serve as a well-compensated arbitrator or mediator. A telephone call to your local American Arbitration Association office or American Association of Mediators is a good starting place.

17. *Employment Agencies.*

a. *Using an Employment Agency.* Often a company with no hiring experience will employ an employment agency to locate a lawyer it needs. Such an agency may be called an executive search firm, headhunter, or a variety of other names. You should consider using an agency to get a job only if no fee is to be paid by you. (The company should pay all fees.)

b. *Working for an Employment Agency.* You may wish to work for an employment agency on a commission basis. Working for an agency is not likely to give you experience you can use in your practice, but it can give you insight into the "hot" areas of law in your region, based on what kinds of lawyers law firms need most.

18. *Consider Moving.* On behalf of the State Bar of California, I did an informal survey of state bar groups to find out who was "importing" lawyers. In the survey, I discovered that some states don't have enough local law school graduates to meet their needs and must bring in lawyers from other states. Although the survey is a bit dated, the results remain the same. States importing lawyers include Delaware, Hawaii, North Dakota, Arizona, Nevada, Colorado, North Carolina, Rhode Island, Idaho, Nebraska, Mississippi, Oregon, New Hampshire, New Jersey, Wisconsin, Alaska, Indiana, Louisiana, and Maine.

Conclusion

The number of jobs available for lawyers in nontraditional areas is extensive. You will have to use imagination and ingenuity. In this chapter, I've tried to give you some ideas to stimulate you to do your own thinking.

As my dear friend, J. Harris Morgan of Dallas, suggests (I consider him the greatest mind on the delivery of legal services):

"Begin! The rest is easy."

Should You Start with Another New Lawyer?

Two new, inexperienced lawyers without an established clientele starting out together are similar to the blind man carrying a legless man on his back with the latter doing the navigating for both. In theory, the combination should work. In practice, it only works on a temporary basis. Therefore, as a general rule, two new lawyers getting together will accomplish very little except to prove that two can starve to death at least twice as fast as one. I recommend against it.

On the other hand, I know from experience that many teams of inexperienced lawyers have set up practice together for noneconomic reasons such as long-term friendships. A few teams will make it. Therefore, although I generally recommend against two brand-new lawyers getting together, I'll give you some suggestions that may increase your chances of success.

1. Don't form a partnership for at least one year. A bad partnership can be financially worse than a bad marriage. Your spouse can only cost you everything you have. Your partner can cost you your future. Get together on an expense-sharing basis. Each of you can be "of counsel" to the other. For example, there could be two sets of stationery as follows:

BRAND NEW LAWYER JONES	INEXPERIENCED LAWYER
123 Main St., Anytown	SMITH
INEXPERIENCED LAWYER	123 Main St., Anytown
SMITH	BRAND NEW LAWYER JONES
Of Counsel	Of Counsel

Check local rules for this situation.

2. Put your expense-sharing, "of counsel" agreement in writing.

3. Pick someone who complements you rather than who merely duplicates you. Remember, you need as much exposure as possible.

a. If you have the same friends, belong to the same church and clubs, have the same interests and hobbies, then you'll make great friends but will lose one of the chief benefits of association, which is multiple exposure to clients and potential clients.

b. Unless you have some reason for trying to start a specialty practice your first day, you should associate with someone who has different legal interests. The most common example I have seen is that one is interested in "Trial Law" areas such as criminal and divorce and the other is interested in "Business Law" areas. Usually, the practice ultimately tends toward the activity of the better business-getter.

c. Be flexible and ready to change your plans. Since the practice will gravitate toward the activity of the better business-getter, the other lawyer may have to readjust career plans. The "Trial Lawyer" will have to start doing corporation formation and leases, or the "Business Lawyer" will have to start getting clients bailed out of jail. If this adjustment doesn't occur, there will be a falling out when the better business-getter realizes that he or she is doing all the work and needs an associate rather than a partner.

4. Be sure your "partner" is adequately financed. You don't want to come into the office one morning and find that you are the "stuckee" on the rent, library equipment payment, payroll taxes, etc., because your good friend couldn't bear half of the burden.

5. Cover in advance the problems of split-up.

a. Telephone number. A telephone number is an exceedingly important asset to a lawyer. Whoever gets the phone number may get cases originally intended for the other.

b. Unpaid payments. Who is going to pay for what?

c. Who moves? Who stays? The office location has a small value. Clients get nervous about lawyers who keep changing address.

d. Who gets the form file?

e. Provide for arbitration of differences. Individual litigation can be expensive and bitter.

In short, if you're smart, you'll have a written agreement.

6. How about a new lawyer getting together with a lawyer with two to three years' experience? In my opinion, this makes much more sense than two new lawyers getting together. The best way to im-

prove your bridge, your tennis or your chess is to play against someone slightly better than you. The same is true in law. A new lawyer can learn a lot from a lawyer with experience, and the experienced lawyer can take advantage of the willingness of the new lawyer to follow instructions and do the work outlined. I recommend this arrangement as opposed to the two-new-lawyer arrangement.

Should You Practice Another Business or Profession While Starting Your Law Practice?

If you can do so, it will probably be in your best interests financially to limit your activities to law until you are fairly well established as a lawyer. In my opinion, your second business or profession is more likely to be a brake than a booster on the development of your law practice. A few people can successfully maintain two businesses or professions with both growing profitably, but they are the exception, not the rule.

If you have another business or profession, I advise you to sell it or become as inactive as possible and devote your full time to the development of your law practice. I know from past experience that my advice will probably be ignored because you'll be afraid to give up your known income for unknown income in a new profession. Three or four years from now you'll say that I was right and you should have taken my advice earlier, but until then you'll hang on to your other practice or business out of fear.

If, on the other hand, you are earning enough from your second business or profession so that you have no immediate interest in creating a full-time law practice, then you can practice another business or profession subject to certain restrictions:

1. *Attorney-Client Privilege Problems.* You must segregate activities as a lawyer from your other activities. When a client seeks legal advice from a lawyer, there is an attorney-client privilege. When the same person seeks nonlegal assistance from the "lawyer" acting in the other, nonlegal capacity, then the attorney-client privilege does not apply. You must take care to protect the client's privilege.

2. *Malpractice Insurance Problems.* Here again you must be careful. For example, if you are both a lawyer and a CPA and you sign a gift tax return as a CPA, your accounting professional insur-

ance should protect you. If you sign as a lawyer, your legal professional insurance should protect you. If you don't identify your capacity, you may find that your accounting carrier will claim you're not insured because you were practicing law, and your legal carrier may claim you are not insured because you were practicing accounting. You can conjure up similar hypothetical problems for the lawyer who is also an insurance agent and gives estate-planning advice, or the lawyer who is also a bank or insurance company director and advises the bank or insurance company.

3. *Advertising and Solicitation Problems.* Disciplinary Rule 2–102(E) of the Code of Professional Responsibility as adopted by some bar associations states: "A lawyer who is engaged both in the practice of law and another profession or business shall not so indicate on his letterhead, office sign, or professional card, nor shall he identify himself as a lawyer in any publication in connection with his other profession or business."

Disciplinary Rule 2–103(A) states: "A lawyer shall not recommend employment, as a private practitioner, of himself, his partner, or associate to a non-lawyer who has not sought his advice regarding employment of a lawyer."

These rules, where they are still in effect, require you to, in effect, hide your second business or profession from your legal clients, and not to recommend yourself as a lawyer when you discover legal problems.

While acting in your nonlawyer capacity, there is significant debate among reasonable people as to whether the prohibitions and restrictions on advertising and solicitation were or are for the benefit of the public or for the benefit of the established law firms who wish to eliminate open competition for clients. There is also an ongoing question as to whether the prohibitions and restrictions are themselves illegal under antitrust laws or as deprivations of the public's "right to know."

The winds of change are blowing strongly in the fields of advertising and solicitation. My personal belief has always tended toward informing the public of the qualifications and fees of a lawyer so that the public can make informed choices when selecting a lawyer. This, however, may not be the state of the law and the new attorney would be well advised to follow the dictates of DR 2–102(E) and 2–103(A) or the applicable local rules unless he or she is interested in a three-to-five-year battle with the organized bar and is willing to bear the expense and stigma attached to such a fight. Each of these rules, in my opinion, represents a compromise between conflicting theories and, for that reason, is worthy of respect.

4. *How to Handle Dual Businesses or Professions.*

a. Maintain two filing systems. Don't mix the legal files with the nonlegal files.

b. Maintain separate bank account systems. Don't mix legal fees with nonlegal fees.

c. Maintain separate stationery and calling cards.

d. Maintain separate billings to the client.

e. Maintain separate phone numbers.

f. If, in the course of your nonlegal representation, you discover a legal problem, bring it to the attention of the client and offer to assist the client's lawyer. Don't offer to handle the legal problem. Explain to the client that you may not have any attorney-client privilege due to having discovered the problem in your nonlegal capacity. If the client insists on your handling the problem as a lawyer, protect both yourself and the client by sending the client a letter indicating:

(1) That the client is not obligated to use you due to your discovery of the problem and your willingness to cooperate with any other lawyer the client might wish to use;

(2) That you will be functioning as a lawyer from that point on at your standard rate for legal fees and that from that point on there will be an attorney-client privilege.

Sole Practice v. Partnership v. Shared Office

1. A partnership can have some economic and psychological advantages over sole practice, especially for a new lawyer. The principal advantages of partnerships are:

a. Each partner can develop an expertise or specialty in specific areas of practice, relying on the other partner(s) to cover the other areas of practice.

b. Someone is earning money for you when you are sick or on a vacation (or vice versa).

c. There is someone to "watch the store" while you are out of the office for short or long periods of time. Your client emergencies can be temporarily handled in your absence.

d. The overhead per lawyer may be slightly less for a two- or three-lawyer partnership than for two or three lawyers practicing solely. (In my opinion this factor is greatly overrated and in itself does not justify forming a partnership.)

e. You have a "sounding board" in the office to discuss your theories or issues. You can easily get a second opinion on a case.

f. A bank loan is easier to get with two signatures.

2. Sole practice (also referred to as *solo practice*) has the following advantages and disadvantages:

a. You don't have to feel guilty about spending large amounts of time on cases that really interest you.

b. You come and go as you wish.

c. You're stuck with all the administrative tasks of running a law firm.

d. You lose the larger or complex cases you have to refer out when you don't have the expertise or personnel to handle the case.

e. Many clients equate small law practices with ability to handle only small legal matters.

f. When you do earn "the big fee," it's all yours.

3. In a shared-office arrangement, you can remain a sole practitioner and still have many of the advantages of partnership in group practice. Normally you are a tenant in the suite along with the others in the suite or possibly you will simply be sharing expenses. The proximity of the other lawyers will give you the second opinion and the coverage you need plus some possible additional referral work.

In the past I was somewhat hesitant about space-sharing, but with ever-escalating costs due to inflation, I now recommend it to the lawyer who wants to be in sole practice but still have the advantages of a partnership without actually having a partnership. I specifically recommend the concept of the "Fegen Suite" (see p. 44).

Part II
Getting Located

Where Is the Best Place to Open Your Office?
(From a Client-Getting Point of View)

If you have a choice, don't practice out of your home. Clients will not appreciate your low overhead. They'll think that you're a lawyer who can't make it. Additionally, clients don't want to be seen by your family or hear a TV set or garbage disposal.

If you really can't get an office, use the attorney conference room of the local law library or the attorney conference room of the local courthouse, or meet the client at his or her place of business. But don't use your home. (However, if you must practice out of your home—see my chapter on "Practicing Out of Your Home.")

Generally, I recommend starting in a suite or area where you can get overflow work from other lawyers.

I know one lawyer who opened his office in a store on a corner by a bus stop which was a major bus transfer point and was across the street from a large phone company office. In a few months he had a very successful practice of telephone company operators and administrative people who had the usual amount of divorces and accident cases. By opening his office at 7 a.m., he also was able to accommodate other people on their way to work between bus transfers.

The lawyer told me that this was all planned and that he bought out the lease of a cleaners after he had concluded that the location was right.

The moral of the above story should be obvious: "Go Where the Clients Are." If you are from a community where you have a lot of friends and family, then this is where you should locate.

If you've gone away from home for college and away from home for law school and you haven't much family, then you should consider moving into an area where there will be a need for you.

As that eminent speaker on law practice management J. Harris Morgan teaches, you should look for a community where there is only one lawyer. As the second lawyer in town you'll get the cases where there is a conflict. Obviously the same lawyer can't represent both the creditor and the debtor or the claimant and the insurance company.

When I first wrote this book I didn't know much about rural or small town practice. I went to Los Angeles High School, UCLA as an undergrad and UCLA Law School. We lived in Los Angeles because that's where the family was.

After presenting hundreds of programs in every state of the Union, I have learned vicariously about rural, small town, and suburban law practices. The problems are very different, but the rewards are often greater in terms of lifestyle and community life and professional growth.

A practice starts with friends, relatives and professional acquaintances. Therefore, the best place to start your career is where they are.

If no one knows you, it's going to be difficult to start your practice. In a small community you become known more quickly.

If you cannot start your practice where people know you, then find a place and make yourself known there. Being unknown can lengthen the time you need to become established.

Geographic Location Checklist
1. Where are your friends and relatives (the best place)?
2. Pick a growing rather than a decaying section of the country. Watch out for blight and decay.
3. Choose urban, rural, or suburban practice. Consider possible changes in economic patterns due to escalating energy costs.
4. Analyze whether you can really be happy in a rural or small-town atmosphere or in an urban atmosphere. This is a matter of your personality and background.

Quality of Life Checklist
1. *Quality of Professional Life.* What kinds of cases and clients can be gotten where you will practice?
2. *Quality of Social Life.* Do you want or need proximity to museums, symphonies, dance clubs, or other young intellectual people?

3. *Quality of Atmosphere.* Smog and pollution or clean air and water?

4. *Quality of Recreational Life.* Do you want proximity to swimming, skiing, boating, hiking, hunting, etc.?

5. *Quality of "Home Life."* Is the area safe for your spouse and children? Will you have to be afraid to go out at night or afraid to sleep with the windows open?

6. *Quality of Economic Life.* What kind of money can you earn? You probably have to compromise some items to obtain others. There is no right or wrong. Think about where and how you wish to spend the next 30 or 40 years of your life.

Where Should You Locate Your Office for Your First Year or Two?
(From a Cost Point of View)

I strongly recommend that for the first year or two you try to locate your office in a suite where there are as many lawyers as possible and in a building which has as many lawyers, law firms, and similar suites as possible.

The other lawyers in the suite and in the building can be a source of legal fees to you.

For purposes of this book, a suite is defined to be a place where more than one lawyer practices, with the lawyers having no economic relationship with each other beyond the sharing of certain common expenses, such as reception space, library, etc.

These suites are more and more available on a commercial basis; there are now companies that set up these suites for lawyers. Even if there is not such a company, you may find in your community one or more suites where there is an association of lawyers, or a law firm that has excess space and wishes to rent it out.

It should be self-evident that the cost per lawyer of a law library is less when there are anywhere from 4 to 20 lawyers sharing the costs than if only one lawyer is paying for it. Additionally, such features as photocopying, receptionist, conference rooms, etc., are much less expensive when several lawyers are sharing the costs than if only one lawyer is covering them. Ask lawyers already in the suite how long they have been in the suite and what they like or dislike about the arrangement. Be careful to control your own phone number.

After you have been in practice a year or two and have gotten over the initial hump of economic survival, you can select an office that you feel fits the needs of your practice.

Additionally, you normally can rent space in suites on a month-to-month basis or with a one-year maximum lease liability. If you find that you've chosen the wrong location or you don't like the other lawyers in the suite, or they don't send you the business you expect, you can cut your losses short and change locations without worrying about a long lease liability.

Neighborhood/Building Checklist

1. Proximity of office to public transportation for staff and clients.

2. Proximity to eating places for client entertainment and meetings.

3. Proximity to law library.

4. Proximity to major anticipated clients.

5. Type of practice hoped for. For personal injury, workers' compensation, and criminal law, proximity to courts and administrative hearing locations or jails may be important.

6. Proximity to other lawyers for advice and possible overflow work and library is important.

7. Will office and building be accessible for people on crutches or in wheelchairs, or elderly people?

Should You Trade "Space for Services"?

The basic concept of "space for services" seems to be a good idea. A lawyer with extra space provides that space to a new lawyer in exchange for a certain number of hours per month. There are various additional services that might be involved, such as office furnishings, telephone answering, client reception, reproduction services, library use, etc. Although secretarial services could be included, they rarely are.

The lawyer with space usually guarantees specified hours of work to the new lawyer and the new lawyer promises to be available for that number of hours.

This system is very appealing to the new lawyer who is afraid to lay out cash for overhead. It is also very appealing for the established lawyer who is trading excess capacity for a part-time associate without cash outlay.

Sometimes this space-for-service arrangement is intended as a "trial marriage" before any job commitment or before any merger.

In theory, this system has mutual advantages and should be a big success. Unfortunately, space for services rarely works for reasons that I will set forth. It usually ends rather quickly with a lot of bad feelings on both sides.

Because this system rarely works, I recommend against space for services. On the other hand, if both the new lawyer and the experienced lawyer face the problems that I've set forth (and others), then perhaps you can make it work.

Typical Problems in Space for Services

1. *Are Hours Cumulative or Noncumulative?* If 20 hours per month is the agreed number, what happens when only 18 are used?

Is there a "debt" of two hours to carry over to the next month? Is reduction in services justified?

2. *Suppose New Lawyer Doesn't Want to Handle the Matter Because of Conflict in Schedules.* Typically, New Lawyer owes five hours and the last day of the month comes and New Lawyer wants to interview a prospective client and Experienced Lawyer wants New Lawyer to handle a matter 70 miles out of town. Who wins this conflict?

3. *Suppose New Lawyer Doesn't Want to Handle the Matter Because of Personal Dislike of the Case or Client.* There may be good or no reason for New Lawyer not to want to handle a matter or client. Does New Lawyer have the right to say "No"?

4. *Are Hours During the Working Day?* Does New Lawyer have to go down to the jail at 3:00 a.m. on Sunday morning or meet with a client when he or she has tickets to take a new client to a Sunday football game? Is there time and a half or double time for nights and weekends?

5. *Who Is to Arbitrate Claims of Excess Time Spent?* When Experienced Lawyer says that 15 hours research was insane, unwarranted and wasted, who is to arbitrate?

6. *Is New Lawyer Obligated to Do Only Legal Work?* If there is time to burn on the last day of the month, can Experienced Lawyer use New Lawyer for tasks such as picking up personal laundry and cleaning? Experienced Lawyer will claim the right to use New Lawyer in any capacity.

Recommended Alternatives

Frankly, I feel that unless the two lawyers can work out the above problems in advance, they should avoid time-for-space arrangements. I recommend, instead, exchanging checks with no promises. New Lawyer pays a fair rental and may accept or reject work assignments as desired. Experienced Lawyer pays an agreed hourly rate (about six or seven times the Federal Minimum Wage) for work performed. If Experienced Lawyer doesn't like New Lawyer's work, the work stops. A 90-day termination period should be provided so New Lawyer can find another situation.

How Do You Get
the Best Space Arrangement?

Make Contacts to Find Space

Sources of information such as your local legal newspaper are very good; nonlegal local papers are all right; local bar association journals are often helpful. A commercial broker may be a good source, if the space you require is not too small. Other lawyers can be of assistance. If there is a particular building in which you want space, try a form letter sent or delivered to every existing tenant and building manager. This is a good source of leads on sublet space when offices move or firms break up, often creating an opportunity for reduced rent.

Determine True Rental Cost in Order to Comparison-Shop Prices

Always ask for the *net* square footage figure from the broker or landlord, and put it into the lease. Divide monthly or annual rent by net total square footage to get cost per *net* square foot, which is the only true way to measure rent cost. There can be a 20% difference between net square footage and gross square footage, due to poles, beams, corridors, window sills, ducts, stairwells, irregularly shaped premises, etc.

Consider Cheap Space in an Expensive Building

Inside, non-window space is very cheap. No one wants it. With imaginative drapes, lighting and decorating, the client won't realize that the offices are inside offices. Cost savings in rent can be very significant. Indicate that you are willing to accept inside space for price or other considerations.

What Size Office Will You Need?

How many square feet do you need for an office? Generally speaking, you'll need about 400 to 600 square feet per lawyer, as follows: Personal office, 150 to 200 square feet (smaller is OK if you have access to a conference room for client meetings). Secretarial area, 150 to 200 square feet (try to defer this for a few months, if possible). Reception area, storage, copy machine, etc., 100 to 200 square feet.

What to Negotiate and Include in Your Lease or Office Rental Agreement

1. Parking for yourself, staff and clients at fixed prices. Don't automatically accept the story that parking is a concession. Buildings often make parking a part of lease if pushed.

2. Access to office at night or on weekends. Will air conditioning, heating and lights be available at no extra cost? Is there any form of building security after hours?

3. Is there any furniture from the outgoing tenant you might have?

4. Right of first refusal on additional space in building if you expand.

5. Air conditioning and heating thermostat controls for your part of the suite.

6. Be sure telephone and electrical outlets are where you need them or get landlord to move them.

7. Carpet cleaning or replacement.

8. Painting or other wall treatment—replacement or cleaning.

9. Drapes often can't be cleaned; insist on new ones.

10. A one-year term, with two one-year renewal options, is best for a starting lawyer. You can stay or move after one or two years' experience.

11. Minimum maintenance such as trash removal, carpet maintenance, etc., and frequency of maintenance (daily, weekly, etc.).

12. Try to delay the effective date of start of rent for as long as possible in order to gain time for delivery of furniture, announcement printing and addressing, etc.

Practicing in a Law Suite

The law suite may be the best way for the solo practitioner or small firm (up to five or six attorneys) to reduce occupancy costs in order to cope with inflation.

By definition, a law suite is a large office where many different attorneys practice. These attorneys may be sole practitioners or they may be small firms, but they are not the tenants of the owner of the building. They are subtenants or licensees of the tenant and they share the cost of reception, conference rooms, library, and common areas through their rent charges.

I must confess that for many years I was opposed to the concept of a law suite. I valued total privacy and possession of my own library, my own receptionist who knew all my clients by name, my own reception room, my own photocopy machine, etc. Times have changed and I have changed with them. Those luxuries were worthwhile when office rents were low and could be planned without cost-of-living increases. Today they are unwarranted luxuries. Inflation in the costs of operating law offices—especially rent, salaries, and library costs—have caused me to change my opinion. I now strongly support the concept of the law suite as a vital tool in reducing costs. I especially recommend the law suite for the attorney starting a practice alone or with a partnership.

It is only common sense that if 25 lawyers share the cost of a receptionist or photocopy machine or library, the cost would be less than 25 attorneys each paying for a receptionist and photocopy machine or library. If the cost of a receptionist increases by $100 due to inflation, it could cost a sole practitioner $100 more to have his or her own receptionist, but only $4 more if there were 25 attorneys sharing the burden of the increase.

In accounting terms, a law suite allows individual lawyers or groups of lawyers to amortize fixed costs over a greater amount of production.

A lawyer who occupies a 225-square-foot office (15×15) in a traditional law office arrangement will need an additional 225 to 425 square feet for secretarial area, library area, reception area, photocopy area, hallways, employees' lounge, conference room and other common areas. The law suite reduces the "common area" by spreading the costs over a large number of attorneys. The additional space drops down in amount to 125 square feet per attorney.

A law suite gives the attorney a flexibility unattainable in the traditional landlord/tenant relationship because the attorney can take additional offices or space in the suite (as available) for associates, partners, paralegals, etc. The attorney can also leave or reduce the amount of space occupied by simply giving a 30-day notice, without having to find a subtenant or worry about a lease liability or liability on library contents, etc.

As an additional benefit, you may get some overflow work or other referral work from other attorneys in the suite. Alternatively, you can refer work to the other attorneys and maintain continuing contact with both the client and the attorney in order to receive forwarding fees (as allowed by the rules of your jurisdiction).

For the new lawyer it is important to be near other lawyers who can help with advice on how to handle new cases or clients that the new lawyer is encountering for the first time. The more experienced lawyers will also be a good source of current information on fee charging and other information. This is always helpful for all lawyers but especially helpful for new lawyers.

Advantages

To recap, the principal advantages of a law suite are:

1. A greatly reduced monthly occupancy expense due to sharing of common expenses.

2. Flexibility to move out (on 30 days notice in most cases) if you find a "better deal" or want to move into another law office.

3. Flexibility to expand within the suite.

4. A known, fixed, monthly occupancy expense subject to your contract.

5. Relief from the administrative problems of maintaining a library, hiring a receptionist, negotiating lease clauses, etc.

6. Close-by temporary secretaries and word processors available on an "as needed" basis.

7. Access to other lawyers for their help in case handling or fee setting in new matters.

8. The possibility of some overflow work and fee sharing.

Disadvantages

There are some disadvantages to law suite practices, but they are relatively minor. They should, however, be noted.

1. Inconsistency of practice mix. Another lawyer in the suite may have a PI or workers' compensation, mill-type of practice. There may consistently be mobs of people in the reception room in factory clothes with their kids because they can't afford a baby-sitter. Your tax and corporate clients may wonder what kind of practice you really have and they may feel uncomfortable in the reception room. Your clients won't be able to distinguish that these people are not clients of your firm or of you. (The reverse may also be true; i.e., your PI and workers' comp clients may feel uncomfortable with the tax and corporate clients.)

2. Receptionist indifference. The receptionist probably won't be able to offer your clients any special welcome or treatment to make them feel comfortable. The receptionist won't bring coffee, soft drinks, etc., out to your client. If your clients or any attorneys waiting to see you want to call their office, count on the receptionist coldly informing them that there are no phones available to them.

3. Access to offices at night and on weekends and holidays may be a problem due to lack of air conditioning or security procedures. This is a problem with all law offices, not just suites.

4. Books missing from the library when you need them will, from time to time, be a problem, but no more or less than the same problem in a large law firm.

5. The interior walls and hallways are bare of decoration, creating a hotel hallway feeling when going from the reception room to the individual lawyer's office.

Paul Fegen (pronounced FEE-jin) is the pioneer in the concept of the law suite. It is to his credit that the law suite is also known as the *Fegen Suite*. Paul and I are contemporaries. I have known him since he first began his concept in Beverly Hills, California, where his headquarters are now located. His company, Attorneys Office Management, Inc., now rents to thousands of attorneys throughout the United States. I would recommend that any attorney considering the opening or the relocation of offices contact Paul before making a move. By visiting a Fegen Suite and getting prices you'll have a rough idea of how low your cost per attorney for occupancy can be.

Practicing from Your Home

Until recently, I have always been opposed to practicing law from your home. I have always advised new lawyers to defer starting their practice until they can get into an office somewhere. Notwithstanding my opposition to practicing from the home, more and more lawyers are, in fact, practicing from their homes. Typically, they practice from their home for a variety of reasons including child-care or elder-care responsibility. Sometimes they just cannot get the money together to get a minimum amount of furniture, first and last month's rent, and telephone costs. Some lawyers simply want to practice out of their homes because of the life style they have chosen, such as practicing in remote mountain or rural areas where there really is no meaningful "downtown." Some lawyers want to be home with their children to share the "growing-up years."

Because of the advent of technology and the personal computer, I have softened and indeed almost dropped my opposition to practicing from the home based on competency and ability to deliver quality legal services. The PC and other office technology gives "David" a bigger and better "slingshot" in the fight against "Goliath." Some have called the PC and modem "The Great Equalizer." Many new lawyers are perfectly comfortable practicing with personal computers. With a PC and a modem a lawyer practicing from the home can have the same research and library resources as the largest firm in the state. With good software packages and a good printer a lawyer operating from the home can turn out the same high-quality documents, pleadings, correspondence, etc., as the big firms. Facsimile equipment makes it possible to transmit documents by telephone line more easily than the larger firms can transmit documents using their messenger services and couriers. The facsimile renders it much less important to be near multiple mail pick-up and deliveries. OCR (Optical character reader) scanners reduce the amount of skilled word processing labor necessary to input data into form files. Automatic dialing telephones make it easier to get hold of another lawyer to exchange ideas on the best way to handle a case or problem. Conference telephone calls reduce the number of face-to-face meetings required to properly represent a client.

In other words, by making full use of computers and modern technology and equipment one can now practice from the home and deliver a competent quality legal product almost equivalent to the product delivered by the largest firms. Accordingly, I am more satisfied that clients can now receive competent legal care from lawyers who practice out of their homes.

My principal remaining objections relate to the circumstances of the attorney-client relationships. How does a client react to the following:

1. A child answers the telephone;
2. A client hears toilets flushing;
3. A client hears radios, televisions, family arguments, or children fighting;
4. A client smells cooking;
5. A client uses a toilet and sees the lawyer's personal toiletries;
6. Children, parents, spouse or a pet walk into a conference;
7. You get up and leave a conference to answer a door for mail or a delivery service or a neighborhood child who wants to play with your child.

Many lawyers who do practice out of their homes tell me that some clients think that the lawyer is practicing law as a hobby and they do not take the lawyer or the lawyer's invoices seriously. Sometimes clients think the lawyers do not "need" the fee income because the client does not see the trappings of overhead.

The lawyer who practices out of the home has to be imaginative. Some suggestions are:

1. Meet clients out of the office whenever possible. Breakfast meetings are good. Use the attorney conference rooms at the courthouse or at the law library or the city hall or other government buildings. Ask another lawyer if you can use their conference room or library.

2. Do not volunteer that you practice from your home, but do not lie about it either.

3. Tell people that you have your office in your home for several reasons, including your being more available to your clients in the evening or on weekends when office buildings have no air conditioning, and being more available to share your child's development (if applicable).

4. Have a separate business-like office in which to meet your clients; have lots of law books and law journals in evidence to keep reminding the client they are in a law office.

5. Be sure your office in the home is soundproofed from other house or neighborhood sounds.

6. Do not let children answer telephones or come into the office area or answer the door.

7. When you are with a client or out of the office be sure your telephones are covered by an answering machine or your secretary, or an adult trained in telephone reception.

8. Have someone available to answer the door when you are with a client.

In most cases, practicing from the home seems to be a temporary or transition phase in starting a practice. Most of the lawyers whom I have met who practice from their homes would rather practice from an outside office and most intend to do so when they can. Often, lawyers who practice from their homes just feel isolated from the mainstream of the professional community and business life and for that reason move their office from their home to an outside office as soon as they can. Many lawyers who practice out of their homes miss the nearby presence of another lawyer to discuss cases and problems for a "backup" or second opinion.

In summary, I have somewhat lessened my opposition to practicing from the home, when there are compelling reasons to do so. I now believe that a lawyer practicing from the home using modern technology can deliver a competent product. I am still greatly concerned by the attitude or reaction or expectations of clients who use lawyers practicing from the home, and I am concerned as to whether lawyers who practice from their homes are truly finding professional satisfaction from their work. Perhaps we will have some accurate data in the not-too-distant future.

Part III
Getting Equipped

How Much Cash Do You Need to Start Your Practice?

Regardless of inflation, recession, boom or depression, the answer to this question remains the same: You need enough cash (or guaranteed income) to support yourself and your family for one year. In other words, assume that even though your practice grows, you will not be able to take any cash out for one year.

You should plan to have some combination of the following:

1. One year's living expenses in a savings account.

2. A working spouse with enough income to support the family for a year.

3. A bank loan of the funds to live on for a year. (This will be almost impossible to get from a bank unless you have the right co-signer or guarantor.)

4. A wealthy parent, in-law or other relative to either:
   a. lend you the money or
   b. give you the money or
   c. guarantee your bank loan.

In addition to the funds for living expenses, you will need money to buy and pay for the following:

1. Announcements, stationery, calling cards, postage, etc.

2. First and last month's rent (possibly, you will need first and last two months' rent).

3. Down payment on modest desk, chair, two or three client chairs and some modest decorating of your office.

4. Initial payment to telephone company for equipment, line charges, directory listings, etc.

5. Malpractice insurance.

6. Used typewriter, or PC with word processing package and printer.

I cannot emphasize strongly enough the necessity of starting with adequate capitalization for your living expenses. It is theoretically possible that you will be able to take cash out from your practice in six to nine months, but an error in calculation here can be fatal. Do not plan for only six or nine months in living expenses. It won't be enough. You'll be forced to leave your practice and get some kind of job to help support your family and this will be the death knell of your practice.

If you can keep your doors open for a year, you'll probably make it, as you'll have a backlog of receivables and work-in-progress that will start producing a steady cash flow. On the other hand, if you go under after six months, you'll take clients with you, and these are the clients who would otherwise have been the foundation of your practice's growth, if you had been adequately financed.

If you open your doors, then close your doors, then open your doors again, you won't get the same clients the second time around. They will remember that you didn't make it the first time and will be afraid to trust you the second time. You will have doomed yourself to perpetual failure with your first failure.

Lawyers have gone under the first time and somehow made it the second time, but this is a rarity. The lawyer who couldn't successfully start a practice the first time probably won't be successful the second time.

Do not neglect your student loan obligations. Try to extend or defer your repayment schedule if you can. In at least one state, being in default on your student loan(s) is considered grounds to prevent you from being admitted to practice.

If I had to choose between opening my doors immediately with only six months' living expenses, or working as a laborer for two years to have enough living expenses for a year, I would choose the latter course of conduct. As a matter of fact, I worked for accountants and as a cab driver to accumulate funds. I also had a working wife, which made it possible to save cash to start the practice.

Even though you are able to make money in your practice right away, this doesn't mean you can withdraw it. You will need cash for many purposes, including:

1. Investigators' fees for personal injury cases.
2. Court filing fees to commence litigation. Even though you may earn a large fee ultimately from a probate or divorce or personal

injury matter, the fee will be received one or two years from the time you get the case started, and you need the filing fees immediately.

3. Law books are exceedingly expensive, as you will soon find out. (See the chapter on "How to Buy Law Books.") There is no end to how much money you can spend on the bottomless pit called a law library.

It is difficult enough to succeed when you are adequately financed. It is almost impossible when you are inadequately financed.

How to Get a Rich Relative or Friend to Finance Your Start-up Costs by Offering Tax Advantages

It's hard to swallow your pride to ask a relative to lend you money for your furniture and equipment. It's no pleasure to ask a relative to guarantee a bank loan for you.

Frankly, the relative may wish to follow Polonius' well-known advice, "Neither a borrower nor a lender be." Additionally, the relative may have serious doubts about your ability to repay the loan or the bank. (You also may have these doubts.)

One way to entice your rich relative or friend to help you is to offer tax advantages as follows:

1. You select the furniture and equipment you want. List the price and where the equipment can be obtained. (You are doing the legwork.)

2. Give your list to your friend or relative.

3. Have your friend or relative buy the equipment in *their name* and deliver it to you.

4. Have your friend or relative lease the equipment to you. (You draft the lease.)

5. Your relative or friend gets the following tax advantages:

  a. Investment credit tax benefits (if the credit is reestablished).

  b. Depreciation expense benefits (technically, cost recovery).

  c. The interest deduction if he or she borrows the money from a bank.

  d. The ability to claim that they are in the equipment leasing business in order to deduct appropriate expenses for use of home as office; telephone expenses; auto expenses; other appropriate expenses. (The amount of these expenses to the extent they are appropriate may or may not be worth the bookkeeping and calculation time.)

e. Assuming both you and the relatives are cash-basis taxpayers (you probably are), the equipment should be acquired and put into use as close as possible to December 31st and the first payment of rent by you should be some time in the following year. Under current tax law your relative gets 100 percent of the investment credit and 6 months depreciation (cost recovery) in the first year, with the rental income starting the following tax year.

You will get the appropriate experience in drafting an equipment lease and become an instant expert on the subject. Be sure to update the current tax law on such areas as:

(1) Length of lease relative to equipment life (for investment credit and depreciation purposes).

(2) Payment of 15 percent or whatever the then current tax law is for operating expenses.

(3) Complying with UCC filing requirements as appropriate in your jurisdiction to protect the relative if things go downhill.

(4) Getting a *dba* or fictitious name for the leasing company.

(5) Deciding whether to expand the indicia of an active business for the leasing company with city license, sales tax number, personal property tax registration, separate employee identification number, etc.

(6) Whatever you as a lawyer would do in advising a third-party client on such a transaction.

As a new lawyer you do not need deductions. They would be wasted. On the other hand, your friend or relative will get immediate tax benefits for helping you.

Checklists of Needs for New Law Office

Get Telephones Ready

1. Estimate number and kind of instruments needed, as well as number of lines needed by meeting with phone company marketing representative.

2. Order equipment (may be delay of 2 to 6 weeks).

3. Order installation date (may require 2 or 3 days to complete installation).

4. Get telephone number reserved in advance of opening office, so you can give it to printer for announcements, cards, and stationery before opening the office.

5. Consider microwave transmission subscription service if you will have a lot of long-distance calls.

6. Get directory publication dates for outlying or other directory listings.

7. Consider yellow page advertising.

8. Try to get low cash deposit on telephone equipment.

9. Get an answering service used by other lawyers or by doctors.

10. Don't forget eventual secretary, receptionist, and client usage of your telephone.

11. Consider getting a cable address (or telex if you can afford it), if you want to attract international clients.

12. Get separate dedicated lines for your fax machine and/or modem, or get switching devices.

Order Furnishings

1. Determine if major items can be rented instead of being purchased.

2. Determine if used furnishings are available (should be about 60% of new furnishing price).

3. Read ads in local legal newspapers for used furnishings.

4. Minimum furniture for office:
   a. Picture of spouse and children for desk;
   b. Lawyer's desk—at least 6 feet wide with overhang in front and treated to protect against scratches and spills;
   c. One "judge's" chair for you. Try it out next to the desk you have selected;
   d. Two to four straight-back chairs for clients;
   e. Wastebasket to match desk;
   f. Clear floor pad for chair if office is carpeted—don't skimp on pad size, or chair will roll off edges;
   g. Floor lamp, if office is not light enough;
   h. Potted plant.

5. *Problem:* Remember that new furniture may take from two to six months to deliver.

6. Keep in mind that subletting an office from a law firm or other lessor may provide a completely furnished office.

7. Second telephone extension for client's usage in office.

8. Bookshelf for those books you need or want in your office.

9. Minimum furnishing for reception room:
   a. Four straight back chairs;
   b. Magazine rack or table;
   c. Reading light for magazines;
   d. Client telephone;
   e. Bookshelf for books;
   f. Coat rack and umbrella stand.

Order Equipment

1. Determine if secretarial service can provide you with dictating equipment as part of its service.

2. Determine if equipment can be rented rather than purchased.

3. Determine if used equipment is available (should be about 60% of new equipment price).

4. Read ads in legal and local papers for used equipment and for equipment specials.

5. Minimum equipment:
   a. Secretarial desk (with return for typewriter);

b. Secretarial chair (if possible, let secretary choose own chair);

c. Small copy machine, unless one is available nearby;

d. Dictating equipment—lawyer unit, transcription unit and two portable tape recorders, one for briefcase and one for car;

e. Typewriter—Buy a used electric typewriter immediately upon opening your office. A used one should cost 30 percent to 40 percent less than a new one. Be sure it has been kept under contract. It doesn't matter what brand or model you buy so long as it's the same typeface as that used by your outside secretarial service. In a rush situation you can make corrections to the work done by the secretarial service if you have the same type, and you can also bring a secretary into your office when necessary and you'll have a typewriter available. (Many new lawyers do their own typing.) During the first few months of my practice I sometimes brought the typewriter home at night and my wife typed my work to save costs of the secretarial service.

f. Word-processing equipment—This requires a whole treatise. Get help from secretaries, administrators, and other lawyers. Read ABA publications. Don't depend on vendors alone.

g. Accurate postage scale and postage meter. This will save you a considerable amount of money over the year.

h. Read my chapter on personal computers, word processing, and office technology later in this book.

Arrange for Supplies

Get some office supply catalogs from two or three nearby office supply stores. Open charge accounts with the stores. Ask for a discount from the list prices in the catalogs. Ask your secretary or another lawyer's secretary to make up an initial "order list" for you. In addition to stationery, equipment and furnishings, consider supplies such as staplers, paper clips, scissors, 2-hole punch, 3-hole punch, telephone message pads, rubber stamps and inking pads, scratch pads, legal pads, paper cutter, felt-tip markers, staple removers, Scotch® tape, desk calendars, pens and pencils, manila envelopes, Rolodex® files, coffee cups and equipment, check protector, fireproof safe for wills, documents, receivable records, etc.

Office Supplies and Procedures

Having good office supplies and procedures makes the practice of law more enjoyable and more profitable. It's frustrating when you are out of supplies or have the wrong supplies. At such times, your attention gets diverted from the client's legal problems to your own administrative problems, and you waste otherwise profitable time on minor administrative matters. Having good supplies and procedures is like having good health. When you have it, you don't think about it; when you don't have it, it's continually on your mind.

Attorney Jimmy Brill of Houston, Texas, one of the finest lawyers you will ever meet, has written a copyrighted article entitled "The Thrifty Fifty," which he also uses as the basis of a delightfully entertaining and informative speech by the same name. "The Thrifty Fifty" is a list of "Fifty time- and money saving ideas that you can begin to implement on Monday morning," to quote Jimmy.

I have heard Jimmy's seminar presentation many times and, like wine, it gets better with the aging. Jimmy's seminar inspired me to add this chapter for lawyers starting a law practice.

Parts of this chapter are based on Jimmy's seminar, modified by me to meet the special needs of a lawyer opening a practice for the first time. You should read this chapter in conjunction with the chapter that includes the checklist for opening your first law office.

Vendor Identification

In some cases you may not know of a source to get the supplies described in this chapter. I've identified some vendors for you with their principal city or phone number. I do not intend to recommend, and cannot vouch for, any of the vendors as being right for your practice and personality, or having better or worse products or services or prices than their competitors. This is a book on how to start a law practice and I'm simply trying to give you a starting point from which you eventually can develop your own sources. I encourage you or your secretary to shop around to find the supplies and procedures best for you.

1. You can buy a "canned" or prepackaged personnel testing kit that includes a dictation test cassette, interview forms, and evaluation forms for screening and testing secretaries, word processing operators, or people who need secretarial or word processing skills. For about $75, you will get enough materials to do about 25 applicant tests (Law Publications, Inc., Los Angeles). Their toll-free number is (800) 421–3173.

2. You can buy inexpensive prepackaged tests for clerical skills (The Psychological Corporation, New York) and general intelligence (Wonderlic & Associates, Northfield, Illinois) to use as hiring aids.

3. If you share a photocopier with other lawyers, there are devices and systems to control who uses the machine and to record usage by user, and in some cases by client. Ask the photocopy machine vendor for recommendations for your particular equipment.

4. Using dictation equipment properly greatly increases the efficiency and cost effectiveness of your office. Most of the equipment manufacturers (Sony, Lanier, Dictaphone, IBM, etc.) offer free-of-charge short guides on dictation procedure, or you can buy a book on effective dictation from the Association of Information Systems Professionals in Willow Park, Pennsylvania. If you want a free 15-minute circus act, ask the vendor to demonstrate all the things you can do with its equipment. You'll feel like you're watching the man demonstrating the vegetable slicer at the county fair—and you'll learn a few things as well.

Portable machines cost from one-half to one-fourth the price of a desktop model. I recommend using a lot of portables instead of buying desk models. You get much more for your dollar using a lot of machines even though the quality of a desktop model is slightly higher.

Don't be cheap by buying and using only a few dictating tapes. You should use a lot of tapes and dictate only one or two items on each one. By using multiple tapes, you can prioritize the transcription of the tapes rather than limit their transcription to the sequence dictated. You also can divide the work up among more than one word processor or secretary, and can use outside dictation services for tapes when you have insufficient in-house capacity. Long tapes can be debilitating psychologically to the transcriber in that they make the job to be done seem more burdensome than does a series of short tapes. Most inexpensive tapes are adequate for word processing dictation even if they are not of concert quality. Be sure to give complete instructions with the tape when you send it to be transcribed.

5. If you are going to use a typewriter as a word processor, be sure all of the typewriters in your office can type the same type styles to enable you to break up a long job with multiple typists. (The same rationale applies to fonts used for typewriters or word processing.)

6. If you are thinking of changing your word processing equipment, you should consider how you are going to get your existing forms and information from one system into the other. When the time comes, you may be able to use electronic disk converters or OCR scanners. The cost of outside disk conversion can be extremely expensive, ranging from $25 to $75 per disk.

7. Choosing the right software is covered extensively in the chapter on computers, but it is worth repeating that the American Bar Association maintains a Legal Technology Resource Center (LTRC) which tests software for ABA approval and distributes the results for review. Additionally, I highly recommend *LOCATE,* a monograph published and updated annually by the Section of Law Practice Management, which provides detailed and current information on software vendors and products for law office use.

8. I advocate using colored file folders and using them in numerical sequence (see my chapter on "Simple Filing Systems for the New Lawyer"). Some lawyers use colored file folders based on the substantive area of law; others use them based on the client.

9. Consider using different colors of paper stock for your photocopy machine (yellow copy to file, green copy to attorney file, blue copy for follow-up, canary for interoffice memos, pink for memos of phone conversations, etc.).

10. For opening a new file, you can design your own new file information form or contact Safeguard (Fort Washington, Pennsylvania), Lawdex (Minneapolis, Minnesota), Law Publications, Inc. (Los Angeles), or All-State Legal Supply (Mountainside, New Jersey) for their printed forms.

11. I do not care to use three-ring notebooks, but some lawyers use them for office files and in some cases for client files. Some trial

lawyers prefer these notebooks for case management. You may want to consider them, too.

12. Ask your stationery supplier to punch holes in your yellow legal pads and in the stationery or paper you use for file copies. Have the supplier punch two holes across the top for standard Acco fasteners for legal files and three holes along the side for three-ring notebooks. You can purchase your stationery from dealers who sell prepunched stationery as a standard catalog item, but any supplier should be able to punch your stationery supplies holes for you at little or no cost. Alternatively, you can buy a two-hole or three-hole punch and waste your time or a secretary's time needlessly punching holes in paper.

13. You can buy recycled cartridge ribbons for about one-half the cost of new ribbons. You also can get recharged and rebuilt cartridges for photocopy and fax machines at a much lower price than new ones. I personally have never used recycled or recharged supplies for fear of a malfunction damaging a machine or voiding a warranty or service policy. But if you are interested, look for ads in your legal paper or journals.

14. You can save stationery when replying to letters received by writing your response in the margin of the original, putting a sticker on it and returning it after making a photocopy for your files. You can get the stickers from Law Publications, Inc., Los Angeles, or other supply houses. I personally would restrict those stickers to situations where I felt the recipient would approve of this procedure. The stickers refer to the speed or convenience of returning the original document with a handwritten response. Sometimes when I receive these stickered responses, I am impressed that the other person is efficient and saves the client or customer money by reducing unnecessary expenses. At other times, I think the respondent can't afford good stationery or a secretary. It depends on how I feel that day.

15. Proper postage procedures and supplies can save you a lot of money over a period of years. Develop your own office postal manual and place it near the mailing area so temporaries and new hires will be able to get the mail out properly.

16. Remember that the second ounce and subsequent ounces cost less than the first ounce for first-class postage. For example, a first-class letter (1991) costs 29 cents for the first ounce but only 23 cents for the second ounce, which means that two ounces costs 52 cents, not 58 cents. You can't use the transitional stamps A, B, C, D, E, F, etc., for international postage.

17. By putting the magic words "Address Correction and Forwarding Requested" on your outgoing mail, the post office will deliver your letter to the addressee and notify you if there is a new address. If you ask only for address correction, you get the new address when they return your letter to you undelivered. It costs only about 30 cents for each such change to keep your mailing lists updated. Put those words on your invoice envelopes and on your "Season's Greetings" mailings.

18. When you send mail, be sure to give the complete address, including the suite number. When mail was addressed to me at 8500 Wilshire Boulevard without a suite number, the postal service often returned it to the sender for incomplete address, even though I had been in this ten-story building for eight years. I encountered a similar problem with my returned outgoing mail. When I moved from the tenth floor to the ninth floor of the same building, the post office returned all mail to senders that was addressed to me at my former location on the tenth floor, even though I had filed a change of address and the same mailman delivered to both floors.

The problem of letter carriers refusing to deliver your mail without a current suite number can prejudice your clients' substantive legal rights seriously if notices are effective when sent.

It seems to me that the U.S. Postal Service has seriously deteriorated at a time when the service and reliability of competitors such as private couriers and fax has greatly improved.

Using a post office box can reduce problems with incoming and returned mail if a post office is convenient to you. You also can get your mail on weekends and evenings with a post office box. Be aware that if you send a letter with both a post office box and street address, the post office will deliver it to the first one you list as the address.

19. Use airmail stickers, stamps, and envelopes. All first-class mail in the U.S. goes by airmail, whether or not you print "airmail" on it. International mail goes by boat unless you mark it "airmail." You can put on all the postage in the world and the letter will go by boat, and train, and mule unless you specify "airmail" on the letter.

20. Express Mail is an overnight service provided by the U.S. Postal Service and is cheaper than couriers (DHL, Federal Express, Purolater, UPS, etc.). It costs about one-half the others' prices. I personally have had very bad results with Postal Service Express Mail. (They lost all of the printed briefs marked for filing with the U.S. Supreme Court. This cost me the time of making a motion and get-

ting new printing done, etc. To add insult to injury, they had no record of what happened to the originals because they didn't make or keep any records of mail going to agencies of the U.S. Government.) I've had fantastically good results domestically with Federal Express and internationally with DHL.

21. Buy preprinted, postage-paid envelopes. If you do not mind waiting a long time (six weeks to two or three months) for delivery, the U.S. Postal Service sells envelopes with both your return address and postage printed on the envelopes. These preprinted envelopes cost you one-third to 40 percent of the cost of getting the same printing done by a print shop. They are great for paying bills and sending invoices. Do not forget to add "Address Correction and Forwarding Requested" on the printing order.

22. Be sure your oversized envelopes have green diamond borders and the words "First Class" printed on the front and back or the post office may treat the letter as a "flat" and deliver the mail with the same priority as bulk-rate advertising.

23. Next to the paper clip, "Post-it™" note pads are the office supply product I most wish I had invented. You can get them printed if you wish with messages, designs, logos, forms, etc.

24. There are at least 20 newsletters and magazines relevant to office management. If you want to start with one magazine, I'd suggest *Law Practice Management,* the LPM Section publication, followed by your state bar economics publications. The others are good, but there is a limit to how much a new lawyer has time to read. If you have delegated office management to a nonlawyer, this individual can join the LPM Section as an associate member and receive *Law Practice Management.* The nonlawyer also should consider joining the Association of Legal Administrators in order to receive its publications. (If you can afford it, you should pay for the nonlawyer's dues.)

25. As noted earlier, Jimmy Brill's seminar inspired me to write this chapter. Jimmy has a printed speech outline of "The Thrifty Fifty" that covers many items not covered in this chapter. You can get Jimmy's entire outline for $8 to cover copy and postage costs by writing to him at P.O. Box 22870, Houston, Texas 77227.

26. Almost all office supply stores have a catalog with list prices in it. There also are several companies that publish catalogs and sell by mail through toll-free numbers. You should get on the mailing list of five or six of these companies and spend a few minutes to flip

through the catalogs to look for new products that can help you. You'll be able to keep up on what's new with a minimum investment of time and no money. If you routinely trash catalogs without skimming through them, you deprive yourself of good information on what's new.

When you are ready to order, compare prices among the catalogs and then ask for your discount. Local catalog list prices are just that—list prices. Discounts run from 10 to 40 percent off that price, depending upon how badly the store wants or needs your business. If you can pay by credit card and also get a cash discount, you may find it both profitable and convenient to do so.

Some catalog companies are:

Stuart F. Cooper Co., Los Angeles
(800) 421–8703

The Drawing Board, Dallas
(800) 527–9530

Law Publications, Inc., Los Angeles
(800) 421–3173

The Reliable Corporation, Chicago
(800) 621–4344

New England Business Service
(800) 225–6380

27. You'll soon learn that time devoted to increasing revenues usually is better spent than time devoted to reducing expenses. On the other hand, that's no reason to ignore expenses or to needlessly waste money. Don't forget that running out of supplies interrupts your ability to generate revenue when you "stop everything" because you've run out of stationery, envelopes, or photocopying machine toner. To avoid this, you, your secretary, or office manager should keep an updated file card for each item of office supplies, indicating cheapest source, fastest source, minimum order vendor will handle, prices (including quantity discounts), and time necessary to fill the order. You should predetermine reorder levels for supplies and inventory your supplies at least monthly. In time, you'll develop your own sources and your own procedures.

Personal Computers, Word Processing, and Office Technology

The typewriter, telephone, dictating machine, photocopier, and facsimile (fax) equipment, have each, in their own time and place, radically affected the way lawyers practice law. Now, the personal computer ("PC"), with a modem and software, has created momentous changes in the way information can be transmitted, stored, and used. The PC and other new technology have caused a renaissance in the methodology of delivery of legal services. We lawyers are using the computer for communication and computation in ways that were considered science fiction only a few years ago. The utilization of advanced technology has enabled us to create a new "golden age" in the delivery of legal services.

In this chapter, I've deviated from my normal writing style of delivering information in "bite-size" quantities. This chapter combines information on computers, word processing, and office technology in general. In addition to describing what is used in a law office, I'm also describing how it is used, what it costs, and how to buy it.

Different readers will have varying levels of expertise in each of these areas. Some will be technology experts or computer "hackers"; others will be computer-phobic or have no idea of what a law office really needs in the way of office technology.

Rather than breaking this chapter into many smaller chapters based on levels of sophistication in each area, as I've tended to do with other subjects in this book, I've put all this information into one larger chapter. I leave it to you, based on your personal level of expertise and experience, to skim a section or to study it slowly.

If you already own and/or can use a PC, you're a long way toward where you need to be. If you don't already own a PC, don't know how to operate one, or are still at the "computer phobia" stage, you should overcome these obstacles. As a beginning, you might start mingling with PC users or join a user group. If you don't have the time or inclination yourself, you must hire people who already have mastered the PC. You must be familiar with the PC and its applications to remain competitive with lawyers who do, and to be able to provide a high level of legal services to your clients.

I'm not a computer or technology expert. I can help you by explaining what you can do with a PC or other equipment and can give you some assistance on how to go about it. I'm the first to admit, however, that I haven't the foggiest idea about the engineering of how or why computers or other equipment do what they do. I can set my wristwatch alarm, but I can't repair a watch.

Why would you want to have a PC as the central point in your law office? Just about anything you do with a computer can be done without a computer, but with a computer you get the job done faster, cheaper, and more accurately. You can cross the continent by flying in an airplane or by driving a wagon and team of oxen. You'll probably get there either way. It's just a question of the time, money and effort needed to accomplish the feat.

Basic Rules for Acquiring Computer Equipment and Office Technology

Before launching into specific uses, I'd like to pass on some general advice on acquiring office equipment, based upon my managing my own practice. These basic rules will assist you not only in opening your first office, but also in managing your practice your entire professional life.

Ask Around

Try to avoid reinventing the wheel. As with other areas of law office management, some other lawyer somewhere has already faced and solved the problems you now are facing. Ask around and locate that lawyer.

Before you spend a huge amount of time talking to vendors and waste a lot of money buying things that won't work for you, see if you can find someone else's solution to copy and use for yourself. Get about two years' back issues of *Law Practice Management* (titled *Legal Economics* before 1990), the periodical of the Section of Law

Practice Management. Also, get about two years' back issues of the *Lawyer's PC, ABA Journal*, and *Law Office Economics and Management*. Get the current issue of the ABA/LPM's publications catalog. Other publications, such as the *National Law Journal* and state and local bar journals also can be helpful.

Read the articles written by lawyers on computer applications you're interested in. Scan the ads to see what vendors claim can be done. The few hours invested in reading these materials will save you many hours in wasted time meeting with vendors. I would estimate that you'll need 10 to 20 hours to do the above research, which could save you thousands of dollars avoiding mistakes. In addition, using office technology you will earn tens or hundreds of thousands of dollars over the years through increased productivity. By reading the articles and the ads, you may find exactly what you're looking for, and you'll get some new ideas, as well. If you're really ambitious, you can go to the quarterly Law Office Information Service (LOIS) indexes and find every article ever published on the subject you're interested in.

LOCATE, a software directory updated and published annually by the Section of Law Practice Management, is essential to review before you spend your money on software. It lists hundreds of vendors of software, including service bureaus and time-sharing.

Many state and local bar associations now have an office management advisory service, available on call with a toll-free telephone number. The Florida, New Jersey, and Colorado bars, among others, maintain this service.

In general, when you start doing your research, give more weight to articles written by practicing lawyers, law firm administrators, or others who themselves have recently practiced law than to consultants, who often may not understand the dynamics of attorney-client relationships or attorney-staff relationships. Some consultants want you to modify the way you practice law to conform to their engineering and accounting precepts. A great deal of what consultants and vendors do is geared to the big firm, big consulting fee situation rather than toward the solo practitioner, small firm, or young attorney starting a firm. This is, of course, a generalization, but in my opinion practicing lawyers best understand the problems of practicing lawyers and can better advise other lawyers on how to solve a problem after having successfully solved similar problems themselves. A lawyer writing an article is usually motivated to help other lawyers by sharing information on what he or she did to solve a problem. A nonlawyer consultant, on the other hand, often writes an article as part of a public relations campaign to get business, and may make promises that are neither realistic nor cost-effective for your particular firm. The ABA/LPM Section's many computer-related Interest Groups have many attorney members who provide help based on "hands-on" situations.

I do not wish to imply that one should never use outside consultants who have not practiced law, but I do feel that the best starting point for a new lawyer is information produced by lawyers who have had to live with their successes and failures.

Don't Wait—Begin

"If it works—it's obsolete." At one time lawyers measured the "useful life" of their equipment at 10 to 15 years for desks, typewriters, etc. (Oversimplified, "useful life" refers to how long you'll be able to use something before it becomes physically worn out or so technologically obsolete as to require replacement.) With the advent of accelerated depreciation for tax purposes, useful life was cut back to 5 to 10 years. Today's high-technology equipment such as computers and software are estimated to have a 30- to 36-month life. Accordingly, when a piece of equipment has been on the market a year or so and has gotten a reputation for being useful, there'll be something newer and better along in about one year.

No matter what you buy, someone will come along and say that some other company has a newer, faster, or cheaper item than the one you just bought. Don't be upset or overly concerned. No matter where or when you acquire your equipment or software, there will soon be something better, faster, or cheaper. No matter when you buy, you'll soon have obsolete equipment. Don't wait forever to take the plunge. If you pick good equipment and a good system, the vendor will update it for many years. Vendors want to sell you something new, so eventually they do stop updating older equipment and software. Make your decisions on today's prices and availability rather than waiting for the next generation of technology or lower prices.

Follow-Up on References, Support, and Warranties

Ask vendors for the names of lawyers in your community who have bought their products. Ask those lawyers if they're happy with the purchase and whether they'd recommend it to you. Lawyers generally will be helpful to, and honest with, other lawyers.

Find out what kind of vendor support you can expect after you buy the product or service. Do they have a toll-free telephone number with someone on line to help you, or will you have to wait hours or days or until after the weekend for a service person to call you to set up an appointment? Is their support facility available during your time-zone requirement? Is there loaner equipment available for you while yours is being serviced?

Don't accept delivery until you're ready to use the equipment. Most equipment has a 90-day parts and labor warranty. There's no point in letting equipment sit in a box unused while the warranty is expiring.

Find out what choices you have concerning service or maintenance contracts. Does the company do its own servicing or does it farm it out to some company that will service your high-tech equipment along with washing machines, water heaters, carburetors, and cheese cutters?

A choice of post-warranty policies may be available to you. Often, there is a reduced-price service contract if you bring the equipment to the dealer or company for repair rather than require the service person to come to your office. Is that service facility nearby?

Ask if you can get a guarantee of trade-in value if the equipment is no longer sold or supported by the vendor.

Stick with brand-name merchandise unless you really know what you are doing. You can waste a lot of time and money trying to correct mistakes and make minor adjustments to get your equipment working. You may have to call in outside people or services to start up the equipment. It can cost you more to get the equipment going than you saved on the price of it. Sometimes clones of brand-name equipment do not accept all the programs or instructions that the original would accept. Buying by mail order can be a big mistake if you buy something you're not familiar with. If the equipment doesn't work properly, you won't know if it is defective or if you just haven't learned how to use it correctly.

Don't Forget to Charge Your Clients for Your Equipment and Technology

If a piece of equipment costs $10,000, the maintenance is $2,000 per year, the equipment lasts 2½ years and will be used four hours per day, be sure to add $6 per hour to the operator's time when you bill your client. ($10,000 + $5,000 = $15,000 cost. Two and one-half years = 125 weeks × 5 days × 4 hours = 2,500 hours usage. $15,000 ÷ 2,500 hours = $6 per hour.) You should add at least this $6 cost figure to the hourly rate charged for the operator.

Use existing equipment and technology as long as it gets the job done for you in an acceptable manner. Don't abandon what you have for something new unless you really need the new product.

Buying Used or Obsolete Equipment

You can save a lot of hard-to-come-by cash by buying used equipment, if you are careful and know what you are doing. You also can make some disastrous mistakes. These suggestions will help you.

1. Try to buy equipment that has been, and still is, under service contract. Equipment that has been under service contract is normally in pretty good condition.

2. Be sure you still can get a service contract for the equipment after you buy it. I've heard of vendors or maintenance companies that service equipment only as long as it's owned by the original buyer.

3. Be sure you can get all of the manuals and or instructions (including tutorials) from the seller or from the company. Without the manuals, you'll waste a lot of time trying to figure out how to make the equipment do a particular task.

4. Find what it will cost to protect your investment in used equipment when you want to upgrade. For example, you may get a fantastic buy on obsolete word processing equipment that works perfectly. You will be proud of the money you've saved until you learn it will cost a fortune to get all of your forms and product and records into the format required for the next-generation equipment. Worse yet, you may find out there is no way to convert or upgrade your system, and you'll have to start all over again or pay a fortune for someone to transfer disks from one format to another.

I was shocked to find that my IBM Display Writer disks were useless in terms of using them for an IBM PC with printer and software package. (One solution to this problem is to print the documents you want to keep onto hard copy and then to feed the hard copy into an optical character reader (OCR) to get the document into the new system.) Accordingly, if I were to sell my old Display Writer system to you, you would buy the equipment at a fraction of the price of new equipment. The equipment would continue to work perfectly for you (under contract), but you would incur a lot of expense getting off Display Writer and onto a different system when you want to upgrade.

5. Do not buy a "boat anchor." Much of available used equipment is bulky, heavy, slow, and nonmaintainable under service contract. Its highest and best use would be as an anchor for a rowboat.

6. Ignore the original cost of used equipment when deciding what price to pay for it. Because of the rapid advance in technology and equally rapid price reductions, it is totally immaterial what someone originally paid for new equipment. What is material is what new, more modern equipment would cost in today's market.

7. Used equipment is great for backup and for expansion. If you have an equipment system that's old but still does the job, you should buy similar or identical used equipment as it becomes available. Since you already have that type of equipment, you can use the spare for backup when your regular equipment is down, for part-time people during busy periods, or for expansion when you add people. The price of used back-up equipment is usually cheap and will more than pay for itself in keeping your production up when your regular equipment is down.

8. You should understand that much used equipment cannot be upgraded to current levels of performance or technology. This is deliberate because the manufacturers want to sell you the new models rather than peripherals or conversions to upgrade old equipment. Although you won't be the first owner of the used equipment, you may be the last owner. Often, you can find a company other than the vendor or original manufacturer that sells the peripheral (or add-on equipment) or programs that the manufacturers won't sell to upgrade your equipment.

Miscellaneous Equipment

Stand-Alone Word Processors

A word processor is just a typewriter with a memory unit. The extent of the memory unit will depend on the equipment and may range from having the capacity to retain a few lines of type to having spelling checked and other features.

The debate over whether one should use a stand-alone dedicated word processor or a PC with a word processing package and printer is over. The PC has won the battle hands down. It is about as cheap to use a PC and printer as to use a stand-alone word processor, and you can do many things beyond word processing with a PC.

There are a few (very few) advantages to using a dedicated word processor, including:

1. They are much cheaper new.
2. They are very cheap used (because people are going to the PC with printer).
3. It is easier to find operators when you have a limited skilled secretarial pool available.

If you are really low on cash and have no choice, then go for the typewriter or stand-alone word processor.

Fax Equipment

Also called facsimile, telefacsimile or telecopier, this equipment allows you to transmit or receive documents through telephone lines from any place in the world to any place in the world. You can transmit a letter, diagram, or photo and receive a copy at the receiving end. Equipment with automatic features can send or receive at any time of the day or night, whether or not your equipment or the other person's equipment is attended. You don't have to rely on mails or messengers. You can get messages to or from your firm or client or the other lawyer instantly. Small machines are available that you can take with you when you travel. Your office can transmit your correspondence or documents from a file to you while you're on the road overnight or on a long trip. Some courts allow service of process by fax. I send all mail of up to ten pages first by fax, then by regular mail for backup.

I highly recommend that every lawyer have a fax machine. If you can't afford to buy one, ask a client or another lawyer if you can use theirs in an emergency. Buy the highest speed machine you can afford. Group III machines will usually communicate with most, if not all, other fax machines. Some Group I (now obsolete) or Group II machines cannot transmit to or receive from other machines. Used fax machines usually work very well because they sometimes have been used only a few minutes or hours a day to send and receive. If you read an article in a legal newspaper or receive an announcement about firms merging, call to see if one firm wants to sell its fax equipment. You should figure on a cost of between $1,000 to $2,000 for a new Group III fax machine. Some of the fax machines have built-in devices to record and report the charges for bills to clients. The three most important features a lawyer needs in a fax machine are (1) automatic receiving (the machine will receive when unattended), (2) Group III capability, and (3) a page cutter for incoming faxes.

I predict that the fax machine will have a greater impact than the photocopying machine on the way law is practiced in America.

Scanners

Scanners are also called optical character readers (OCRs) or optical scanners. A scanner is sort of a reverse photocopy machine. You put a sheet of paper into or under a scanner and the scanner "reads" what is typed or printed on the paper. It transfers that information into your computer (technically, it transfers the characters onto the medium) at about a page a minute, or faster.

An inexpensive scanner can cost $2,000 to $3,000 or less and can read most typewriter printing, allowing you to copy almost any legal document produced by another lawyer. Scanners costing $10,000 and up can read just about any print, including almost any form found in a form book.

In addition to the scanner, you must buy some peripheral equipment to integrate into your word processing system.

With a scanner, you can copy other lawyers' product into your system and then print it out on your own printer. This enables you, without keypunching, to use other lawyers' forms or the parts of them you like better than your own, or to use their forms in addition to yours. Scanners also are useful for copying the other lawyers' documents into your system so that you can print the final version of a document for your client to sign. This gives you control over the possibility of the other attorneys' "accidentally" omitting a word or phrase in a long document. (Incidentally, there are word processing packages such as CompareRite which will permit you to compare your copy of the document with that of the other attorney, and then will highlight discrepancies between the two documents.)

I once drafted four 75-page settlement agreements for four consolidated cases. The cases were similar yet differing from case to case, as were the settlement agreements. I took the documents to the other lawyer's office to negotiate various aspects of the agreements. While we were discussing the first agreement, his staff was feeding the other three agreements to the scanner(s), and then later they input the first agreement into his word processing system. We made the agreed-upon changes and I left his office with finalized documents produced by his word processors, having used my documents as the starting point.

Tax and court administrative forms also can be read into your word processing system without inputting by keyboard. The forms then can be filled in and printed out on your system.

Paper Shredders

I was shocked to learn that police agencies and private investigators routinely go through the garbage produced by lawyers to look for evidence or information that can be used against the lawyers' clients. It is my understanding that in most states no warrant is necessary to search a lawyer's trashed documents once they leave the lawyer's office. If the possibility of police agencies or your client's competitors or adversaries having access to your trashed documents concerns you, you should consider a paper shredder for use when appropriate. Proper document and file disposal procedures are part of a lawyer's ongoing obligation to maintain client confidences, even after the case is closed or the client no longer is a client.

Telephones

There is no limit to the number of features you can add onto a telephone system. You can have features such as redialing and music for callers on "hold" built into the instrument, and you can get features such as conference call capability from the phone company. The important features to you are the number of instruments and lines the system can handle. Leave room for future stations and lines. You cannot depend on being able to get additional equipment later on because companies quickly discontinue one line to start a newer line with more sophisticated technology and features.

A car phone allows you to return client calls and to be in touch with your office while commuting or going to and from court. I recommend them. Try to get a car speaker phone so you can keep your hands on the wheel while driving and talking.

Telephone Answering Machines

I am generally opposed to answering machines for after-office hours and prefer answering services with live operators who are trained to handle hysterical callers. If you *are* going to use an answering machine, there is a new feature available that I like. The new feature is called remote call transferring. When a caller leaves a message and hangs up, your answering machine dials your remote beeper, your remote home telephone, or any other number. You then call your own number to get the message that was left on the machine. This system can give you 24-hour availability and coverage using a machine.

Overcoming Computer Phobia

If you already are a hacker, skip this part and go on to the next one. If you are not a hacker (or don't even know what a hacker is), then continue reading.

If you have the ability to operate a car, you have the ability to operate a computer, but you first have to learn how. Just as you aren't born knowing how to drive a car, no one is born knowing how to use a PC. It takes a certain amount of time and practice.

If you are at the overcoming computer phobia stage, the atmosphere and circumstances at the place you take classes can have a significant effect on how quickly you learn to use a PC generally or learn to use a specific application, such as time billing and accounting or word processing.

It's important that you take your lessons with students of equal or lesser ability. If you progress at the same rate or faster than the others, you'll feel good. If you are significantly slower than the others, you'll feel foolish and give up. No one wants to appear slow or dense and if you feel "out of it," you'll probably quit the class.

After all, you went through high school, college, and law school with good grades because you were a fast learner. To appear to be a slow learner is a big blow to your ego. It's because of this fear of appearing slow that many lawyers prefer to learn in private using tutorials. These are software programs that interact with the students so that they advance at their own pace without others knowing how slow or fast they learn.

Try to find a class of students about your age. Learning speed is to some extent more a function of your generation than of your education. A person who has been playing video games at home since early childhood will learn to use a PC much more quickly than someone whose skills never got past the two-finger hunt and peck on a manual typewriter. If you are in a group significantly younger than you, you may get left behind quickly, become discouraged, and quit the class. In addition, if people in a computer class are from the same firm, the attorneys senior in age and experience may be ashamed if younger firm members outperform them.

Some experts feel the best way to learn is for two people of approximately equal age and position to sit side by side and share a computer. The two students encourage and help each other and are more apt to advance at the same speed.

If you want to learn to use the PC, look for classes sponsored by your local bar association. You also can call Bob Wilkins at RPW Learning Center in Lexington, South Carolina (803/359–9941), to get his recommendations.

PC Software for the Sole Practitioner or Small Law Firm

This information is fairly current as of 1991, which means you probably can use it for about three to five years, at which time some of the information may be obsolete in the sense that, although the software described will still do the job, there probably will be other better, faster, and cheaper packages available.

Throughout this section I'll cover the applications most important to a new practice or a newly started office. I will mention several different packages. It is not my intention to recommend any of them or to downgrade their competitors. I feel that by giving you the name of a system already used by lawyers, or which vendors claim will work for lawyers, I'll be helping you in two ways:

1. You'll have an idea of *what* can be done with a PC;

2. You'll have a starting point of at least one specific package that you can look at and with which you can compare others.

Some software is free or low cost and can be obtained by "downloading" bulletin board services. Other software packages can cost between $70 and $3,000. Most software that a new lawyer would want or need is in the $100 to $350 range.

Some lawyers have their own favorite software or hardware and will be concerned that I did not mention something important. If you feel I've neglected some system that's three times as good, four times faster, and one-tenth the cost of those I mention, you're right and I apologize in advance.

The Law Practice Management Section annually publishes a monograph called *LOCATE,* a directory of software available for law offices. *LOCATE* lists about 40 different areas of application and usually comes out in August of each year.

Word Processing

Choosing a word processing software package is very important because lawyers tend to stay with the first system they learn. The lawyer (or word processor) who becomes used to a system does not want to change, and compares all other packages to that one.

If a lawyer achieves success and comfort with a word processing system, the lawyer is more likely to go on to other PC software packages and systems. A bad result with word processing tends to make the lawyer hesitant to use a PC for new applications or to maximum advantage.

The Law Practice Management Section has Interest Groups organized by computer hardware and by software applications. It will take some time to find the users who can help you, but they will help you when you ask for help. Call (312) 988–5619 to get more information on how you can join Interest Groups.

WordPerfect is one of the most popular software packages currently used by lawyers. It is reported by the experts to be easy to learn and use. It has good support and does most of the things lawyers need from a word processing package, including (according to many lawyers) good document appearance, page and paragraph numbering and renumbering, underlining, title centering, spell checking, and automatic creation of tables of contents and/or index of words used. Microsoft Word also is a very popular software system used by lawyers, according to those who review software packages. WordStar and MultiMate also are used by lawyers. Other word processing packages which can be used with a PC include Displaywrite, Samna, Easy Writer II, and PC Writer.

The Law Practice Management Section's Word Processing Interest Group publishes its own publication, *Word Progress,* which keeps lawyers up to date on available packages and specific applications.

The ABA's Legal Technology Resource Center (LTRC), in conjunction with the IIT Center Software Testing Laboratory, provides evaluations of law office software. The ABA does not specifically recommend software for individual firms, but it does certify software that meets its rigid criteria. A telephone call to 312/988–5465 will get you further information.

CompareRite is a system that is supposed to eliminate or reduce the need for two people proofreading to compare documents. You can input by scanner or by keypunching (the fancy word for typing on a computer) your original document via an OCR scanner into your PC. CompareRite will highlight the differences between the two documents, giving you the equivalent of a blue line or red line version of the document and covering the possibility of the other lawyer's "inadvertently" forgetting to tell you about changes made in your document.

Spell Checking and Thesaurus

If you don't get a software package which contains spell checking, you can buy a spelling package very cheaply. Typically, the dictionary contains about 75,000 words. If a word in your document doesn't match up to a word in the list, the package highlights the differing word and gives you a choice of possible correct words. Some stand-alone word processors contain this feature. I strongly recommend this feature. It is especially important if you are going to rely on a high-school graduate secretary or word processing operator to do your post-graduate spelling.

Some software packages have a thesaurus. This package brings up synonyms to the screen to help you compose a letter or document when you can't find just the word you need.

Cite Checking

If your legal work includes a lot of law and motion or appellate work where you'll be citing a lot of cases, there are software packages that check cites against the Harvard Blue Book. CiteRite is a relatively well-known product.

Form Creation and Retrieval

When you input a form, you can retrieve it to use again when you need it. You can input your forms much the way you would on a typewriter, or you can input other lawyers' forms using a scanner. Wills, trusts, pleadings, discovery, and myriad commonly used forms can be created and stored in your PC on a disk unit ready to use.

The ABA/LPM Section publishes a *Model Partnership Agreement* for lawyers and *Law Office Staff Manual* on diskettes with accompanying text. Each of these provides you with a skeleton form to be tailored to your law partnership or policy and procedures.

Mailing Lists

You can use a PC to maintain your mailing lists for seasonal greeting cards, client newsletters, announcements, etc. All of the above can be done with your word processing functions.

Litigation Support

If you are fortunate enough as a new lawyer to get a big case, then litigation support systems using a PC, scanners, etc., may enable you to handle a case competently that you otherwise would have to refer to a larger firm. You can keep track of thousands of documents and be able to find what you need when you need it. You can project and calculate damages using a spreadsheet. You can analyze and organize a deposition with a PC by using key words and phrases.

Office Management

Your PC can be used to run your office. Some examples of what the PC can do for your office include:

1. *Calendar and Docket Control.* Your PC can be used to maintain a calendar to manage your office and docket controls. You can schedule appointments, court dates, conferences, depositions, etc., with reminders before the events take place and follow-up dates after they pass. You also can schedule birthday cards, anniversary cards, will revisions, reminders of lease renewals, reminders of directors' and shareholders' meetings, probate and trust accountings, tax returns, etc.

2. *Accounting and Billing Systems.* Many different accounting and billing systems are available. Some are ABA-certified (call ABA's Legal Technology Resource Center at (312) 988–5465 to get an up-to-date list of ABA-certified packages). Ask your CPA to suggest reports you need from the system.

3. *Time Recording.* Some lawyers recommend Timeslips III as an easy-to-learn way of keeping good time records for the purpose of preparing a bill to the client and reviewing the status of work in progress.

4. *Check Writing and General Ledger Accounting.* Some systems allow you to write checks and distribute the checks through the accounting system all the way to the general ledger.

5. *Electronic Mail (E-Mail).* This is an electronic mailbox system. Using your computer and modem, you can send a letter through

over a telephone line to another electronic mailbox. The letter is received at the mailbox the instant it's sent. You can check your mailbox for mail at any hour of the day or night from your computer and modem. The ABA maintains its own e-mail system on ABA/net. My own ABA/net I.D., for example, is ABA1428. Many lawyers use ABA/net to work from their homes.

6. *Telex, Fax, and MCI Mail.* These and similar communication systems are all accessible through your PC and modem.

7. *Conflicts.* You can use a PC to check every potential new client against every current and former client to find potential conflicts of interest.

8. *Telephone Directory and Dialing.* You can program a computer to look for a client's telephone number (after you've input it). You punch a key and the computer will dial the client's number through a modem.

Research and Databases

You would have to be living in a cave on a remote island not to know about LEXIS and WESTLAW and the research that now can be done on these two systems through your PC with a modem.

In addition to doing classic legal research, you also can reach about 95 percent of all the printed information that's been printed in the last decade. This information is in electronic databases which are accessible via a PC, modem, and software package. There are somewhere between 3,000 and 4,000 of these databases. These include newspapers, trade publications, technical journals, etc. You can find out every time your client or adversary has appeared in a press release or interview. You can check out witnesses, the judge, opposing counsel, nonlegal facts, etc., all through the PC. Lockheed (with its DIALOG) and Mead Data Central (the creators of LEXIS) are the biggest middlemen to accessing these databases. You normally would go to the middleman who goes to the database directly. There are hundreds of different vendors of database information accessible to lawyers, but DIALOG and LEXIS are the most commonly used by lawyers.

The ABA also maintains a database, AMBAR, which gives you access to ABA publications and products. AMBAR can be accessed through LEXIS or WESTLAW. Whole law libraries can fit on a few CD-ROM disks accessible from a PC. World Book Encyclopedia's

Information Finder™ fits on one CD-ROM disk. One 5″ CD-ROM holds 12,000 pages of information. This technology is still expensive and normally is not economical in a new law practice.

Bulletin Boards

With a PC, a modem, and a communications software package, you can sign on to a bulletin board. Computer hackers call the bulletin boards "BBSs," an acronym for "bulletin board systems." The person or company that sponsors or maintains the BBS is called the SYSOP (for system operator). Your computer dials a BBS telephone number through your modem and you "log on" to the board. The board subscribers typically are other lawyers who are willing to share what they do and what they know by making information available to other lawyers. The BBS is usually free (you must pay for the telephone call), but sometimes there is a nominal two- or three-dollar per month charge to defer expenses. There are an estimated 50 different BBSs in the U.S. for lawyers. Some are maintained by sharing, caring lawyers as a service to the profession. (Richard T. Rodgers of Campbell University School of Law is such a lawyer.) Others are sponsored by law book companies or law libraries.

Typically, the lawyers' bulletin boards share information on specific legal subjects. Rick Rodgers' BBS is called Frolic & Detour and contains hundreds of files that can be downloaded, as well as the North Carolina Supreme Court's new decisions. Rick's number is (919) 893–5206. The Law Practice Management Section periodically prints an updated list of BBSs in *Law Practice Management*.

Desktop Organizers

Lawyers often scribble time records and notes on random pieces of paper. A desktop organizer does all that through a keyboard without paper all over the desk. You simply input (type) the data you used to scribble, and it's in form for filing and bill preparation.

Spreadsheets

Among many things you can do with a spreadsheet is to set up your computer to accumulate data, organize it, and list it in any sequence you wish. You then can ask the computer what-if situations and the computer will give you the answer based on the way you set up the spreadsheet.

Substantive Law Systems

Starting with admiralty and administrative law and going alphabetically down to veterans' benefits, wills and workers' compensation, there are software packages designed for almost every area of law. Many continuing legal education suppliers sell software for substantive systems. Wills, corporations, bankruptcy, taxation, and litigation management commonly are available. There is more commercial software for federal practice areas than state practice areas because of the larger market. On the other hand, much of the information for state practice areas can be obtained for free or at low cost through BBSs.

Miscellaneous Computer Equipment

Computer Tables and Cabinets

Specialized furniture to accommodate a PC, manuals and peripherals is available.

Flat Wiring

If your landlord or contractor wants a lot of money to bring electrical or telephone wires in conduit through the roof, ask about flatwires for electricity and telephones that go under pressure-sensitive, easy-release carpet tiles.

Modem

The modem is the device that connects your PC to the telephone for both incoming and outgoing information. Modems typically transmit data at speeds ranging from 300 baud now obsolete), to 1,200 and 2,400 baud (now common), to 9,600 baud (still relatively rare).

Since you pay by the minute for telephone time and access time on databases, you want to be able to send or receive quickly. What you spend on a modem you'll usually save on time access charges. What would take four minutes of telephone access time to offload (copy from) a database with a 300-baud modem would take one minute with a 1,200 baud modem. (Some databases charge by the line instead of by time when you unload with a faster modem.) The most common modems are 1,200 baud and 2,400 baud, and these are recommended if you plan to send/receive large quantities of data via telephone lines. Some modems are external (they connect to the outside of the PC); others are internal and, accordingly, out of sight.

Printers

There are various types of printers available at prices ranging from a few hundred dollars to several thousand dollars. Laser printers are small desktop machines, and produce letter-quality documents that you can send to your clients and opposing counsel without embarrassment. You should use different stationery for laser printers. This type of stationery is called "low impact." In large volume reproduction, it is often cheaper but slower to use laser jet printers than to use photocopying machines.

Should Your Office
Furnishings Be Lavish?

Any ten lawyers are likely to have at least thirty opinions on this subject. Perhaps there is no answer. My advice is for you to do whatever makes you feel comfortable, and whatever you personally think your clients will like. I have been in offices of lawyers who make well into six figures a year. Some offices appear to be "Early Salvation Army," and others are garish with rare and expensive furniture and works of art. I have also seen the offices of lawyers who went under and found the same discrepancies. I therefore have come to the conclusion that your office furnishings will not determine your success or failure.

I will repeat here some "maxims" that I have heard over the years and leave it to you to make your own decision.

1. In a "neighborhood practice," heavy with divorce, criminal, and accident work, the prospective clients want a "successful" lawyer, and will be impressed by your success if you have garish, obviously expensive furnishings.

2. In a "neighborhood practice," heavy with divorce, criminal, and accident work, the prospective clients will be frightened away if they see expensive furnishings. They will be afraid of being charged high fees, knowing that in the final analysis, their fees pay for the furnishings.

3. Business executives don't want to pay for your unnecessary overhead. They know that the quality of the furnishings is unrelated to the quality of the legal services.

4. Business executives want a successful lawyer, and they will expect high fees when they see expensive offices.

There are many, many more "maxims." Frankly, I don't believe any of them. Do whatever makes you feel comfortable.

I do recommend, however, that during your early practice you avoid buying expensive furniture for a year or two. You can anticipate several office changes during your first few years, and a piece of furniture that fits perfectly in one office may not fit at all in your next office.

Also, give serious consideration to buying used furniture. Your local legal newspaper will have ads from lawyers who learned the hard way that they no longer need the furniture they bought.

I recommend the following furniture for your office:

1. Formica-top lawyer's desk, at least six feet. Be sure the desk has an overhang in front, so that your client can come up close to the desk without banging knees.

2. One judge's chair for you.

3. Two to four straight-back clients' chairs. Remember that clients who are old or who have injured bodies have difficulty getting out of soft chairs.

4. Wastebasket to match your desk.

5. Potted plant.

Don't buy items for your desk such as memo pads, ash trays, clip holders, pen sets, desk radios, etc. You will be deluged with gifts of these items from well-meaning friends and relatives.

Diplomas, Degrees, Admissions to Practice, Etc.

Your parents were very impressed with all of your certificates. Your clients won't be. They will assume that you have graduated from law school and are admitted to practice. It's not necessary to prove it to them or to reassure them. It may, however, be reassuring to you to put these on a wall in your office. If so, do the following:

1. Put them on a wall behind your desk. This will be close enough for the clients to see you have them, but far enough away that they can't see the dates.

2. Get them framed in glass, rather than sealed in plastic. I learned, to my dismay, that the fancy gold seals of the Court and university were permanently squeezed flat beyond recognition by the heat-pressure combination. If you want to preserve the lettering on the seals, get the certificates framed or at least investigate what you are doing when a relative, such as your mother, offers to pay the cost of the plaques.

Announcements, Stationery and Professional Cards, Christmas Cards, and "Mailing Lists"

Stationery in General

Your stationery is a legitimate form of advertising and you should use only the very highest quality of engraved stationery. Clients, prospective clients, adverse parties, adverse attorneys, judges, etc., may never see you face to face, but they will see your stationery.

I shudder when I see the cheap heat-process stationery where the ink chips off or causes the paper to stick together. I mentally downgrade the lawyer, and I suppose I also downgrade somewhat that person's client and that client's case. Whether this reaction is or is not a proper reaction is immaterial. The important thing is that you, your clients, and your clients' cases may be judged in part by your stationery. So use only the highest quality. Saving money on stationery is a false economy.

It has been estimated that it costs about $6 in secretarial time and overhead to type a letter, fold it, put it in the envelope and carry it to the mailbox for mailing, as well as getting the copy into the file, etc. The postage stamp will cost 29¢ or more, and the letter may be the only tangible manifestation of your legal work (besides your bill) that your client will ever get.

Your client will probably never throw your letters away. Your client (mentally) may be paying from a few dollars to hundreds or even thousands of dollars for the one letter from you, or for a few letters from you, embodying your sage advice.

For a lawyer to use cheap stationery, to me, is comparable to a jeweler's wrapping a fine diamond ring or watch in an old newspaper.

Legal services, like jewelry, are a relatively expensive commodity to the consumer, and, in my opinion, should be well packaged when sent out. Please keep in mind that I am referring in this section to your letterhead, letterhead envelopes, billing stationery, and professional cards. I am not advocating this high-cost stationery for scratch pads, forms or other similar materials.

You will need engraved letterhead paper, "copy" paper (stationery identical to the letterhead with the word "copy" on it), envelopes, professional cards, and statement paper. In order to save the cost of die cutting, the printer may try to sell you an introductory "package" of some of each of the above, using the identical die which looks like this:

BRAND NEW LAWYER
ATTORNEY AT LAW
123 Main Street—Suite A
Anytown, USA 00000

Telephone 312–123–4567

The die is used on all your cards and stationery except that the telephone number is left off the return address. It is very tempting to order this package due to what appears to be a special price. And the printer may tell you that if you order the package you can get delivery in ten days, but it will take four or five weeks to get a special die. Often there is nothing "special" about the special price. It only appears special because you are ordering everything at one time instead of ordering piecemeal at intervals. The major cost of printing is the labor cost of set-up. Once the presses are set up, the cost of feeding additional stock is negligible. You should keep this in mind and try to order several stationery needs at the same time wherever possible. In other words, if you are about to order letterhead stationery, check all your printing needs.

My objection to the package is that it is obvious to other lawyers that it is a package. I recommend not using the package and instead having something prepared which makes it obvious that you are *not* using the package.

Die Costs

Depending on local custom and law, the die the printer makes for you may legally be your property. If so, don't be embarrassed to ask for the die if you change printers.

Time Lag in Printing

When considering opening or changing your office, remember that printers are worse than lawyers when it comes to delivering their work product. Time delays of two weeks to two months are not unusual. Asking your printer for your die to give to another printer can sometimes decrease the waiting time for an order.

Announcements

To whom you send announcements is largely a matter of local custom. See DR 2-102(A)(2) or whatever is your local equivalent. As a general rule, you can, and should, send your announcements to anyone with whom you have a pre-existing relationship. Again, the acceptable practice varies greatly from jurisdiction to jurisdiction. For a new lawyer, announcements accomplish the dual purpose of telling people that you passed the bar and where your office is. You may find a substantial delay due to printers and getting your phone numbers confirmed. Don't be concerned if the announcements don't arrive until after you've moved in. Order some extra announcements to send to people you overlooked on your first list. For a decent interval of time, you can send these overlooked people your announcement.

When people receive your announcement, they will read it and say, "That's nice." They may then put your phone number and address in a book and throw your expensive announcement immediately into the waste basket. (Except for your parents, who may frame it or put it in a scrapbook.)

I personally think you will be doing more for your friends and relatives if you include a professional card with your announcement. The small card can be easily placed in a wallet to be available when your client needs you right away.

Announcement Mailing List

Your announcement mailing list is a valuable asset. Keep it updated with new addresses and clients. Eliminate people with whom you have no contact. Announcements to people you have not had prior contact with may be a form of improper solicitation.

Christmas Cards

Every year I send personal "Season's Greetings" cards to my clients. Invariably, the cards serve as a reminder to some of them to take care of some legal matter such as updating a will. A divorce lawyer told me that couples stay together during Christmas and New Year's and start divorce proceedings in January and February. If this is so, then I suppose "Season's Greetings" cards are a very good investment, as you may be reaching two potential clients.

Here again, local practice varies from jurisdiction to jurisdiction, and you should ask other lawyers what is permissible. In some areas, you cannot use a firm name on the card and in some you can.

Part IV
Getting Clients

How to Handle Friends and Relatives

It is a fact of life that many, if not most, of the new lawyer's clients and sources of clients will be friends and relatives. If the new lawyer can't be trusted by friends and relatives to handle a legal matter then who will trust him or her?

Most lawyers have unhappy experiences representing their friends and relatives, and it is usually the fault of the lawyer. No matter how hard the new lawyer works on the case, no matter how fantastic a job the new lawyer does, no matter how successful the result, friends or relatives honestly believe that they are the recipients of third-rate legal services. They honestly believe they did the new lawyer a favor by giving him or her the case "for experience." Regardless of the fee, friends or relatives think they are being overcharged.

Face reality. You had better satisfy your friends and relatives if you expect to make it as a new lawyer. They will be the source of much, if not most, of your practice your first few years.

There are several things you can do to improve your image with them:

1. *Be friendly* when they seek free legal advice at social events and on the telephone at night.

2. *Get them into the office.* Don't conduct your law practice in an atmosphere of blaring television, screaming children, or orchestras at weddings. Tell them the case sounds very interesting, and if they can please come to your office, you'll be able to concentrate on their problem and get the facts down correctly. Tell them you don't like to interview clients outside the office because you can't make the notes essential for the proper handling of their case.

3. *Don't reveal confidences.* Go out of your way to tell the client

that you can't or won't discuss the case with your mutual friends or relatives. Tell your cousin Mary that you can't and won't discuss her case with her mother, Aunt Jane, or your mother who is Mary's aunt. Tell cousin Mary that if she wants Aunt Jane to know about the case, that she'll have to tell her because you won't. This touch of professionalism goes a long way toward solidifying the attorney-client relationship.

Early in my career, I represented some very close friends in the early stages of an adoption just before and just after the baby was born. I never told my wife. A few weeks later we went to the friends' house for a long-planned social gathering. At the party my wife found out for the first time about the new baby, and promptly let out a stream of not-too-kind comments for my not having said anything about the baby. (All the other couples had brought baby gifts and we hadn't.) The adopting parents tried to alleviate my wife's embarrassment by saying that they assumed I would tell my wife about the adoption and hadn't called her with the good news. I stated that I couldn't say anything about the new baby because I couldn't disclose a client's confidence. Over the years, I've gotten a lot of business and a lot of referrals from the people at that party and that couple. If my friends had doubts about my professionalism before this episode, the doubts were over afterward.

4. *Billing friends and relatives*. It is very important that you bill friends and relatives properly. Suppose $450 is a reasonable fee for your services, but your friend or relative only has $150 to pay you, and you are willing to take this case for $150 because:

    a. You want the experience;

    b. You are tired of playing solitaire in the office;

    c. The phone company is threatening you about your unpaid bill.

The proper way to bill someone like a cousin is as follows:

Flaky Cousin
123 Main Street
Anytown, USA
RE: Professional Services Rendered
    Cousin adv. People
    Case C123456

One-half day trial in traffic court to defend charges of speeding violation of Vehicle Code Section 5976. Preparation of trial brief to exclude improperly obtained confession and attempting to exclude eye witnesses. Obtaining letter from employer asking court not to suspend driver's license.

Services rendered January 3, 7, 11 and 14, 19___.

Total Fee	$450.00
Less family discount	300.00
Balance now due and payable	$150.00

Thank you.

The reason for showing the $450 price and $300 discount is to let the cousin know the value of what was received. He or she has no way of knowing your services were worth $450 unless you say so. A relative will think they were only worth $85 and you were over-charging. (Remember, they think they did you a favor by letting you get experience.)

Additionally, you want relatives and friends to refer you $450 cases, not $150 cases. If they don't know the value of the services, they'll recommend people to you telling them you only charge $150. Your cousin will be grateful to you for the $300 "discount."

In summary, friends and relatives will be the beginning of your legal practice. Treat them professionally, and they will recommend clients to you. Treat them with scorn and disdain, and your practice may never get a good start.

How to Market Your Services

Start on Announcements

1. Prepare mailing lists:

    a. Law school class (get addresses from Alumni Association);

    b. Undergraduate classmates (get addresses from Alumni Association);

    c. High school classmates, if appropriate (get addresses from Alumni Association);

    d. Church members, if appropriate;

    e. Family (your mother will be glad to help you);

    f. Organizations you belong(ed) to—sports clubs, social clubs, philanthropic clubs (get addresses from club secretary);

    g. Professional associations you belong to.

2. Get sample announcements from printer.

3. Get time and cost estimates from printer.

4. Decide on style of announcements (listing or not listing areas of practice).

5. Remember to order professional cards and enclose one with announcements.

6. Don't use cheap announcements or cards (be sure you get them engraved, on good stock).

7. Get cost and time estimate from professional addressing service for addressing, stuffing, and mailing announcements.

8. Start addressing envelopes while announcements are being printed.

9. Consider buying old postage stamps from stamp dealer for postage to attract attention to the announcement when it is received.

Order Stationery

Allow up to two months delivery time for high-quality stationery. Get a catalogue with samples from a national supplier such as Stuart Cooper, or a local company. Order letter-size bond letterhead, and second sheets. Also blank letter-size bond, letter-size envelopes, professional cards, announcements, Will paper, and Will covers.

If your state allows or requires letter-size pleadings, don't use "contract" or "pleading size" stationery.

Also get "cheap" envelopes for bill-paying from post office. Order billing stationery and window envelopes.

Cost-Effective Media Advertising

In this chapter, I wish to touch upon lawyer advertising as it affects the lawyer just beginning a practice.

What is in this chapter is my experience in discussing advertising with tens of thousands of lawyers all over the United States. A particular lawyer in a particular community may have contrary experiences but I believe that on balance these observations are correct.

1. *Yellow Page Advertising.* Yellow page telephone directory advertising is probably the most cost-effective advertising there is for the new lawyer, if done correctly, because the persons looking believe they need a lawyer. If done improperly, however, the cost-effectiveness is questionable.

Improper (least cost-effective or non-cost-effective) advertising is too general and tells the potential client too much. A poor advertisement might read like this:

JOHN DOE

123 Main Street		555–1234
Business law	Probate	
Family Law	Workers Compensation	
Criminal Law	Civil Trials	

FREE INITIAL CONSULTATION

The proper (cost-effective) advertising lists the principal types of case(s) you hope to get from the advertising in simple individual ads:

JOHN DOE	JOHN DOE	JOHN DOE
Drunk Driving	Divorce and	Auto Accidents
555–1212	Family Law	555–1212
	555–1212	

JOHN DOE	JOHN DOE	JOHN DOE
Will and Estates	House Purchases	Purchases and Sales
555–1212	555–1212	of Business
		555–1212

The "one-inchers" are extremely cost-effective according to the people who use them. I haven't done any formal marketing research into specialization, but I believe that the American public wants lawyers who specialize in the kind of problem that they have. Thus the "one-incher" is cost effective.

2. *Newspaper Advertising*. Here again there is cost-effective and non-cost-effective advertising.

Metropolitan newspapers, generally speaking, are not cost-effective. I believe that when people read the metropolitan newspaper they skim it and have no time to study or remember lawyer advertising.

Smaller newspapers, such as neighborhood papers, shopping news, and local throw-aways, are extremely cost-effective according to the reports I get. For some reason, college newspapers and newspapers in college areas are very effective. It is my personal opinion that the people who have the inclination to read this type of publication apparently have the time to read the paper or study it carefully.

It appears that in newspapers the display ad is not any more effective than the classified ad. (Again, those people who have the time to read these papers have the time to read them carefully.) It would appear that it is sufficient simply to state:

JOHN DOE
ATTORNEY AT LAW
555–1234

a. *Frequency of Ad*. Very few ads are worthwhile, however, on a one-shot basis. To be successful, almost all ads must run over a period of time. People will look for a lawyer when they need one. Therefore your ad must run continuously until there is a matching of your availability and the client's need for a lawyer.

3. *Radio Advertising*. I have no experience or history reported to me on radio advertising, so accordingly I make no suggestions. If you have any first-hand experiences, I would appreciate learning about them from you.

4. *Television Advertising*. For reasons that I don't understand,

people just don't want to believe the truth about TV lawyer advertising. I continually tell groups of lawyers my observations in the area and then immediately encounter reservations or disbelief from the lawyers in the group. When I ask if anybody can report contrary evidence no one raises a hand. When I ask who in the audience has tried TV advertising a few hands go up and then they tell me their experiences. Their experiences match the experiences of other lawyers throughout America, yet the rest of the audience still seems hostile and disbelieving.

With two possible exceptions, TV lawyer advertising is not cost-effective and should be avoided. Many lawyers have related to me that the TV advertising money they spent was totally wasted. The two exceptions are as follows:

First, sponsoring a public service television program. Recently a San Diego, California, law firm spent about $8,000 to sponsor a program on PBS television. (I believe that technically the sponsorship was termed a "grant.") The TV station is well respected in the area. The newspaper accounts indicated that the sponsorship was extremely well accepted by the firm's existing conservative business and financial clients. It is not known whether this ad resulted in any new clients or work.

If I were to spend money on TV advertising I would follow the leaders and sponsor a series or a special.

Second, there is one law firm I know of which claims that TV advertising is cost-effective for developing new business. They sell what, for all intents and purposes, amounts to a franchise for a neighborhood law office and then promise to spend the investor's money on TV ads (at least they did so in the past). I am not aware of any independent verification of their claims, and I don't doubt that the investor's money was spent on TV ads, but I don't know if there is any benefit to the investing firm from a cost-effective point of view. I have my doubts about the cost-effectiveness, but I repeat the claim that at least one firm has found TV advertising worthwhile.

In summary, in my opinion, I wouldn't spend my precious dollars on TV ads when I could spend the money in yellow pages and neighborhood newspaper classifieds.

The Importance of Accepting and Returning Telephone Calls

I needed a lawyer.
I couldn't reach you.
I reached another lawyer.
I don't need you anymore.

In terms of good public relations, this may be the most important chapter of this book. Unless God made you clairvoyant, you won't know in advance why people call. When Mrs. Jones calls, you don't know if she's pestering you about her complaint about the apartment owner turning off the hot water, or if she is trying to reach you because her husband fell down the unlit stairwell and has two broken legs and a broken back.

Most clients feel that lawyers' telephone calls are excessively screened. Failure to maintain communications with clients is the single most common complaint to bar associations. Increasingly, lawyers are being disciplined for ignoring clients' calls and letters.

Unless you have a storefront office, most if not all of your new clients will call you before coming in. Your telephone is your lifeline to new clients and new matters. If you can't return a call, have your secretary or another lawyer return the call for you so you won't lose that new client who is trying to reach you.

I think it's good public relations for you to return calls at night and on Saturdays and Sundays. Tell the client you are concerned about his or her call and didn't want to wait until the next morning or until after the weekend to return it. The client will really appreciate your concern.

Be sure you use a duplicate phone message system for *all* telephone messages to protect yourself from the client who claims to have called you ten times and you didn't return any of the calls. When you try to return the call without success, note on the message itself your efforts.

Sample notations would be:

3/1/89	10:04 a.m.	BY—Busy
3/1/89	10:30 a.m.	BY—Busy
3/1/89	1:00 p.m.	N/A—No Answer
3/1/89	5:00 p.m.	N/A—No Answer
3/2/89	9:00 a.m.	WCB—Not in, left message will call back

You might even send the client a speed letter or form letter by fax and by mail as follows:

Dear Client:
   I tried five times to return your call of March 1. Please call me or drop me a note so that we can help you if necessary.

                                        Very truly yours,

                                        John Novice

Logging Incoming Telephone Calls. I don't. Some lawyers do. If the client connects on the call, I have notes in the file and my time records to verify the call. If the client doesn't connect, I have my return message carbon copy. I've never needed a log of incoming calls. In some situations they might be worthwhile, but I doubt it.

Telephone. Telephones are your lifeline to new clients. Use a speaker phone so you can take notes during conversations and can go through files for information while talking on the phone. Get an extension phone in your office so your client can listen in. Get multiple lines. Three to four lines should be adequate during your first year. A client who gets a busy signal may call the next lawyer on the list. List yourself in as many phone books as your local ethical rules permit. Never use another lawyer's phone number. Get your own number. Clients often will take the first lawyer they can get hold of. Don't use mechanical answering devices. Use an exchange instead.

PETERS VS JONES

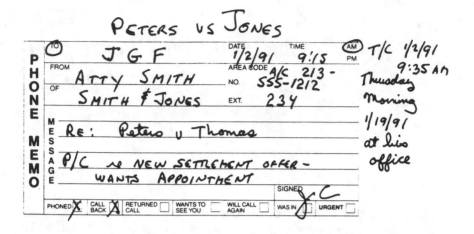

PHONE MEMO

TO: J G F
DATE 1/2/91 TIME 9:15 AM/PM
FROM: ATTY SMITH
OF: SMITH & JONES
AREA CODE A/C 213-
NO. 555-1212
EXT. 234

MESSAGE
RE: Peters v Thomas
P/C re NEW SETTLEMENT OFFER –
WANTS APPOINTMENT

SIGNED JC

PHONED X | CALL BACK X | RETURNED CALL | WANTS TO SEE YOU | WILL CALL AGAIN | WAS IN | URGENT

T/C 1/2/91 9:35 AM
Thursday Morning 1/19/91 at his office

PHONE MEMO

TO: J G F
DATE 1/2/91 TIME 10:30 AM/PM
FROM: MRS PETERS
OF:
AREA CODE 213
NO. 652-5010
EXT.

MESSAGE
HAD 2ND ACCIDENT OVER WEEKEND
HUSBAND HAS BROKEN RIBS –
IN HOSPITAL
HIT BY DRUNK RUNNING RED LIGHT
SURGERY TODAY

SIGNED JC

PHONED X | CALL BACK X | RETURNED CALL | WANTS TO SEE YOU | WILL CALL AGAIN | WAS IN | URGENT X

1/2/91 10:45 AM NO ANSWER
1/2/91 11:00 AM NO ANSWER
1/2/91 11:25 AM BUSY
1/2/91 11:30 AM - Operator says line out of order
1/2/91 11:45 AM Sent Fax to client asking client to call us because we cant read her

PUT MESSAGE FORM IN CLIENT FILE WHEN CALL IS RETURNED.

Can You Get Clients from Organizations?

Can you get clients from social, civic, or charitable organizations? The answer to the question is simultaneously "Yes" and "No." If you join an organization solely to get clients, you will be wasting your time and money. The other members will see through you, and you won't get anything from them.

On the other hand, if you belong to an organization because you sincerely believe in its purposes and you work hard for the organization, the other members will be impressed by your efforts and how sincere and dedicated you are, and they will come to you with their legal work.

If you are going to pick an organization to work for with the hope of getting legal work, stay away from organizations which are heavily constituted of lawyers. It should be obvious that if 65 percent of the members of an organization are lawyers, there won't be as much legal work as there would be if you were the only lawyer. Some charities are so heavy with lawyers that they have a "Lawyers Division."

Some lawyers claim that you can get business simply by belonging to clubs and occasionally attending a meeting and making some noise so people know who you are. I think this was true years ago when very few people knew even one lawyer and would go to the lawyer they knew. The number of lawyers has more than doubled in the last 20 years and most people now can choose from many lawyers. Perhaps in some lower socio-economic organizations you can get business from the members simply by being the only lawyer and making some occasional noise, but it will be difficult.

The advice, "Above all, to thine own self be true" applies in this area.

Insurance Claims Adjusters:
A Source of Clients

Insurance claims adjusters can be a very profitable source of clients in the personal injury and casualty fields. Insurance adjusters frequently are asked by their insured to recommend an attorney to represent them against the other parties. Sometimes the adjuster will recommend an attorney, and sometimes not.

You must be very careful in your dealings with, and relations with, insurance adjusters.

Honest insurance adjusters will recommend an accident case to you if they think you are sincere, hard-working and competent, and if they like you. Adjusters will not ask for, or expect, any remuneration for recommending a client. Stay away from dishonest adjusters. Remember, all the dishonest adjuster has to lose is a job. You have a license to practice law to lose.

The best way to meet insurance adjusters is in connection with the cases you already have. When an adjuster makes first contact with you on a case, ask him or her to join you for lunch. You owe it to your client to meet the adjuster. Impress upon the adjuster that you are ready, willing, and able to fight for your client to get your client what can reasonably be expected. Remember that impressions of you and your office may end up in the case file and may affect the amount of the settlement you can obtain for your client.

If the adjuster is impressed by you, you will obtain a better settlement for your client, and new cases may be referred to you. Remember that the recommendations of an insurance adjuster carry a lot of weight with accident victims. Work as hard and rapidly as you can on the referred matter. Remember that the first matter the adjuster refers to you may be a "real dog," as he or she may be testing you.

A lawyer can build a very profitable law practice on the referrals and recommendations of a single insurance adjuster. Just be very careful not to trespass the ethical prohibitions against soliciting.

How to Accept
Personal Injury Cases

I have written a special chapter on accepting personal injury cases because all lawyers, and especially new lawyers, run the risk of being called "Ambulance Chasers" if they act too quickly and "Negligent" if they act too slowly.

To begin with, the lawyer, when talking to the prospective client or family of the prospective client, should give the following advice (an exception to my warning about giving advice to people who are not yet your clients):

1. Engage a lawyer (whether it be you or somebody else) as rapidly as possible.

2. Do not discuss fault or facts with anybody except police officers until *after* they've consulted with a lawyer. (Usually there is a police report long before any lawyer is contacted.) If there is any possibility of criminal liability, then tell them not to talk to police officers either.

The client or potential client must be made to understand that it is essential for your investigator to photograph vehicle damage *before* the damage gets repaired. The adverse parties' statement must be gotten *before* they are instructed not to give statements. Third-party witnesses must be interviewed while their memory is fresh and before they move away. The scene of the accident must be examined and photographed *before* it is altered. Torn and blood-stained garments must *not* be thrown away at the hospital. Bruised and broken bodies should be photographed *before* healing.

The client or potential client must be made to understand that insurance companies have millions of dollars available for investigators and it is reasonable to assume that the insurance company will be into the case as soon as the other party reports the case to his or her insurance agent.

Criminal suspects get a Miranda warning advising them of availability of counsel. Personal injury victims don't get any such advice. If anything, overzealous insurance adjustors sometimes tell the injured party *not* to get a lawyer, misrepresenting that the insured party will get a good recovery without the lawyer and that the lawyer is taking money which would otherwise go to the injured party.

The injured person must be made to understand that the insurance company's primary concern is to *defend* a claim for damages rather than getting any funds for their insured for personal injury. The injured party must also be made to understand that a personal injury claim must be valued and that the injured party doesn't have enough experience or knowledge to value it properly.

How to Protect Yourself

1. *Don't quote numbers or promise recoveries.* Tell the client orally and again in writing, "Based on the facts as they appear at the present time, it appears that you have a meritorious case. It is impossible to value the case until the full extent of injury, treatment, damages, and losses are known." Tell the client orally that anybody who promises or guarantees any specific recovery without knowing the extent of injury, etc., is either foolish or stupid or fraudulent.

2. *Get the client to sign more than one document.* We ask the client to sign and date the fee agreement and also to sign and date four "Authorities to Release Information." A client might say he didn't know what he was doing if he signed only one document, but he is hard pressed to make this claim when he has signed five times in five different places and dates his signatures five times in five different places.

3. *Try not to be present when the client actually signs and dates the fee agreement and authorities.* Have the client sign them out of your presence and either mail them back to you or have a friend or relative bring them back to you. If possible, have a friend or relative be with the injured party when the documents are signed. That friend or relative can later testify to your absence during the signing.

If necessary, leave the room yourself. Tell the injured party that you're going down the hall to the bathroom so that he or she can think about which lawyer to use without your presence. Knock on the door when you come back even if it's your own office you've left and come back to. Give the prospective client every reasonable opportunity not to use you.

4. *Begin work on the case immediately.* This is necessary not only to protect the client's own best interests, but also to substantiate the need for immediate legal help. If you told a client he or she needed a lawyer immediately and then did nothing for two weeks, you were either unethical for pressuring the client to sign or you were negligent in the conduct of the case, or both.

Re: Accident of _____ (date) _____

Dear Mr. (or Ms. Client):

This letter will confirm the details of our telephone discussion (our discussion in my office on ____ (date) ____.

Our firm will represent you in your claim for damages as a result of the above accident. Our fee will be one-third (1/3) of any amounts obtained by settlement if a lawsuit is not necessary or forty per cent (40%) of all amounts received by settlement or judgment if filing of a lawsuit is necessary. If there is no recovery for you, there will be no fee.

We are enclosing herewith several authorities to obtain information. Please sign each where indicated by the red "X" as we need the authorities to obtain police reports, medical reports, etc. Additionally, please sign the enclosed copy of this letter and return the copy along with the authorities in the enclosed envelope. We cannot begin work until we have received back the copy of this letter and the authorities.

Very truly yours,

FOONBERG, CHAYO & GARDNER

by JAY G. FOONBERG

JGF:ak

(On Copies Only)
THE ABOVE IS UNDERSTOOD AND AGREED TO.

_____   _____
Signature   Date

SHORT FORM LETTER TO ACCEPT A PI CASE

AUTHORITY TO RELEASE RECORDS

TO WHOM IT MAY CONCERN:

    This is authority for you to furnish to my attorneys, FOON-BERG, CHAYO & GARDNER or their representatives, all medical, police and financial reports pertaining to my accident which occurred on or about _____, 19__ at or about
_____, _____, Calif.
       Street   City

_____   _____
        Dated   Signed

(Signed by _____because victim is minor/
            (Relationship)
physically unable)

_____
     D.R. No.

FOUR COPIES OF "AUTHORITY" FORM SHOULD BE SENT WITH FEE LETTER

How to Communicate Settlement Offers to Clients

Be sure that the client understands the difference between the *gross settlement* and the *net settlement* after costs, unpaid medical bills, and your fees. Send the client a letter explaining the breakdown and the *net* settlement. Clients are concerned about what *they* get, not about the gross settlement. When the insurance company sends a draft, get the client into the office to sign it. If you have to mail it to the client for signature, be sure to tell the client that it's a draft, not a check, and cannot be honored until *after* the insurance company compares your signature on the draft to your signature in their files. If you're stupid enough to endorse the draft before the client does, then you deserve to be deprived of your fee. Be careful about unpaid medical bills that have to be paid.

Failure to observe these rules is a very good way to get a complaint filed against you with the bar association. A sample letter follows.

Ms. (or Mr.) Client

 Re:

Dear Ms. Client:

 This letter will confirm our previous telephone conversation of _____. We have an offer from (insurance carrier) in the gross amount of _____.

 The gross settlement would be disbursed as follows:

Gross Amount		$
Less: Property Damage	$	
Out-of-Pocket Costs		
Police Report		
Medical Reports		
Filing Fee		
Service		
Total	$ _____	
	Balance	
	$ _____	
Our Fee (as agreed)	$ _____	$ _____
	Balance	
Liens		$ _____
Dr.	$	$ _____
Net to You		$ _____

(Opt.) Please understand that the doctor bills are your responsibility and must be paid by you.

(Opt.) As we related to you by telephone, it is our opinion that your case has substantially more value. However, you would not realize this value for a significant length of time and we shall comply with your wishes to settle the case now. The case is your case and we undertook to prosecute it fully and had you wished, we would have rejected the offer and tried the case to judgment although this would have caused a substantial delay in your obtaining funds.

(Opt.) If the above is acceptable and agreeable to you, please sign and date the enclosed copy of this letter and return to me in the envelope provided.

(On Copies Only)—THE ABOVE IS UNDERSTOOD AND AGREEABLE TO ME.

Date:_____   Signed:_____

Can You Get Clients by Running for Political Office?

I really can't answer this question for you. The answer will depend on your area. I've listed this question solely to call the possibility to your attention.

Running for office will give you exposure. You will address many groups and may get radio, TV, or newspaper coverage. You will get good insights into what people feel are the significant issues in your community. People who see and hear you or read about you will learn your views. Some of these people may identify with you and wish to use you as a lawyer.

On the other hand, if you run and lose, people may avoid you and want to go to the winner. The time, energy, and money you invest in an unsuccessful political campaign may have been much better spent in your practice.

If you are thinking of running for political office with the plan or hope of increasing your practice through publicity whether you win or lose, I would suggest some homework on your part before you start.

Contact some of the lawyers in your community who ran for office and lost during the last few years. Ask them if, on balance, the campaign exposure enhanced or damaged the development of their law practice. Ask them if they would do it again.

Based on my very limited questioning, I believe that running for political office and losing might help you in rural areas but might be disastrous in an urban area.

Getting Paid Work from Lawyer Referral Services

List yourself with every lawyer referral service that will accept your listing. The listing fees are nominal (usually $5 to $25 per year), in addition to the cost of the bar association dues, and the lawyer referral service will refer you many matters over the years.

Lawyer referral services are allowed to advertise to the laity in phone books and in other places. People new to a community often turn to such lawyer referral services for help in selecting a lawyer.

Not too many years ago, people went to a bar association for referral because they simply didn't know any lawyers. Today, I suspect people go to bar associations for referrals because they know too many lawyers and don't know how to select one. They believe that the lawyers who list themselves as being available through the bar association are likely to be the better lawyers, or they believe (sometimes erroneously, sometimes correctly) that the bar association lawyer referral service will refer them to a lawyer most likely to be able to help them. The public is aware of the fact that all lawyers specialize to some degree and that not all lawyers are willing or competent to handle all cases.

There is no way of knowing or guessing whether you'll get your first significant matter in weeks, months, or years. However, sooner or later you will get a significant matter, and the investment will be repaid handsomely. Additionally, you are helping the public by making lawyers (including yourself) available.

I recommend that you make the financial investment in the lawyer referral services.

Getting Legal Fees and Work from the Government

With the recent huge increase in the number of new lawyers, this kind of work is becoming increasingly difficult to obtain. How much of this work is available and how well or poorly it is compensated depends upon your local situation.

All I can do is to give you some typical examples and typical sources and you'll have to get the information yourself.

Types of Work

1. *Conflict of Interests.* It is common where there are multiple defendants that a single lawyer or department cannot represent some of them, and either the court or the government agency appoints and pays for the representation of the others.

2. *Juveniles.* It is common for a probate or juvenile court to appoint a lawyer to represent the interests of a child or unborn child.

3. *Appeals.* Commonly, because of indigency or conflict of interests, a lawyer can be appointed for the appeal even though another lawyer or government agency represented the appellant or respondent at trial.

4. *Indigents.* Indigents generally are entitled to free representation (meaning someone else is paying), both in civil and criminal matters. There are various agencies that pay for private lawyers for indigents.

Sources of Work

Getting this type of work may be very easy or very difficult, depending on how profitable (or unprofitable) it is and depending upon the method of lawyer selection.

1. Judges (federal, state, and local) are the most common sources of appointments. Sometimes each judge has his or her own list or own system of choosing lawyers and sometimes judges are obligated to use a master "approved" list. Ask the judge's clerk how the judge picks or selects a lawyer when a court-appointed lawyer is necessary. If the judge makes the selection, make an appointment to see the judge to tell him or her you are available. If there are too many judges, ask around to see which judges or departments make the largest number of appointments. See those judges and mail a résumé to the other judges. Tell the other judges that you are a new lawyer available for appointments. Ask them to keep the letter for several months even if there is no immediate need for you.

2. Public defender and legal aid (federal, state, and local) attorneys. Contact responsible people in the offices to find out how outside lawyers are selected in conflict cases and how you can get on the list.

3. Contact appeals court clerks (state and federal) to find out about getting appointed for indigent appeals.

4. Contact various state, federal, and local administrative agencies that seek private practice attorneys. Naturally, you won't know which ones do until you ask. In some jurisdictions, this conduct may not be permissible. Therefore, you will have to ask how to ask the agencies ethically.

Be Persistent

Getting some of this work may be difficult. Sometimes clerks will tell you that the judges have no time to see you. This may be true, but possibly the clerk has some favorites and wants to keep you off the list. These government appointments might be someone's private political slush fund. You may step on a few toes, but you may also end up with some cash fees and experience right away.

Getting Legal Work and Fees
from Other Lawyers

Can you get legal work from other lawyers? You not only *can* get legal work from other lawyers, I recommend that you *should* seek work from them.

Solicitation of work from another *lawyer* is perfectly proper. Solicitation from the laity is improper. Ethical consideration EC 2–22 and Model Rule 1.5(e) allow a lawyer to associate with a lawyer outside of his or her firm with the consent of the client.

DR 2–103's *only prohibition* is recommending yourself for employment to *nonlawyers*. There is no prohibition against recommending yourself to *lawyers*.

Many lawyers, especially sole practitioners, have low-fee legal work that they don't want to handle, or can't economically devote the time to. Additionally, overburdened and underpaid lawyers, particularly sole practitioners, are an excellent source of immediate legal fees and immediate work for the new lawyer. The problem is one of making your availability known to sole practitioners. They frequently are so busy that they have no time to see you even though they need your help as badly as you need income.

Most sole practitioners dislike leaving their office for minor matters. Most have a backlog and an ongoing flow of relatively low-pay, low-profit matters that they are only too happy to refer out to you if they know you exist.

The following kinds of cases can be obtained from overburdened lawyers:

1. *Low-pay domestic relations matters*. There are many people who just don't qualify for legal aid or other public lawyers but who need legal services and can pay a little. Five hundred dollars may be a reasonable fee for default divorce, but the client may only be able

to pay $175 or $200. The established practitioner with established overhead can't economically handle this case. You can, because you don't have the overhead yet. It's a quick fee and some legal experience for you.

2. *Landlord-tenant disputes.* No lawyer or client enjoys this kind of work, representing either the landlords or the tenants. Here again you can handle an eviction proceeding for a relatively low fee due to your lack of overhead and need for experience, and at the same time relieve another lawyer of an unwanted matter.

3. *Out-of-office minor court appearances and minor proceedings.* Lawyers don't like leaving their office for a whole morning for some simple matter that will take a short time. Typical examples are: perfunctory court appearances for such matters as continuances or minor judgment/debtor examinations. Attendance at depositions (where the deposition is a great distance from the office) and attendance at medical examinations are other examples.

In short, you do both yourself and the sole practitioner a favor when you handle a relatively minor matter at $25 an hour plus 25 cents a mile. The $75 you are paid for the morning will enable a solo to earn $300 or more in the office.

4. *Research, pleadings, investigations.* These areas are covered by professional organizations and, unless you are in a geographic area where they don't yet exist, you shouldn't try to sell yourself to other lawyers on this basis. Once you "get your foot in the door" with the sole practitioner, you will get work of this nature, but you are competing with nonlawyers such as law students, etc., who actively solicit this business.

5. *Minor low-pay criminal and traffic court matters.* Here again there are people who want to contest a speeding ticket, but who can't pay more than $200 to $300. The established practitioner can't handle the matter at this price, but you can and should, both to fulfill the client's need for legal services and to earn some money as well as get experience. To obtain this work, you have to make the other lawyer aware of your existence and availability to do this kind of work. The easiest way is to locate yourself as close to as many sole practitioners as possible. Locate yourself in a suite of sole practitioner lawyers or in a building with sole practitioners or in a block or in a neighborhood or town with as many sole practitioners as possible, as close as possible. Introduce yourself to each of them. Sit next to them at the bar association meetings. Tell them plainly and

simply of your availability to do the kind of legal work described above.

Don't steal clients. Remember, you are being selected by the lawyer, not by the client. You want more work from the lawyer who is paying you. Therefore, when the "client" asks you to handle another matter, you are obligated to refer the client back to the referring lawyer.

Remember, the overburdened sole practitioner wants to give you the work to get it off his or her desk. You must be aggressive and make yourself known to these lawyers as being available. Get close to them physically by being in the same suite, building, block, or area. Take them to lunch. Walk in on them and announce yourself. You have nothing to lose.

At least one state bar is attempting to match the new lawyer's need for fees with the overburdened sole practitioner's need for help in a statewide service with a view toward giving the low-fee private practice client good service. In my opinion, this "matching" process may be the greatest impetus to private practice growth since casualty insurance.

Minority Work and Money

Minority Work

In this section I only wish to suggest a concept. The particular fact situation is so complex that all I can do is make some general suggestions and give you a few examples and then it's up to you to start making telephone calls and writing letters. The availability or non-availability of what I call minority work changes according to your particular locality and the politics of your particular minority or location.

What I call "minority money" is also called "set-aside" money or "affirmative-action" money or by other names. Many agencies' rules require private companies and semi-public entities such as public utilities and investment firms to set aside funds to use minority firms.

Many federal and state appropriation bills contain clauses that a certain percentage of the work must be awarded to minority-owned or operated businesses depending on the particular person administering the particular program at the particular time. This may or may not vary to include awarding contracts to minority law firms to do some of the legal work. Sometimes this minority legal work is awarded as a matter of policy rather than a matter of law, so you'll have to dig around until you find the person in the government agency or the company who is responsible for "affirmative action" programs. You may find that the company or agency has a well-defined policy or program that includes attorneys or you may have to convince them that you should be the first attorney firm hired under a new program that you will help design.

Minority Money

Again depending upon the time, the place, and the facts, there may be minority money available to you if you can qualify.

Often banks as a matter of company policy or the Small Business Administration or other agencies may loan or guarantee loans to minority businesses. I have heard of white lawyers going into partnerships with black lawyers or Spanish-surname lawyers to get access to the money for starting a law practice.

If you are a minority lawyer, or know a minority lawyer, you should consider this avenue of financing. Unfortunately, you'll have to do the legwork to get more information.

American Bar Association Commission on Opportunities for Minorities in the Profession

The Minority Counsel Demonstration Program, sponsored by the ABA's Commission on Opportunities for Minorities in the Profession, brings together minority firms and majority firms and corporate counsel. (The commission does *not* function as a job placement service for individuals; minority firms participating must have at least two attorneys.) The commission is very successful in its effort. Contact the commission at (312)988–5643. I personally have delivered many programs for the commission designed for minority lawyers starting their own practices.

Ethnic and Minority Bar Associations

There are dozens of ethnic and minority bar associations at the national, state, and local levels. I recommend supporting them and being active in their membership (if you qualify). They are excellent for networking with other attorneys. I'm proud of my two decades of service to minority bar groups.

The Hispanic National Bar Association, of which I am an honorary member, services hispanic lawyers. The National Bar Association is a leading association for black lawyers. The National Asian Pacific American Bar Association was created to address the concerns of Asian attorneys. The American Indian Bar Association serves American Indian lawyers. The ABA Commission can help you locate appropriate associations to support.

How to Get More Legal Work
from Existing Clients

A satisfied client will produce more clients and generate more business for you than any other single source. There are two ways in which existing clients can generate business:

1. *They can bring in new clients.* A satisfied client is your most likely and probable source of new clients. Clients who have been well served have all of the zeal of missionaries. They can't wait to brag to friends and relatives and co-workers about what a great lawyer they have. They will recommend many clients to you over the years.

2. *They can bring you their own repeat business.* As a general rule, clients want more attention, not less attention from their lawyer. They are willing to pay for legal work if only the attorney is available to do it.

The attorney who shows a genuine interest in the welfare of a client will find that the client will want the lawyer to do "whatever is necessary" to keep the client's legal matters in order. The attorney who stays in close touch with clients will get a telephone call from the client ("Before I sign this lease, I want you to look at it"), which will not happen if the attorney is inaccessible to the client.

After 10 years in practice, I set up a 20-year follow-up calendar. I wish I had started my first day. The following are examples of "follow-up" legal work, often required by clients, and commonly neglected by lawyers:

1. *Corporate Minutes.* Most corporations have periodic meetings of their governing bodies, at least annually, if not more often. You should send a reminder letter about 30 days prior to meetings. There is nothing unethical in reminding the client of the meetings requirement. In most instances, the client will ask you for help in

setting the agenda and preparing the minutes. The client will be happy to pay you and will be grateful to you for the reminder. In some instances, the client will ignore your letter. In my opinion, anything more than one letter starts bordering on solicitation.

2. *Lease Options.* Whether your client is the owner or the tenant, the lease may have options for renewal or for purchase. A letter to the client about 90 days before the option date will often lead to your doing legal work for the client.

3. *Wills.* A letter should be sent to the client about five years after the will is drafted, reminding the client that five years have elapsed, and that a will review would be appropriate.

4. *Judgment Renewals.* A letter should be sent about a year before a judgment becomes unenforceable.

5. *Minors Becoming Adults.* Minors often are entitled to receive funds upon attaining majority. The funds may be from previous settlements, inheritances, trust terminations, etc.

6. *Annual Statements of Officers for Corporations.* In most states, an annual statement of officers of a corporation must be filed with the Secretary of State, and a letter reminding the client of the deadline is appropriate. In some cases, the form may be sent directly to you, if you have formed the corporation for the client, in which case you will send the form to the client for signature, with a short note of explanation.

7. *Fictitious Name Statement.* A periodic letter to your business or corporate clients reminding them to file fictitious name statements for their various entities is often in order. Additionally, reminding clients that businesses which are no longer doing business should file an Abandonment of Fictitious Name could be an important reminder for the client, and additional legal work for you.

8. *Expungement of Prior Criminal Records.*

The above list is not intended to be exclusive. Depending upon your local practice situation, and your desire to be of service to your clients, there are many more possibilities.

The important things to remember are:

1. When you finish a particular assignment for a client, close the file, and calendar future work that the client may need. (See Closed File form in chapter on "Simple Filing Systems for the New Lawyer.")

2. Remember that the client welcomes your reminders.

3. Don't send more than one reminder (thus avoiding the problem of solicitation).

4. Don't worry that your reminders may generate work for another lawyer; you'll get your share.

How to Recognize and Handle Conflicts of Interest

Any time you are representing more than one person in a matter, ask yourself if there is a conflict of interest. Remember that corporations and partnerships are "persons" for purposes of conflicts of interest. If there appears to be a conflict, explain the potential conflict to the client *in writing* and get permission *in writing* to continue the representation. If you can't do this, pick one client at the beginning and tell the other to get another lawyer.

New lawyers are especially prone to problems involving conflicts of interest for the following reasons:

1. They don't recognize the problem when they see it.

2. They don't know how to handle the problem when they recognize it.

3. They are afraid to broach this subject for fear of frightening the client away and losing a fee.

4. They don't realize they can still do the work and gain a fee if the conflict problem is properly handled.

The importance of recognizing and solving conflicts of interests at the beginning has two aspects:

To you as the lawyer: If you don't recognize and solve the problem:

1. You may have to withdraw from the case.

2. You may not be able to collect any fees due you.

3. You may have to refund any fees previously paid you.

4. Depending on the extent of the problem, you may be disciplined or disbarred for your stupidity.

To the client: The client will have to obtain a new lawyer and waste a lot of time and energy locating and educating the new lawyer. This delay might even prejudice the case.

How to Recognize a Conflict of Interest Problem

Simple Conflicts

These are conflicts between you and the client. To the extent that lawyers are compensated by clients and clients compensate them, there is always a theoretical conflict between the client and the lawyer. This theoretical conflict comes close to being actual when the lawyer is compensated by "a piece of the action." This problem, however, is normally treated by bar associations under the category of "unreasonable" or "excessive" fees rather than conflict of interests.

These simple conflicts also can arise when you have two clients unrelated to each other such as:

1. Client A wants you to collect $1,000 from X and Client B wants to collect $3,000 from the same X. X only has or is even likely to have $500. Who would get it? Client A or Client B or both A and B in some ratio?

2. Client A wants you to argue as a lawyer for a debtor that involuntary repossessions are unconstitutional and Client B wants you to argue to the same or a different court in a different matter that involuntary repossessions are constitutional. Do you take both cases on the theory that the court makes the law and not the lawyer?

Complex Conflicts

These are the more common situations and arise out of the fact that multiple parties want to use only one lawyer, typically to save fees. The most common situations are:

1. *Partnerships*. Each partner and the partnership are independent entities and there are conflicts and potential conflicts in the situation.

2. *Corporations*. Each incorporator, each director, each officer, each employee, and the corporation are independent and could have conflicting interests.

3. *Divorce*. Usually the husband and wife have conflicting interests in a divorce. In theory, the court represents the children. In some jurisdictions another lawyer is appointed to represent the children.

4. *Multiple Defendants or Potential Defendants in Criminal Cases*. The defendants may later wish to turn on each other or try to get immunity in exchange for testimony.

5. *Auto Accident Cases.*

a. Insufficient insurance or assets. There may not be sufficient insurance or assets to cover all of the injured parties. For example, suppose the defendant has a $15,000-$30,000 policy and there are four parties seriously injured in your client's car. Suppose that the claims of each are reasonably worth $20,000 or more. Suppose further that the defendant is an indigent who can successfully go bankrupt on personal injury judgment debts. Suppose further that the insurance company is willing to pay in the entire $30,000. If you take all four cases, how do you divide up the insurance money? Can you take all four cases? Which client(s) do you keep or reject? If you advise one or more people to get independent counsel (probably the lesser value cases), should you explain why? Would an explanation be a conflict with the clients you keep?

b. Passenger or driver. Can you represent both the driver and the passengers? Is there a possibility of suing the driver/owner for negligent operation or maintenance of the vehicle, or under a guest statute?

6. *Other Conflict-of-Interest Situations.* Obviously, there is an infinite number of possible conflict-of-interest situations. Any time you have or may have more than one client in a matter you should ask yourself, "Do I have a conflict-of-interest situation here?" If you are not sure, call another lawyer for an opinion or call the local bar association and get the name of a member of the ethics committee. (Some ethics committees will only answer requests of the bar association itself, however, as opposed to individual members of the bar association. And some ethics committee members will only respond to written questions for fear of misunderstanding of the facts.)

You should get another lawyer's opinion of the situation to protect both yourself and the client. The opinion of an older, more experienced lawyer can help you decide whether or not you have a conflict, and the fact that you were concerned over the possibility of a conflict and took steps to get another opinion or other opinions would probably be of help to you in the event of a subsequent problem.

How to Handle the Problem

Be honest, be forthright, and put everything in writing!

The Model Rules of Professional Conduct do *not* prohibit your representing clients when there is or might be a conflict of interests. The lawyer may represent more than one party provided the client understands the conflict and waives it. Below is a form letter for conflict-of-interest problems (I use the same or similar language in my oral discussions in the office):

Name and address of Client

　　　Re: (Matter involved)

Dear _____:

　　　I am writing to you to repeat in writing what I told you earlier in the office. I cannot commence work on your case until you have returned the enclosed copy of this letter indicating your preference.

　　　As I explained to you in the office, a lawyer cannot be on both sides of a fence; nor can a lawyer ethically represent people who may have conflicting interests unless they understand they may have conflicting interests and still wish to use the same lawyer to do the work by waiving the conflicts.

Partnerships, Corporations, Business Ventures

　　　Each of you is a legal entity and in the eyes of the law, the partnership is a legal entity. Theoretically, each of the three of you should have a different lawyer to protect your respective interests.

　　　I can draft your partnership agreement to conform to what you have agreed to and can raise additional problems which have to be solved by you, but I cannot take sides.

Alternative 1:

　　　In the event of a dispute between you I shall have the right to withdraw from the case and not take either side.

Alternative 2:

　　　In the event of a dispute between "A" and you, you must understand that I would have to represent "A" since "A" is actually my client.

Alternative 3:

In the event of a dispute between you, you have agreed that my client will be the partnership and you understand that I would not represent either of you personally.

Alternative 4:

In the event of a dispute between you, I will choose a client between you.

I would not intentionally favor one of you over the other but you may feel more comfortable with a lawyer who is actively representing your individual personal interest.

Divorces

You asked me to represent both of you in order to save legal fees and costs.

You told me how you wanted the assets and liabilities handled and the amounts you have agreed on for alimony and child support. I explained to you that if you wished to fight in court, a judge might give either of you more or less assets or more or less alimony. I explained that the issue of child support cannot be bargained solely between you and that the court keeps jurisdiction to decide child support and custody regardless of what you have agreed to. I have also cautioned you on the necessity of making full disclosure of all assets, liabilities, income, expenses, etc., and that the intentional or negligent omission of important facts might cause a court to overturn the whole agreement in future years.

I also explained to you that in later years it may be relevant who was the plaintiff and who was the defendant in the divorce action and that it was possible for each of you to sue the other for divorce.

You indicated that notwithstanding your rights, you wished to proceed with the divorce as a default proceeding and to make the provisions you have agreed upon.

Multiple Defendants in a Criminal Proceeding

You have indicated that you wish to be represented together and I indicated to you that you are each entitled to individual, separate counsel and that if you can't pay for separate counsel, a public defender may be available. I also informed you that you may wish to "finger point" at each other or that one of you may be able to receive immunity from prosecution for testifying against the other.

Multiple Plaintiffs in Auto Accident Cases

I explained to you that there may not be enough insurance or assets for all of you to recover what you are entitled to and you indicated that if this should happen you would divide the total proceeds between yourselves as you will agree and that if you can't agree, the funds will be held in my trust account while you arbitrate between yourselves to determine the share that each of you is entitled to. I would not represent either of you in any such arbitration, which would be at additional expense to each of you.

How to Keep Clients

What do clients want from you? There is often a difference between what people want and will pay for as opposed to what they need.

Often a person will happily pay for what is *wanted,* but resents paying for what is *needed,* if the two differ. Think of your own situation when you are sick. You'd pay anything within reason for a physician to make a house call. It is much more efficient and economical for you to go to the physician's office, but you'd still prefer a house call. You need a $35 office visit, but you want and would pay for a $100 house call. The supply-and-demand situation between new physicians and patients is such that new physicians can turn down business they used to welcome. Unfortunately for you, the supply-and-demand situation between new lawyers and the need for legal services is in a different balance, and you must give clients what they want.

The purpose of the comparison is solely to emphasize the difference between providing a client what is *wanted* and providing what is *needed* (these are not mutually exclusive).

Therefore, the gist of this chapter is to teach you the things that clients *want* in *addition* to your efforts and in *addition* to good results.

1. *Effort vs. Results.* New lawyers think that clients want results more than they want effort. Believe it or not, the reverse is true. Clients *need* favorable results; they *want* effort. Don't misinterpret what I am saying. I am *not* saying that clients don't care whether they win or lose. They care very much. I am saying that whether they come back to you when a matter is over with, or whether they recommend other clients to you or pay your fee willingly, or not at all,

is determined more by their opinion of your efforts than their opinion of the results.

2. *How to Project Efforts.* Listed below are things you can do to let the client know you are putting forth effort. It is *not true* that the practice of law is like the proverbial iceberg, with 90% hidden. It *is true* that there are lazy lawyers and lawyers who really don't care about their clients, and who obscure under a basket 90% of what they are doing.

a. Send your client a copy of EVERY document you produce, including correspondence, pleadings, briefs, etc., as you produce it.

b. Send your client a copy of all incoming documents as they are received, including pleadings, correspondence, etc.

c. Return your client's calls immediately, or have someone else return them. Remember this:

(1) I needed a lawyer;

(2) I couldn't get in touch with you;

(3) I got another lawyer;

(4) I don't need you anymore . . .

d. If you work on your client's case in the evening or on a weekend, call him or her at home to ask some questions, so that he or she knows you are devoting your "personal" time to the matter.

e. Bill monthly.

f. Make "house calls."

g. One of the most effective techniques I employ is to visit clients at their places of business.

(1) Visit your client's place of business to understand that business. Don't charge for the time you spend going through the factory, but do charge for the conference at the place of business to the same extent as you would have charged for the same conference in your office.

(2) Go with your client to the scene of the accident in personal injury and worker's compensation cases. This will really impress your client as to your effort.

(3) Go to the medical examination with your client when the defense doctor makes an examination.

h. Inform clients of new cases or statutes which come to your attention that affect their affairs. They will appreciate your concern. They will feel you care about them and are putting forth effort for them.

How to Lose Clients

Why Do Clients Leave?

According to a national survey,

1% die;

3% move;

5% dislike the product;

24% have some dispute that does not get adjusted;

67% leave because they feel they were treated discourteously, indifferently, or simply were not given good service.

Cases and Clients That Should Be Turned Down

Abraham Lincoln reputedly advised a new lawyer on passing the bar, "Young man, it's more important to know what cases not to take than it is to know the law."

As a new lawyer with relatively little case load, you'll want to take almost any case from almost any client. The more experienced lawyer knows better. It is most crucial that you recognize that you need cash, as well as satisfaction in helping the downtrodden, if you intend to be in practice the second or third year. Therefore, I am going to list cases and clients that you should turn down during your first year or two. After you're established and can afford the luxury of laying out your time and money to be a "swell person," or to gamble on profitability, then you might wish to take these cases.

This list is based upon my personal experiences and you may wish to expand or contract it as time goes by.

When You Are the Second or Third Lawyer on the Case

Be very careful. There may be honest personality differences between the client and prior lawyers but multiple lawyers often indicate:

A nonmeritorious case;

An uncooperative client;

A nonpaying client.

Check with the prior lawyers before accepting the case. Ask the prior lawyers if there is an unpaid bill involved. If, after checking, you believe in the client and the merits of prosecution, then by all means accept the case if you want to.

If you do take the case, you should—whenever possible—communicate with the adverse lawyer or party to make clear the reasons for multiple lawyers, if you can do so without violating attorney-client privilege and without further damaging the case. The other side may, and probably will, equate multiple lawyers with the three problems stated, and your coming in as lawyer number three may harm your client's case and your economics. If you can't explain the multiple lawyer problem to the other side, then keep in mind that you'll have a more difficult and perhaps impossible task reaching a fair settlement without a trial to judgment.

"Hurt Feeling" Cases

This type of case usually has wrongful conduct by the defendant, but no provable special damages on the part of your client, or nominal damages at best. The case and your compensation are dependent on either presumed or punitive damages. Examples of this type of case are:

1. Libel and slander;
2. Barroom brawls;
3. Most assault and battery cases.

Landlord-Tenant Cases (Unless You are Paid in Full in Advance)

It makes no difference if you represent the landlord or the tenant, your client will never be happy and will never pay you *after* the case is over. Landlords greatly resent having to pay you money to evict someone who is already delinquent in rent or who is busting up the place, or driving other tenants away with such activities as drag racing in the driveway at 4 a.m., or having all night pot and bongo parties. Tenants often want to leave, but want to blackmail the landlord into paying them something to leave. Sometimes tenants can't leave because they haven't got the first and last month's rent to move into another place. Sometimes tenants feel they are being unreasonably evicted because they made what to them is a reasonable request that the landlord ignored, such as fixing the leaky, noisy toilet.

Landlord-tenant disputes are often more vindictive than divorce suits, and each side wants to use the lawyer for revenge if they can use the lawyer for free.

Divorce Cases for People Heavily in Debt (Unless You Are Paid in Advance)

Please remember that poor people can get divorces through legal aid. In most—if not almost all—cases, divorce is an economic disaster for everyone involved. There is rarely enough money to support the parties and children living apart. I am not a qualified expert on the subject of causes of divorce cases, but I believe that economic insecurity is a major factor in divorce. In accepting or not accepting divorce cases it is safe to assume that the retainer money up front may be the only money you'll see. Be firm in getting the money up front. Court orders awarding you a fee of one-half of the fair amount at the rate of $15 a month if the breadwinner sticks around aren't worth much. Don't blame the court. Blame yourself for accepting a case legal aid would have taken.

Criminal Cases (Unless You Get Paid in Advance)

A person in prison doesn't earn much more than cigarette money. Don't take clients that should be represented by the public defender.

Slip Falls (Unless There Are Substantial Damages)

Even the most meritorious slip fall is hard to settle for a fair amount short of trial. You'll spend huge amounts of time and have very little to show for your efforts.

Bankruptcies (Unless You Are Paid in Advance in Full)

It was embarrassing when my client amended his bankruptcy schedules to include the unpaid balance of the fee due me.

Clients Who Loudly Proclaim That You Can Have All the Money Recovered; They Are "Only Interested in the Principle"

These cases fall into the same category as the "Hurt Feeling" cases.

Clients Who Want to Use Your Telephones, Secretary, and Offices to Do Their Business

I don't know why, but this type of client always seems to end up "trouble." Be forewarned.

Clients Who Ask for a Loan of Money Against Their Case

You'd be surprised at how many new lawyers get stuck lending small amounts of money to clients. When clients say that if you don't lend them some money they'll have to go to another lawyer who will lend them money, then you're better off without those clients.

Cases Where "They'll Settle Right Away Because They Can't Afford the Publicity of Litigation"

When a prospective client makes this statement, I cringe. Usually the person honestly believes what is said. Unfortunately, it never happens this way. For some reason the adverse party in this type of case will consider discussing a possible settlement as soon as the United States Supreme Court denies *certiorari*. When you hear these magic words, convince the client that a noncontingency hourly rate payable in advance is best for him or her. Convince such a client that a contingency fee in such a case would overcompensate you as the lawyer in view of the early anticipated settlement of the case.

Cases Totally Without Merit

If a case has no chance, be honest; tell the client you won't handle a case totally without merit.

The next chapter will give you some techniques for saying "No" to the prospective client.

Keep in mind that you are not obligated to take cases that could and probably should be handled by publicly funded lawyers such as those in legal aid and public defender offices. Remember also that if your fee agreement is properly drafted, you can withdraw from the case. But don't forget that you cannot hold onto the client and stop working due to an unpaid fee.

How to Say "No" to a Client or Case

For a new lawyer, cases and clients are hard to come by. You'll be afraid to say "No" when a case or client should be turned down. Lawyers by nature like to be "nice people." Lawyers also want as many clients as possible and don't like to get rid of clients or cases. The suggestions of this chapter may help you in a difficult situation.

Tell Your Client the Truth

Ninety-five percent of the problems will disappear when you tell your client the truth.

1. *No Merit to Case.* Tell your client that, in your opinion, the case is without merit. Tell the client that you'd like to take the case and make money, but there just isn't a case.

2. *Uneconomical Case.* Tell the client that although he or she is legally in the right, the economics of the case just don't warrant the use of a lawyer.

Suggest Alternatives

1. *Small Claims Court.* Suggest in the smaller cases that the client use the services of the Small Claims Court and keep all the money without sharing it with lawyers.

2. *Other Lawyers.* Suggest that the client seek the opinion of another lawyer who might disagree with your evaluation. Give the client the phone numbers of legal aid, public defender, bar association referral system, consumer advocate offices, etc., so that the client will know where to go for help.

3. *Suggest that certain clients represent themselves.* In some sit-

uations, such as landlord-tenant conflicts, you can teach landlord clients what they have to know to represent themselves. Let them know they are paying you for their education.

Put It in Writing

After you decline the case or client, send a follow-up letter confirming what you told the client, including the suggestion to contact another lawyer and repeating the phone numbers. This will be of great help to you in protecting yourself if the client denies the conversation.

Ask Your Client for "Money Up Front"

Asking clients to put their money where their mouths are will help get rid of unwanted clients who know a case is nonmeritorious.

Believe it or not, the honest, legitimate client wants the truth. The client won't be angry with you for hearing bad news. You'll be respected and that client will come back in the future.

Damage Control If You Are Fired

Sooner or later, you will be fired by a client. The most usual form of notification is a letter from another lawyer asking for the files, accompanied by an authorization signed by the client.

If you handle the situation properly, you will protect the client's rights and you will protect your own rights.

While you normally will not feel good about being fired, you need not overreact by looking for a tall building from which to jump off. You cannot be all things to all people. Sometimes, no matter how hard you try and no matter how good a job you do, the chemistry just will not be there between you and the client (often the situation in divorce cases).

There are several things you should do upon being fired.

1. Immediately call the new lawyer and confirm you have received the letter and will immediately send over the files. Offer to answer any questions the lawyer might have concerning the case or the client. (You do not want to make an enemy of the next lawyer. You may need his or her help if there is a subsequent fee dispute, malpractice claim, or disciplinary complaint.)

2. Confirm your call in writing and repeat your offer in the letter.

3. Review the files before you send them over to be sure they do not contain any materials relevant to other clients' matters that got misfiled, or any other sensitive information that you feel does not belong there.

4. If you suspect that you will become the object of a fee dispute, malpractice claim, or other problem, photocopy the entire file to have your own copy to protect yourself at a later time.

5. Immediately send a letter to the client. Your letter should:

(1) Identify legal matters covered.

(2) Indicate that you are acting immediately.

(3) Tell them you still have some information on the file in the event they want to come back to you in the future in connection with this or other matters.

(4) Let clients know you are still trying to protect them even though they fired you.

(5) Get permission to destroy what you do not want to store.

(6) Establish the fact that you are *not* the lawyer.

(7) Establish the date from which to measure all possible statutes of limitation in case the client later wants to sue you for malpractice.

(8) Establish that if the next lawyer loses the case or gets a result unfavorable to the client, you are not accepting responsibility for what the next lawyer does.

(9) Set the record straight what fee disputes, if any, arose *after* the person no longer was a client.

(10) Let the client know that you expect to be paid immediately.

(11) Offer arbitration. Many state bars require an offer of arbitration as a condition precedent to litigation. This letter can become the offer of arbitration.

(12) Let the client know you are willing to sue to get your fee, if necessary.

(13) Keep the door open for the client to return if you really mean it. I have had clients fire me and come back later when they subsequently did not like the next lawyer(s). Some clients who have fired me have nonetheless later recommended me to other clients who had good cases and with whom I have had good professional relations.

(14) You may wish to send a survey to help you ascertain WHY the client left you. Remember, a former client who fired you is still part of your client base and can still return to you in the future or recommend new clients to you if you treat the former client properly when they leave.

The following sample letter demonstrates the points listed above:

To: Disgruntled Client
      123 Main Street
      Any Town, USA

(1)   Re: *Files on Client v. Jones and Client adv. Smith*
Dear Mr. or Ms. Client:

(2)   As requested by Mr. Jones in his letter of January
___, 1989, and your authorization of January ___, 1989, we
are in the process of immediately transferring your files to
Mr. Jones. It will take a few days, as we must go through
the files to be sure the file does not contain materials rele-

(3)   vant to other clients that might have been accidentally
placed in your file. We are also copying parts of your file
for our insurance and tax needs.

(4)   We have telephoned and written to Mr. Jones to offer our immediate help should it be required. You have
some other files and we would appreciate hearing from
you as to whether you want us to return them to you, send

(5)   them to Mr. Jones, or destroy them. If you do not instruct
us, we shall destroy them when we next periodically remove all files that have been inactive for five or more
years.

(6)   I am sure that you understand we are no longer
(7)   your lawyers in this case, and that as of _____,
(8)   Mr. Jones is now responsible for the conduct of the case. If
you have questions about the case, it would be appropriate
for you to contact him and for him to contact us, if he
wishes, rather than for us to discuss the case with you directly. It is possible that his office wants to treat certain
aspects of the case differently from the way our office
would treat them and we would not want to be in a position of giving you conflicting advice.

(9)   Until this point, you have never indicated any dissatisfaction with the fee arrangement or the amount of the

(10)   fees and I assume that you have no disagreement over the
fees. Immediate payment of the outstanding balance of
$____ would be appropriate at this time as we are no
longer
the lawyers and there is no reason to defer closing the
file.

        In the event you do have a fee problem, our profes-
sion recognizes that honest, sincere people can have bona-
fide differences of opinion relative to fees and, accordingly,

(11)   if you do have a fee dispute, I am hereby offering to arbitrate that fee dispute in accordance with the Rules of the
State Bar of California and the procedures of the Beverly
Hills Bar Association, which professional rules require us
to notify you of the opportunity to arbitrate any fee dis-

(12)   pute as an alternative to litigation. You can obtain information from the bar association directly, if you wish.

This letter may end up being Exhibit B in your complaint for fees (if your state requires proof of an offer to arbitrate as a condition to precedent to a suit). You may, therefore, be able to get all of the information which is in the letter into the court record and before the trier of fact as an exhibit.

Most of the information contained in the letter is self-serving and will be of great help at a later time if the letter comes into evidence in court in a suit for fees or before the State Bar on a client complaint.

It is important that you remain professional when you are fired. Be firm. Protect yourself and leave the door open for the client to come back or refer you to other clients. If you overreact or are uncooperative, you may not get paid what is owed you. You may get a disciplinary complaint filed against you by either the client or the next lawyer, and you will have lost possible future return work and referrals.

Part V
Setting Fees

The Fee and Representation Letter

The importance of the fee-representation agreement cannot be overemphasized. It will help eliminate disputes between you and your client more effectively than any other procedure.

The fee letter can best be explained by using an all-inclusive example and then exploring the importance of the various parts:

John Client
123 Main Street
Anytown, U.S.A.

(1)   RE: Jones vs. Smith; breach of contract
        Dear Mr. Jones:
                     This letter will confirm our office discussion of
(2)   Thursday, January 4.
                     It was a pleasure meeting with you in our office. As
        I explained to you, it is my opinion that you definitely need
(3)   the assistance of a lawyer, whether it be our firm or an-
(4)   other lawyer. In my opinion, the matter is too complex for
        you to represent yourself.
(5)   As I explained to you, if you wish us to represent
(6)(7) you, our fee will be $1,500 to prepare the complaint, do
        written interrogatories, take the deposition of Mr. Smith if
        necessary, and appear for the first day in court. If any ad-
(8)   ditional work is required for such things as motions, addi-
        tional depositions or additional days in court, you will be
(9)   charged at our hourly rate of $115 per hour. If the case is
        settled short of trial, the fee will still be a minimum of
(10) $1,500.
(11)   The above does not include any out-of-pocket costs

which may be incurred, such as court filing fees, sheriff's fees, deposition costs, photocopying, etc. We estimate, but cannot guarantee, that these costs will run between $250
(12)   and $350, and, as explained, these costs are in addition to our fee and are not included in the $1,500 fee.

(13)   You indicated that you wished to pay in installments of $350 fees and $100 costs to begin work, and $150 fees and $50 costs the first of each month until you are current, and then, additional fees and costs will be paid monthly, as billed.

This schedule is acceptable to us, so long as you understand that if you terminate payments, we may termi-
(14)   nate our services and withdraw from the case.

(15)   As I indicated to you, based on the facts as you related them to me in the office, you should win, and you should be awarded a judgment of between $9,500 and $15,000, unless the case is settled at a different sum. Obviously, depending upon the facts as they are developed, our opinion could change and you could be awarded more or less, or even lose. You also understand that getting a
(16)   judgment is not the same as getting cash and that you may have to expend additional costs and fees to collect the judgment.

(17)   You asked me if spending money on legal fees in this case is throwing good money after bad, and I told you that at this point, I couldn't give you an answer, and that you should understand that there are no guarantees of winning or collecting.

It is my opinion, however, that whether you use our firm or other lawyers, you should proceed with your
(18)   case. Please do not delay. If you delay the commencement of your suit, you may at some point be barred from bringing it.

(19)   If the above properly sets forth our agreement, please sign and return the enclosed copy of this letter,
(20)   along with a check in the amount of $450, payable to my trust account. I will draw $350 toward my fees, and leave $100 toward costs as outlined above. A self-addressed, postage-paid envelope is enclosed for your convenience.

If we do not receive the signed copy of this letter, and your check, within 30 days, I shall assume that you have obtained other counsel, and shall mark my file
(21)   "closed" and do nothing further.

(22) If any of the above is not clear, or if you have any question, please do not hesitate to call.

Very truly yours,

To be typed on the copy of the letter:

The above is understood and agreed to, and my check in the amount of $450, payable to Jane Attorney Trust Account is enclosed.

(23)   Dated:_____

John Client

Essential Points to the Fee and Representation Letter

Obviously, the fee-representation letter must be tailor-made to the particular facts of the matter and the fee. Whatever form you decide to use, your letter should include the following:

(1) *The Matter Involved.* Perhaps your client has several legal matters, and has not told you about any of them except the Smith matter. This should prevent a later claim that you were responsible for *more* than this matter.

(2) *Your Interview Date.* This establishes when you had an interview to get the facts. This is for your protection in the event you are sued by your client or another party.

(3) *Whether or Not a Lawyer is Required.* This avoids the interviewee claiming that you said no lawyer was necessary and that he or she should "forget about it."

(4) *Suggesting Other Lawyers.* Suggest that the client may wish to see another lawyer. This relates to not representing the client until the agreement is returned. (See point 21 of this chapter.)

(5) *If You Wish Us to Represent You.* This reinforces that you are not yet the lawyer, and don't yet have responsibility.

(6) *The Amount of the Fee.* This establishes what I call the "Basic Fee."

(7) *Describing the Work the Fee Covers.* This discusses what you will do for the Basic Fee.

(8) *What the Basic Fee Does NOT Cover.* This describes what is not included in the Basic Fee.

(9) *Additional Work Fee Arrangement.* How you will charge for the work that is *not* included in this Basic Fee.

(10) *Minimum Fee.* What the minimum fee will be.

(11) *Out-of-Pocket Costs.* The client will not understand the difference between costs and fees, unless you explain it. This reinforces your explanation.

(12) *Addition to Fees.* Reinforce that out-of-pocket costs are in addition to fees.

(13) *Payment Schedule.* Set forth the cash flow that you have agreed upon, to avoid later misunderstandings.

(14) *Right to Terminate Services.* It is important that the client understands your right to terminate services for nonpayment. In some jurisdictions there may be ethical considerations in domestic relations and criminal matters. This portion should satisfy the requirements of DR 2–110(C)(1)(e) so that you can withdraw when the client stops paying.

(15) *Your Opinion of the Merits of the Case.* Repeat in a letter what you told the client in the office, and that what you said was based upon the facts which were given you. (Obviously, you may use this part of your letter to state that you are not yet in a position to express an opinion as to the outcome, or that you won't be able to express an opinion until research is done or until discovery is underway or completed.) In some types of work, you can quote dollar amounts. In some types, such as personal injury, you should not. Always repeat in writing what you did or did not say in the office to prevent later problems when the client claims you quoted a large recovery.

(16) *Explain Judgments.* Be sure the client is aware that winning a case and getting a judgment for fees and costs is not the same as getting cash, and that many judgments are uncollectible.

(17) *No Guarantees.* The client should understand that you have *not* guaranteed the outcome, and that it is possible that the funds expended on legal fees won't guarantee results.

(18) *Tell Client Not to Delay.* Warn the prospective client in lay language not to delay. Warn the prospective client that laches or a Statute of Limitations can prejudice the case if there are delays. *Do not* express an opinion on the statute

date, unless you are engaged to do so. If you gave the client the wrong date, you could have malpractice liability.

(19) *Signing and Returning Copy of Letter.* Obviously, the signed copy in effect becomes a fee contract when returned to you.

(20) *Repeat* that both letter and check should be returned.

(21) *Set Date for Return of Engagement Letter.* Clearly indicate that you will assume the "client" has obtained other help to prevent the "client" coming in two years later claiming you undertook the case even though you never heard from the client again. Let there be no misunderstanding that you are doing nothing further until you receive the signed fee agreement and the check.

(22) *Clarify Any Loose Ends.* Give the client an opportunity to ask if anything is not clear.

(23) *Have the Client Sign the Fee Agreement, and Get Your Retainer for Fees and Costs.* Upon execution and return of the fee agreement, you have a client, and the client has a lawyer.

The Section of Law Practice Management of the American Bar Association has published a book which may be helpful in expanding the scope of this chapter: *Legal Fees and Representation Agreements* (1983). It is available from American Bar Association, Order Fulfillment, 750 N. Lake Shore Drive, Chicago, IL 60611.

Balancing the Public's Need for Legal Services and the New Lawyer's Need to Eat

Society as a whole has an obligation to provide legal services to those who need them. Lawyers as a part of society should bear their proportionate share of this burden.

There are some ignorant, misguided people (including some new lawyers) who feel that lawyers alone are obligated to bear the entire burden of society. This is not now, and never has been, the case.

The lawyer who feels that each lawyer is obligated to do free legal work for anyone who wants it should not go into private practice unless he or she can get a subsidy from some organization.

Ethical Considerations 2–16 and 2–26 from the Model Code of Professional Responsibility state the situation as fairly as possible and are submitted here for your consideration.

Financial Ability to Employ Counsel: Generally
EC 2–16 The legal profession cannot remain a viable force in fulfilling its role in our society unless its members receive adequate compensation for services rendered, and reasonable fees should be charged in appropriate cases to clients able to pay them. Nevertheless, persons unable to pay all or a portion of a reasonable fee should be able to obtain necessary legal services, and lawyers should support and participate in ethical activities designed to achieve that objective.

Acceptance and Retention of Employment
EC 2–26 A lawyer is under no obligation to act as adviser or advocate for every person who may wish to become his client; but in furtherance of the objective of the bar to make legal services fully available, a lawyer should not lightly decline

proffered employment. The fulfillment of this objective requires acceptance by a lawyer of his share of tendered employment which may be unattractive both to him and the bar generally.

Keep in mind that when a private practice lawyer does free legal work, another lawyer may be deprived of a job in a publicly funded agency.

I submit that private practice lawyers should earn a good income and then devote some portion of that income to activities which simultaneously provide work for other lawyers and provide lawyers for people who can't afford them.

I also believe that during the first few years the new lawyer should concentrate on building a solid financial basis for a practice so that in later years there will be resources available for charitable enterprises. If the new lawyer does not first build up a practice, there never will be a later time or later resources to devote to society as a whole.

How to Set Your Fees

No matter how long you practice law you'll make a lot of mistakes when you set fees. As a new lawyer you are obviously more vulnerable to making mistakes in fee setting than the more experienced lawyers.

There are no simple formulas for fee setting. Platitudes are plentiful and concrete advice is hard to come by. Acknowledging in advance my inability to give you a simple panacea, I'll try in this chapter to give you general rules for fee setting, emphasizing the problems you'll encounter in the early part of your career. Hopefully you won't quote $3,000 for a fee when you should have quoted a $300 fee, or vice versa.

Fee Surveys

The Law Practice Management committee or section of your state or local bar association probably conducts periodic surveys of prevailing fees being charged by firms for given types of work. These fee surveys are typically done by firm size. Bar associations don't like to disseminate these survey results for fear they will be equated with the old minimum fee schedules, which are generally not used any more. You may have to ask the Economics Chair of your bar association to get this information.

Other Lawyers

In my opinion the smartest thing you can do to get a handle on fee setting is to ask another lawyer. The other experienced lawyer will be able to give you some help in ascertaining the important factors that will affect fees and costs. If you explain to the other lawyer that you don't know what you are doing he or she will help you. Obviously you will get only generalizations. These generalizations are much better than nothing.

Contingency Fees

Contingency fees are common in some types of work such as personal injury and are absolutely prohibited in other areas such as criminal or domestic relations.

1. *Personal Injury—Auto Accident.* Fees are commonly quoted by formulas such as "one-third if no lawsuit is necessary or 40 percent if a lawsuit is necessary" or "one-fourth if settled before filing of suit or 40 percent if settled after suit is filed but before 30 days of trial date and 50 percent if tried or settled within 30 days of trial."

2. *Personal Injury—Assault and Battery.* Fees of 40 percent to 50 percent with a cash minimum fee of $300 to $600 or more paid in advance are common. Collection of judgments is difficult as there is often no insurance.

3. *Personal Injury—Slip Fall.* Fees of 45 percent to 50 percent are common due to difficulty of establishing liability.

4. *Personal Injury—Medical Negligence.* Usually slightly higher than personal injury auto accident due to high cost of preparation of case and difficulty of settlement until you are "on the courthouse steps."

5. *Worker's Compensation.* Depends on local practice. Private fee contracts not permitted or valid in some jurisdictions. A private fee agreement may even be illegal.

6. *Commercial Collections.* Usually 25 percent to one-third of collections, based upon amount involved.

Lump Sum Fees

This involves setting a lump sum fee regardless of how little or how much work is involved. This is very common in criminal matters and domestic relations. Although this method has the greatest potential for being grossly unfair to either the client or the attorney, it seems to be the most desired by clients who prefer a fixed fee. Since both you and the client will be relatively unsophisticated, this method is probably best for both of you.

A word of advice. If you grossly underestimated the fee, that's your mistake, not the client's. Continue doing the very best job you can on the case. When you finish the case tell the client what you should have charged. About one time in 25 a client will offer to pay the difference to bring the fee to the proper amount. Be careful not to suggest that the difference be paid. As with friends and relatives, the client has no way of knowing the value of the services unless you tell him or her. If you did $4,000 of work for $1,500 tell the client. The client should know the value of what has been received and that you're a person of your word. The client will respect you and use you again.

Minimum-Maximum Lump Sum Fees

For the new lawyer this method is also good when you can't get an accurate handle on the exact amount. Give the client a range of minimum to maximum. For example: "I cannot give you an exact fee quotation at this time since the amount of work required will depend upon how aggressively the other side fights. The minimum fee will be $500 and the maximum, to and including trial, will be $5,000."

Hourly Rates

I don't recommend the use of hourly rates in the first several months for new lawyers for two reasons:

1. The time you devote to a matter in many instances will be inordinate due to your inexperience. It's not unusual for something to take you 12 hours the first time, including research and drafting, because you are starting from ground zero. The second time, using your form file as an aid, it may only take six hours; the third time perhaps only three hours and the fourth time one hour or less. There are many things I can do now in an hour which took me from 10 to 30 hours the first time I did it. Based on purely hourly rates the inexperienced lawyer will be more highly compensated than the more experienced lawyer.

2. You'll frighten the client away. It is difficult if not impossible to quote an hourly rate of $100 per hour to someone who earns $65 per day. There simply is no communication between you. If you estimate that the work should reasonably take 10 to 15 hours and you

want $100 per hour, then tell the client the cost will be between $1,000 and $1,500 and don't mention time.

Sophisticated business executives are used to being charged on an hourly rate; lower- and middle-class people are not used to paying on an hourly rate.

After you've been in practice six months or so you'll have enough background to be able to quote hourly rates where appropriate.

Fee by Stages

There will be cases where you simply cannot quote lump sum fees and where you don't want to quote hourly rates. You should try to break the work into "stages," estimating the work for each stage and then setting a fee for each stage as you go. An example would be as follows:

1. Research as to merits of case and written opinion: $350.

2. If I believe the case is meritorious and collectible, our fee will be one-third of recovery, giving you credit for $350 paid.

3. If I believe the case has uncertain merit or uncertain collectibility, you may use other counsel with no further obligation to us or you may proceed further as set forth.

4. Drafting of complaint: $350.

5. Law and motion appearances (prior to answer): $750 (includes two appearances if necessary; additional preparation and appearances $300 each if required).

6. Propounding or answering written interrogatories (four anticipated): each $100.

7. Deposition preparation and attendance: $300 per deposition of less than four hours, or $650 if more than four hours and less than 10 hours.

8. Trial estimated (five days): $750 per day.

9. All other services not covered above: $100 per hour.

10. You may stop using our services at any stage simply by so notifying us. If we accept the case on a contingency basis and you subsequently discharge us, our fee will be the *greater* of one-third of any offers received prior to or within 5 days of being terminated or $100 per hour. If we decide not to proceed further after taking the case on a contingency, then you will have no further obligation past the $350 and out-of-pocket costs advanced.

Bonuses

I personally believe that fees should be related to results. I pay substantial bonuses to employees based upon money they earn for the firm or money they save the firm with management suggestions and secretarial productivity. I also believe in billing clients *over and above* the agreed hourly rate when we accomplish unusually good results for the client. On the other hand I sometimes reduce a fee *below* the agreed hourly rate when the results are poor for the client. I have rejected substantial fees based upon purely hourly compensation where the client was not agreeable to a bonus. I have refused to accept a case based on a purely hourly basis, where I would have earned between $25,000 and $50,000, because the client was not agreeable to a bonus of 10 percent of the amount saved. The amount in the case was in excess of $1,200,000, with another $300,000 in interest and penalties involved. I was not about to accept professional responsibility for $1,500,000 for 2 percent to 3 percent of the amount involved. I would have been happy to accept the fee arrangement if the amount involved had been about $500,000.

While the numbers involved here may be beyond what you can reasonably expect in your first year or two, the concept is the same for smaller amounts.

It goes without saying that the "bonus" must be agreed to in concept if not in exact amount as soon as possible in the case. The concept of a fee predicated in part upon the results obtained and the amount involved is recognized by most existing state bar rules.

Setting Fees after the First Year or Two

After you've been in practice a year or two, much of the mystery in the fee-setting process will be removed, although some will always remain. You may wish to use different methods, examples of which follow (these methods are not necessarily recommended):

1. *Supply and Demand.* Charge all you can get in each case, subject to the fee not being unconscionable or "clearly excessive."

2. *Follow the Leader.* Charge what your contemporaries charge on the theory that they know what they are doing (a premise of doubtful reliability).

3. *Take What the Client Pays and Be Grateful.* This is a sure way to bankruptcy court (your personal bankruptcy). Remember that

even churches doing the work of God have to close when their parishioners don't give enough.

4. *Decide Your Own Value:*

a. Estimate the number of chargeable hours you work per year (Factor CH).

b. Set the net dollar profit you wish to earn per year (Factor P).

c. Estimate your overhead per year (Factor O).

d. Hourly rate = (P + O) divided by CH.

Legal Fees and the Code of Professional Responsibility

The Model Rules of Professional Conduct cover fees in Model Rules 1.15(a) and (d). Unfortunately, the code is of limited help to the new lawyer. It is very helpful in analyzing a situation in retrospect, but isn't very helpful to the new lawyer who wants to quote a fee to the client sitting across a desk.

I suggest you read Model Rule 1.15 and try to apply it within the context of the suggestions in this chapter.

Should You Charge for the Initial Consultation?

Our firm does not charge separately for the first consultation. We feel that the public should not be afraid to see a lawyer when they want to find out if they need professional help. After we have gotten the facts we advise them that they do or that they don't require professional help. (See points 3 and 4 in sample fee representation letter in "The Fee and Representation Letter" chapter.) We include the initial consultation services in the first bill if we do further services for the client.

Other lawyers tell the prospective client to bring a check to the initial interview. I feel that demanding a fee in advance for the first consultation leaves the public and potential clients with the impression that the lawyer is more interested in making money than in helping the client.

I have no proof, but I feel that our method gives the clients respect and confidence and encourages candor in relating the facts. I also feel that the client understands that we are sincerely trying to help.

Don't Quote Fees or Give Legal Advice over the Telephone to New Clients

In discussing charging for the initial consultation in the last chapter I said that some lawyers do ask the client to bring a check in advance of the initial interview, and that others don't require a check in advance of the initial interview. Both schools of thought have one thing in common, which is: *"Get the client into the office for the interview."*

Don't be seduced into the trap of quoting fees or giving legal advice over the phone. As a new lawyer you'll want to talk to a prospective client all you can to impress him or her with your legal knowledge and ability to handle the case.

Be wary of the "client" who won't come into the office for an appointment and who is trying to pump you for legal advice by telephone. In addition to pumping you for legal advice, such clients will continually try to get a price quotation over the telephone. When you ask these people how they got your name they'll typically be very vague. They'll say that someone—whose name they don't know—at a bank or at a party recommended you. They may claim they were referred by the bar association, but they'll never be recommended by any client you know of.

This type of person will absolutely refuse to come into the office even when you say there's no charge for the consultation. You'll get some story about being in town for a few hours or some other crazy excuse. When you ask for a phone number of address to contact him or her, you'll get another long story, giving neither address nor phone number.

This type of person has absolutely no interest in using you for a lawyer. He or she may have gotten your name from a phone book or some client who owes you money. In most instances this person already has a lawyer and is trying to use your advice and fee quotation to get the other lawyer to reduce a fee.

You are a fool if you give legal advice to this unknown voice over the telephone. When you get sued for malpractice two years later by this "voice" you'll have only yourself to blame.

Be firm. Tell the "voice" that you can't quote fees or give legal advice until *after* you've interviewed the client to be sure you have all the relevant facts and have examined the relevant documents. Don't waver. You'll be better off. If this person never comes, you won't have lost a client; you'll have lost a freeloading problem. It's hard to say "No" when you're a new lawyer who wants all the clients possible, but believe me, it's the best thing.

Getting Money Up Front from New Clients

Abraham Lincoln is reputed to have said, "The lawyer should always get some part of his fee in advance from the client. In this way the client knows he has a lawyer and the lawyer knows he has a client."

Whether you call it a "retainer fee" or an "advance," or any other name, the concept is still the same. Before doing a significant amount of work for a new client, the lawyer should always obtain part, if not all, of the fee in advance. It is not fair to the client or the lawyer for the client to undertake legal services that he or she cannot afford. I advocate that it is better for the lawyer not to do the work and not get paid than to do the work and not get paid.

Most people who seek the services of a lawyer expect to pay. A responsible client will not start expensive litigation if it is known that you will have to stop work if the fee is not paid as agreed. The client who cannot afford to pay for the services is not likely to pay the retainer fee in advance, thus saving the lawyer a lot of unpaid work. The prospective client who asks, "Don't you trust me?" should be answered: "No, why should I? I don't know you yet. If I can't protect my own legal interests, then what kind of job could I do protecting yours?" The same client who would be angry or insulted over paying some money in advance is usually the one who will be angry and insulted over your bill after you have done the work.

I am *not* advocating that you not do *pro bono* public legal work or just plain free legal work for experience. I *am* saying that *you* and *not* the client should decide when you are going to do nonpaying legal work. Being the most-loved lawyer in town won't help when you are evicted from your home and have to list your secretary's salary on a bankruptcy. We are dealing with an economic issue.

Cash Fees

When a client offers you cash fees, call in a secretary to count the money and to give a receipt to the client. Deposit the cash intact in the bank with the deposit ticket indicating the source of the fee. Be very careful about the client who makes some sort of remark to the effect that the cash is "hot" or that he or she is not keeping any record of payment of the fee. When the client says that only two people will know, the two of you, tell the client that that's one too many, namely, him or her. This type of client is a good candidate to try to blackmail you at a later date. He or she will threaten to turn you in to the IRS if you press for a unpaid fee. Such a client may also threaten to turn you in to the IRS unless you "loan" him or her money. When you get cash fees, go out of your way to let the client know that you've recorded the fees in your books and will report them in your income tax return. (As a new lawyer you won't have the problem of being in too high a tax bracket.)

Client Costs

The subject of cost advancement is subject to debate and disagreement in many jurisdictions. The purpose of this chapter is not to take any position, but to caution the new lawyer that you can go broke advancing costs. Costs should always be considered and handled from a cash flow point of view, keeping in mind your economic survival from a profit or loss point of view and also from a case acceptance or rejection point of view.

Never be afraid to ask an experienced lawyer what out-of-pocket costs and fees should be anticipated in a given type of case and at what stage of the proceeding they will have to be paid.

If at all possible, you should not have to finance client costs. You are not a bank or financial company. You should *always* ask the client for estimated costs in *advance* to place in your trust account to be used as needed and replenished as used. You should ask for costs in advance even in contingency fee cases.

The reality of life, however, is that you will be financing client costs for a number of reasons, such as:

1. Indigent client with meritorious case.

2. Convenience. You "lay out" the money for the client because it is more convenient, especially with smaller amounts such as long distance telephone calls, court fees, etc.

3. The competition. Other lawyers in your community don't ask for or get costs up front and you're afraid of losing the client if you insist.

In some cases you should *ask* the client for costs up front, but indicate to the client that if necessary or convenient, you can advance them subject to monthly reimbursement or reimbursement at the end of the case (meritorious accident cases, corporate formation, etc.).

In some cases you shouldn't take the case unless the client puts the costs "up front" (slip falls, doubtful recovery cases, etc.)

In some cases the amount of costs required on a meritorious case is so large that neither you nor the client can afford the costs, in which case you should associate in a well-financed law firm that can advance the costs for cases that require large amounts of investigation or outside experts (antitrust, medical malpractice, etc.) and cases where the pretrial, the trial, and the appeals will take years.

The Importance of Cash Up Front
for Survival
(Also Known as "Foonberg's Rule")

The concept of "cash up front" is a critical one for two reasons:

1. The case selection process for all lawyers new and experienced.

2. Economic survival for new lawyers.

Foonberg's Rule of "cash up front" can also be stated in three additional ways:

1. The client who can't or won't pay you cash up front at the beginning of the case is the same client who can't or won't pay you cash during the case, and is the same client who can't or won't pay you cash at the end of the case.

2. As I said earlier, if you choose between doing the legal work and not getting paid or not doing the legal work and not getting paid, you are better off not doing the work and not getting paid.

3. A bona fide client who seriously cares about his or her case will give you a cash advance for costs and/or fees to the best of their ability. A flaky client or one who is holding back on telling you everything will not advance cash on his or her own case because they know things either about the case or themselves that would affect your accepting or rejecting the case. (There will be some exceptions in criminal cases.)

Financing Your Practice with Bank Credit Cards

Credit is like medicine; properly used when and where appropriate, it can alleviate pain and discomfort and/or cure a temporary ailment. Improperly used credit, like improperly used medicine, can become addictive and even dangerous, to the point of doing permanent damage.

Financing your new practice for short periods with credit cards, in whole or in part, can be done, but it must be done very carefully and only as a last resort—when you have no alternative.

The secret of financing yourself successfully with credit cards is to get as many credit cards as possible that allow cash advances or equivalent traveler's check purchases. The cash advances can be used just as loans from the bank to pay office bills that must be paid in cash. The cash advances also can be used to make payments on other credit card accounts to keep them current when you previously have used them for cash advances or for purchases.

Shop Around for Merchants Who Accept Credit Cards

Merchants accept major credit cards to give them a competitive advantage over those merchants who do not accept them. It is a form of promotion. It often is cheaper for the merchants to pay a bank a small percentage of a sale than to maintain their own credit departments.

When ordering merchandise or services, or when establishing relations with a vendor, always ask, "May I pay by credit card?" Often, although a company will accept credit card payment, it does not advertise it, preferring to ship C.O.D. or prepaid.

You may have to be imaginative or creative. For example, a book publisher may not take a credit card for payment, but you may be able to special order the same book at the same price through a book store that will accept credit cards. Your insurance company or agent may sell you insurance with monthly payments. When the company or agent offers you this payment schedule, it is called "premium financing" if they charge interest. You may wish to accept their financing and use credit card cash advances for the monthly payments, although this could cost you double interest—once to the insurance company and again to the bank. On the other hand, you should shop around. You may find you can buy an identical insurance policy or coverage through an agent or company that does accept credit cards for payment. If you can find such an agent, you can bypass the insurance company's financing. If prices, quality, and service are otherwise about the same, always use a vendor who accepts credit cards so you can use them when it suits you.

Getting Bank Credit Cards

It is much easier to get credit cards than to get equivalent bank credit. The same bank that will give you $2,500 credit on a credit card might turn you down if you asked for a $2,500 loan. The bank's credit requirements on credit cards are more liberal than the credit requirements for a loan.

How Banks Earn Huge Profit on Credit Cards

(You either can take my word for it that credit cards can be an extremely profitable business for a bank, or you can read the rest of this paragraph to understand the mechanics.) When you buy a $1 item from a seller and pay with a bank credit card, you technically are signing a sales draft, which is something like a check. The merchant deposits your draft the same day and receives instant credit for the $1, less a discount that can run from one to eight percent, but which is normally about three percent. The bank gives the merchant cash or credit to an account when it deposits your draft. Assuming a three percent discount, the merchant gets $.97 cash. You are expected to pay the bank the $1 within 30 days. Therefore, when you pay as agreed, within 30 days, the bank has earned $.03 interest from you on a $.97 advance to the merchant. Thus, the bank will earn about 37.11 percent interest on an annual basis. If you pay the bank over a period of time, you will pay an interest charge of about 15 to 19 percent per year on the $1 you signed for, even though the bank gave the merchant only $.97. Assuming you pay 18 percent on the $1, this is actually 18.56 percent on the $.97. Accordingly, the bank will earn from 37.11 percent (if you pay your credit card bills within the interest-free period) to 55.67 percent (if you pay their bill in installments). The bank could charge you only about 16 percent on a normal loan of cash based on prime rate loans. (All prices are based on 1991 information.) To protect this high interest income and to push credit card use, merchants sometimes are prohibited by law or by contract from giving cash discounts to non-credit-card users.

Why Banks Give Out Cards Readily

Banks, as demonstrated, earn very high interest rates on their bank credit card business, whether you pay within the time limits without interest (euphemistically called service charges) or over a period with interest. In a May 1988 *Wall Street Journal* article, it was estimated that 94 percent of all Americans who want a bank credit card already have one. Accordingly, banks must push their cards onto the few people who do not already have one, using very low, if any, credit standards. Alternatively, the soliciting bank must try to get you to accept a second or third card when you already have one or two from another bank. If you had to go through a difficult procedure to obtain a card, you would not bother if you already had a good card. This is why banks send out unsolicited, pre-approved credit card applications. You may receive these applications from banks you have never heard of, in places you may never have been. To get help "pushing" the cards, the bank will give a kickback to bar and other associations, airlines or other groups for help and recommendations in the marketing of the cards.

Get All the Cards You Can

Consider the annual credit card membership fees as a form of "standby credit" expense. Large corporations often pay a bank a "standby fee" for unused credit. If you have to pay $50 per year to get a $3,500 line of credit, you are paying a 1.4 percent standby fee. If you pay no annual fees the first year, you are paying seven tenths of one percent standby fee the first two years. You ultimately may want a large number of credit cards, depending on the credit limit of each and the amount you eventually will need.

If you buy supplies or equipment using credit cards, from a large variety of vendors, you actually may have an offsetting savings through the reduction in the number of checks you have to write each month—and you may save bookkeeping time, costs, and bank service charges, based on the number of checks written.

Never Go into Default

Whether you pay in full on a current basis, without interest charges, or whether you pay in installments—never miss a monthly payment. As long as you pay timely, whether it be in full, within the non-interest period, or monthly with interest, the computer will show you are paying "as agreed." Paying "as agreed" will enable you to increase our line of credit and will result in a favorable credit rating when you seek additional cards and use the existing cards as a reference. Always use each card each month. Although it may be a nuisance to use all those cards and to write a lot of checks, use of the card creates an active status, which further improves your credit.

Seek the Maximum Line of Credit on Each Card

After you have received the card and used it for a period of time, call the bank (usually a toll-free number) and ask what is involved in getting a slightly larger line of credit. In some cases, you can obtain additional credit simply by asking for it by telephone. In other cases, you will have to request it in writing. Sometimes, the bank will treat your request for additional credit as a brand new credit application and ask for references, financial statements, etc. Surprisingly enough, the same bank that gave you a $3,500 line of credit without checking you out when they wanted you to take a card might consider you an unworthy credit risk when you submit financial information requesting $500 more on your line of credit.

Once you have a higher limit, you have what amounts to a line of credit and don't need to reapply for a loan every time you need cash.

Never Use Any Card to Its Maximum Credit

Always leave a margin of unused credit on each card. Your payment check could get lost in the U.S. mails, lost in the mailroom of the bank, or applied to the wrong account. If this happens, you could make a subsequent purchase that, unbeknownst to you, brings your total debt beyond your credit limit. The bank's computers will be alerted and you'll be placed on a special list that could cause forfeiture of the card and negative or derogatory comments on your credit standing.

Understand the Interest Rates You Are Paying

When using credit cards, you should understand that you may be paying an interest rate of from 15 to 36 percent, that you are paying an annual fee which may be considered as just more interest, and you may be foregoing cash discounts or lower prices that might be available if you do not use a credit card. When you add up all of these costs, you will see that credit card interest can be very expensive.

On the other hand, when you learn the true interest rates you pay on an automobile loan, a second mortgage, or on a small personal loan from your friendly finance company, you may be surprised to learn you are not paying much more for credit card interest than for the other forms of interest.

The difference in rates between credit card interest and that of alternative forms of financing (if you can get the alternative financing) is not so great as to make the difference between success and failure as a lawyer. A lawyer pays rent for the use of an office and pays a rent called interest for the use of money. There are high-rent districts and low-rent districts, both for money and for offices.

Never, Never Use a Credit Card Without a Clear Plan on How You Are Going to Pay for What You Purchase

Before you use the card, decide how you are going to pay for the projected purchase, even if you have to plan on getting a cash advance from that card or another card into your checking account to write the check to make the minimum monthly payment(s). Using a credit card with the intention of not paying the resulting debt is obtaining money or credit under false pretenses (fraud), and can result in jail or denial of discharge in bankruptcy. A criminal conviction or bankruptcy can cost you your license to practice law.

Improper credit card usage is a common factor in bankruptcy. Debt counselors often have an advisee symbolically cut all credit cards in half with a pair of scissors as the first step toward financial stability. By overuse of credit cards, at some point you simply will overextend your credit and end up in serious financial difficulty. As I said at the beginning of this chapter, credit is like medicine and must be used properly.

In conclusion, when planning your cash flow for the first year, you might wish to consider credit card financing if you can't get sufficient financing from a relative or bank—at no interest or at low interest. In the final analysis, although credit card interest rates are high, the difference between credit card interest rates and other interest rates available to you is not going to make the difference between your making it and not making it as a lawyer. You must discipline yourself to use the cards properly and never to abuse your credit. Properly used, credit card financing enables you to get your practice off and running and to keep it running.

How to Get Cash Up Front to Reduce
Bad Debts and Increase Cash Flow
and Avoid Going Under

As a practicing CPA, I quickly learned that the most common cause of new business failure is under-capitalization. Over the years, the statistics put out by the Small Business Administration bear this out. In other parts of this book, I have emphasized the importance of minimizing overhead and cash outlay in the beginning of your practice. I have also dwelled heavily on how to borrow money. I have also indicated the importance of the concept of cash up front (Foonberg's Rule) in the case selection process.

In this chapter, I will cover how to *use* the cash-up-front concept. Perhaps you will be able to modify these examples to fit your own situations. First, things you can say at the interview:

1. "Mr. Jones, it is office policy to ask new clients for a cash retainer. This retainer will be placed in a trust account and used for payment of fees and costs to other people. Each month we will send you a statement and will draw upon the trust account for payment of these fees and costs."

Alternative 1. "When we have used up the funds in the trust account, we will then bill you monthly and will expect you to pay upon receipt of the bill."

Alternative 2. "Each month we will expect you to send a check payable to the trust account to replenish the funds used."

2. "You can discharge me at any time and I will simply refund the unearned funds to you." (This reassures the client who is afraid you won't do the work after the funds are paid.)

Other things you can say and do:

1. "I tried to pay my secretary with accounts receivable, but the supermarket wanted cash from my secretary."

2. "Mr. Smith, you appear to have a meritorious case and I am

willing to invest my time and overhead in your case and get paid my fee when the case closes, but I'm not a banker. I don't loan money to clients or anybody else. I expect you to advance $_____ to my trust account to be used for out-of-pocket costs. None of the money will go to me for fees, but I expect you to advance your own costs."

3. "Mr. Smith, neither you nor I want you to start the case, then have to abandon it or postpone it in the middle because you can't pay your bill. It's better for both of us for you to pay the legal fees in advance so you won't have to worry about it if you run out of money one or two years from now during the case."

There is no substitute for simply asking for the cash up front in a simple, forthright manner.

How to Word Invoices That Clients Are Happy to Pay

The basic secret in invoicing is to tell the client everything you did. There is no such thing as an invoice that is too long. If you do a good job of preparing invoices, clients will think they're getting a bargain and will be glad to pay them before you reconsider how little you seem to be charging.

Source of Information for Invoices

The source of information for invoices is your time records. If you recorded everything you did, then preparing the invoice will simply be a matter of transferring the services rendered record from your time records to the invoices.

How to Word the Invoice

The most important thing in invoicing is to list every single *document* you prepared or reviewed. Clients often think that lawyers are in the stationery business. They ask, "How much for a will . . . or a partnership agreement . . . or a lease . . . or a lawsuit?" List every single letter, court form, document (including the number of drafts or revisions) that you worked on. Also indicate whether you reviewed the document or prepared it or revised it. Also list the forms your secretary prepared, including such documents as summonses, declarations or returns of service, and instructions to the clerk of court. Examples of three invoices are included at the end of this section.

Billing for Telephone Calls

Clients despise paying for telephone calls. Even our most sophisticated clients grit their teeth and mumble when charged for telephone calls. However, the same clients gladly and willingly pay for correspondence or other tangible "stationery."

When clients call and ask a question about legal rights in a given fact situation, they balk at paying for that advice. ("All I did was ask a simple question about mechanics' liens that didn't require any work" is a typical response to the bill.)

On the other hand, if you immediately sent a letter repeating the facts given you and your opinion, the client will gladly pay for "correspondence and telephone conference concerning Mechanics Lien Law." As an added benefit, you decrease your malpractice exposure by repeating the given facts or questions in the event the client later claims he or she gave you different facts.

Show Dates of Services

Your invoice should show every single date you worked on the matter even if only a minor service was rendered on a particular date. A client will usually be impressed by the fact that you worked on his or her case on six or seven different dates during a month. This technique lets clients know you are giving their cases continual attention.

Do *NOT* list the date opposite the service rendered. List the dates at the end of the invoice. If you worked on a single document on two different dates, the client erroneously may think that you are double billing if you show the same or a similar description twice.

Show Litigation

If there is a pending lawsuit, always show the name(s) of the case(s), the court(s) where the matter is pending, and the case number(s). Clients know that litigation is expensive (because you warned them at the inception of the matter), and by listing the court information you remind them monthly that the matter is expensive because litigation is expensive and not because you are expensive.

Don't Show Number of Hours of Service

Unless your fee agreement requires you to spell out the time devoted to each part of the work, don't do it. Listing each and every service and time often upsets the client over some minor aspect of the invoice.

If your fee agreement requires showing the hours worked, show the hours at the end of the invoice after all services are set out. Do not show every time detail alongside the work done unless the client asks for it.

Sample Invoices

Which invoice do you think your client would be most willing to pay?

Invoice 1

Re: Professional Services Rendered $450.00

Invoice 2

Re: Professional Services Rendered. Motion for Change of Venue and Answer to Complaint. $450.00

Invoice 3

Re: Professional Services Rendered. Jones vs. Smith, Los Angeles Superior Court Case No. 123456: Analysis of Complaint; office conference with Arthur Smith to obtain facts of case and to discuss strategy of defending; preparation of Motion for Change of Venue, including Notice of Motion for Change of Venue, Points and Authorities in Support of Motion, Declaration of Arthur Smith in Support of Motion; Declaration of Attorney in Support of Motion; preparation of Proposed Answer to Complaint; preparation of Declaration of Service by Mail of various pleadings. Telephone conference with Arthur Smith and opposing counsel concerning no settlement of case. Telephone conference with clerk of court and opposing counsel to obtain hearing date for Motion; preparation of Order Granting Change of Venue. (Services rendered January 4, 5, 7, 9, 11, 13, 15, 16, 25, 26, and 28, 19__.) $450.00

The Importance of Monthly Billing

Invoices should be sent out monthly. You pay secretaries and clerks two to four times a month. You pay rent, telephone and bank loans monthly. You need income on a monthly basis. You cannot pay payables with work in process or accounts receivable. Monthly billing lets you match your income against your expenses.

Monthly billing lets the client know you are constantly working on his or her matter.

Monthly billing allows you to determine when a client cannot or will not pay a bill.

Clients prefer to make progress payments as the case progresses rather than be shocked with a big bill at the end of the case. You are not doing the client any favor by letting bills run up that can't be paid. If the client is not happy with the results of the case, there may be an unwillingness to pay the last bill.

If the client cannot pay legal fees "as you go," you should consider handling the case on a contingency fee basis. If you have a low opinion of the merits of the case or the collectibility and don't want to proceed on a contingency basis, then you should be fair to the client and try to dissuade him or her from the litigation. Encourage the client to seek other counsel who may disagree with you as to the merits or collectibility, and who will take the case on a contingency fee basis. If there is no possible recovery and a defense is necessary, the client should be directed toward an agency with publicly paid lawyers.

(See chapter on "Cases and Clients that Should be Turned Down.")

Final Billing on Completion
of a Matter

Even though you have been billing your client monthly, there will be a final bill. This bill is usually a fairly large one because of the work normally incident to the conclusion of a legal matter. You will have put in a lot of time in trying the matter or in negotiating the settlement and drafting the documents.

There are two basic reasons for getting in the final bill as soon as possible after the matter is concluded:

1. *The Client's Financial Condition*. Often the client is about to receive or pay a large amount of money as a result of the conclusion of the case. If the client is going to receive funds, you want to be paid before they are dissipated. If the client is going to pay the money (or go bankrupt) this may be your last chance to get paid.

2. *The Client's "Curve of Gratitude."* My version of the famous Client's Curve of Gratitude is based on an article in *Law Office Economics and Management* and is found on the following page. Obviously the time to send the bill is between points 8 and 9.

After studying the Client's Curve of Gratitude you'll understand the importance of sending a final bill when the matter is concluded.

The Client's Curve of Gratitude

1. *Day Complaint Is Served on Client*
"Boy am I in big trouble. I never should have sold those pulleys without checking them out. I didn't know they were defective and would be used in a jet airplane which crashed."

2. *Next Day*
"I forgot I cancelled my products liability insurance."

3. *2 Days Later on First Meeting with Lawyer*
"I'll lose this case I'm bankrupt."

4. *After 8 Days of Deposition of Adverse Party*
"I don't know how you learned so much about pulleys and jet airplane hydraulic mechanisms. You really studied hard."

5. *At Trial*
"Do you really think you can keep the copy of the contract from being introduced by using 'The Best Evidence Rule?'"

6. *After Motion Sustained and Motion for Directed Verdict Taken Under Submission*
"You've got them running scared—try to settle."

7. *After Settlement in Hall*
"You did it! You did it! I can't believe it. I'm getting a cashiers check right now to pay the settlement before they change their mind."

8. *Day of Settlement*
"He's a fantastic lawyer. No other lawyer could have done what he did. I owe him my business, my career, everything."

9. *10 Days Later*
"He's a great lawyer and did a good job, but the law and the facts were on my side."

10. *3 Weeks Later*
"He's a pretty good lawyer but the judge and the jury were on my side."

11. *1 Month Later*
"He did his job but there was no way I could lose."

12. *6 Weeks Later*
"The case was cut and dried. I could have argued it without a lawyer and won easily."

13. *2 Months Later*
"I never needed a lawyer to begin with. He made a big deal out of a simple matter just to build up a big fee."

14. *10 Weeks Later*
"He's crazy if he thinks I'm going to pay his bill."

15. *3 Months Later*
"That shyster S.O.B. sued me. I'm filing a complaint against him with the Bar Association and I'll cross-complain for malpractice."

How to Make Clients Happy to Pay Legal Fees by Selling Them Stationery

Clients often have difficulty understanding that you are selling your professional advice. Professional advice is intangible. You can't see it or feel it; there is always a natural reluctance to pay for things that you can't see or feel. I have given this and similar advice in other parts of this book, because I feel the advice is important enough to be repeated.

Clients believe that lawyers are in the stationery business. They will ask you, "How much do you charge for a will . . . or a lease . . . or a lawyer's letter . . . or a lawsuit . . . or a partnership agreement?" Clients rarely ask you how much per hour you charge. Therefore, try whenever possible to convert your advice into stationery.

For example, a client calls and asks you a question about garage mechanic's liens. You tell the client that the mechanic at the garage has a lien on his or her car for up to $300 for parts and labor. If you send the client a bill for the telephone call for $10 you will get an angry response over being charged for a "telephone call." ("All I did was ask a simple question about mechanic's liens that didn't require any work," is a typical response to the bill.)

On the other hand, you should immediately send the client a letter repeating the facts given you, and your opinion. Send the client a photocopy of the applicable statute. He or she will gladly pay $35 for "correspondence and telephone conference concerning Mechanic's Lien Law." As an added benefit the lawyer decreases (or increases) malpractice exposure by repeating the given facts or questions in the event the client later claims different facts were given.

Many clients save forever anything they receive from a lawyer. Make the client happy. Bombard him or her with copies of the paperwork. Clients can understand paying for paperwork. They often can't understand paying for "advice." Send copies of checks, correspondence, pleadings, statutes, cases, etc. Clients want the paperwork and stationery and will pay for it.

What to Do with the Huge Fee

Occasionally, lawyers start their own law practice because of a single huge case that they can take with them from the old firm. I know of one lawyer who started his career with a $2.5 million fee on a single antitrust case. (He tried the case and gave his old firm one-half of the fee.) I know of another lawyer who started his career with a probate case with a fee of over $1 million.

Even if you don't start your career with a huge fee, you may get one at some point in your practice. The whole world will stand in line to sell you tax shelters. At one time hustlers of tax shelters were promising 4-to-1 write-offs on oil wells and 6-to-1 write-offs on lithographs. I believe that for a high enough fee someone would have created a tax shelter package of a lithograph of an oil well with a resultant 24-to-1 write-off.

The safest, most secure, risk-free way I know of to shelter as much income as possible, and still have the cash available, is through the use of a professional corporation and a corporate benefit plan.

If your motivation for starting your own law practice is a single huge fee, then I implore you to consult a competent tax lawyer before you do so.

How to Make Money by Reading Advance Sheets and Technical Journals

I spend about an hour a day reading advance sheets and journals for the following reasons:

1. To be a good lawyer by keeping current on the law;
2. To make money;
3. To impress clients that I care about them and their legal matters.

I read the journals with a red pen in hand. When I find an article or new case that affects or may affect a case in the office, I circle it and write the case name and client name on the face of the journal as well as the page number where the materials can be found. I then dictate a letter (you can do it the next day at the office or if, like me, you read advance sheets at home or on airplanes or during commuting, you can use a portable machine, as I do, to dictate it immediately).

A sample letter would be as follows:

Ms. Mary Jones
123 Main Street
Hometown, USA
      RE: Jones vs. USA USDC Case #_____
            Smith vs. USA decided June 1, 19__

Dear Ms. Jones:

I am enclosing a copy of the decision of the Second Circuit Court of Appeals in the case of *Smith vs. USA*. This case was decided on May 15 and was just reported in the May 25, 19__ issue of the *Daily Journal*. A copy of the case is enclosed for your files.

The facts and legal issue of the Smith case may have an

effect upon your case. The case was decided by the Second Circuit Court of Appeals in New York. We are in the Ninth Circuit here in Los Angeles, but nonetheless the Department of Justice (the trial lawyers for the government) will be aware of the case and it may affect the Judge's decision in your case.

You will note that one of the principal issues in the Smith case is the principal issue in your case (deduction of travel expenses for spouses).

No response on your part is necessary. We thought you would appreciate receiving this information.

Very truly yours,

Typical Client Costs

If you are handling a certain type of case for the first time or are not quite sure of yourself, ask an experienced attorney for help in estimating the kinds of costs to be anticipated in a given case. The costs listed here are simply some of the typical or "classic" costs you are likely to encounter in any given type of case.

Litigation

Police reports, court reporter minimum appearance fee, transcript costs, deposition appearance fees, medical examinations, medical opinions and reports, medical testimony, investigations, photocopy costs, record copying costs (employer and hospitals), expert opinion and testimony costs in addition to nonmedical, including accountants, actuaries, engineers, etc., sheriff's fees or other process fees, and travel expenses.

Business Formation and Businesses Generally

Advance payment of franchise or income taxes, filing fees for secretary of state or for county clerk, permit fees for stock issuance, transfer taxes, certified copies, recording costs (per page), newspaper notices and advertising, stock certificate, corporate seals and books, notarial fees, travel costs, long distance telephone calls and telex costs, title searches and reports, and out-of-state attorneys.

Again, these are only typical costs to be considered and you should always, when necessary, ask for help from other attorneys in estimating costs.

Can You or Should You Pay or Receive "Forwarding Fees" or Referral Fees?

Can You Pay Such Fees?

To Lawyers?

As a general rule, you *can* pay or receive forwarding fees if you follow certain rules as set forth in Disciplinary Rule 2–107 and Model Rule 1.5(e). These rules are as follows:

1. The client knows there will be a division of fees and consents. This consent should be in writing.

2. The total fee of the lawyers is no more than the reasonable value of what the client received. This is not usually a problem if the receiving lawyer charges a usual and customary fee and the lawyers share that fee. This restriction is intended to prevent overcharging the client to cover the fee splitting. For example, if a personal injury lawyer normally charges a contingency fee of 40 percent of recovery for a certain type of case, but increases the fee to 50 percent to cover the forwarding fee, then this fee conduct is probably improper.

3. There is a division in proportion to the services performed and the responsibility assumed by each. This is easier preached than practiced. I don't know how to divide responsibility proportionately. I suppose a written agreement between the two lawyers stating that they agree to divide responsibility proportionately is as close as you can come.

To Nonlawyers?

No, you may not. Fee splitting with nonlawyers is the second fastest way to get disbarred, running second after improper use of clients' funds. Fee splitting with nonlawyers is absolutely prohibited and there are no ifs, ands, or buts. Indirect fee splitting schemes are just as wrong as direct payments. Sample illegal fee splitting devices are: paying "investigators" a percentage of fees; paying "landlords" or "business managers" a percentage of fees.

Should You Pay or Receive Such Fees?

From a purely economic, short-range point of view, forwarding fees may be a very desirable policy for a young lawyer for the following reasons:

1. It encourages getting the client over to a qualified specialist rather than leaving the client with an inexperienced lawyer who is afraid to lose a fee.

2. On an hourly rate, both the sending and receiving lawyer get relatively well compensated at no increase in price to the client. This is particularly true in percentage and standard fee situations. The specialist can accomplish the task in fewer hours and will get the fees more quickly.

From a long-range economic point of view, referring clients to others may be detrimental to the growth of your practice, since you've given up the major portion of your fee and since the client may refer other clients to the specialist rather than to you. Although a receiving lawyer should decline to accept employment on other matters from a previously referred client, this restriction does not apply to the people the client refers.

To illustrate: Suppose Ms. Client comes to you, Mr. Swellperson, with a case, and you refer Ms. Client to Mr. Specialist, who satisfactorily handles the matter. Two years later Ms. Client calls Mr. Specialist on an unrelated matter. Mr. Specialist should refer Ms. Client back to you rather than accepting the employment. In theory, this is simple. In practice, it often does not work. Ms. Client will usually say something along the line of, "I don't want to go back to Mr. Swellperson. It's you I have confidence in. If you won't accept my case, then I'm going to a third lawyer because I don't want to go back to Mr. Swellperson"; or the conversation may be to the effect, "I don't want Mr. Swellperson because he didn't want me." However you dress the package, the results are the same: Mr. Swellperson never sees the client again nor does he see the people referred by the client. Whether this result is good or bad or right or wrong is beyond the scope of this book.

Is There an Acceptable Middle Ground?

I believe there is an acceptable middle ground that is fair to the client and fair to you. I engage a specialist to work for me. I pay the specialist by the hour out of my own funds to get advice on how to handle the case and upon the merits or value of the case. Often the specialist has no contact with the client at this point. The specialist should be paid a consultation fee "up front" by you and then be given the facts by you. The specialist will tell you if he or she thinks the case can be handled by you with assistance, or if the matter is so far over your head that both you and the client would suffer if you tried to handle the matter without the assistance of a specialist.

For example, products liability cases or aircraft crash cases may require tens of thousands of dollars for investigators and testing. A difficult medical malpractice case may require expertise possessed by few lawyers. A first-degree murder case is no place to get some experience before a criminal jury. There are many types of cases where you simply will not have the bankroll or expertise to handle a case simply because it's too big or too complicated.

On the other hand, if you can handle the case with the help of a paid specialist, you will have the best of all worlds in that you will still earn the major part of the fee, keep a well-served client and his or her referrals, and receive experience under expert tutelage.

In the Final Analysis, Should You Pay the Referral Fees?

On balance, during the first year of your practice, you should pay referral fees as asked for. Referrals from other lawyers can be a significant source of cases, experience, and fees in the beginning of your career. The case you get from the other lawyers will not be any bargain from a fee point of view, but if you play it straight and honest with the referring lawyer, he or she will gain confidence in your integrity and refer more cases to you. In most cases, the referring lawyers who send you the low-pay cases will *not* want a referral fee, but they might, and if so, pay it following the rules set forth in Model Rule 1.5(e).

Caveat

As a general rule, neither courts nor legislatures are concerned about fights between lawyers over fees.

The advice I have given here is general advice. It behooves you to make inquiry of local lawyers to modify this general advice to your local situation. The rules and law in this are changing rapidly, and you must be sure you are current. Some of this advice may be totally inapplicable to your local situation and, in fact, may even lead to unethical conduct judged by local standards.

"Bedside Manner" in Setting Fees

1. *Be Firm.* No matter which method of setting fees you use, be firm. If you are uncertain or wishy-washy, clients will rapidly lose confidence in you as a potential lawyer to handle their cases. After all, if you can't set a value on your own services, perhaps they have no value.

2. *Use Words Like "Per My Standard Fee" or "The Standard Fee" or "In Cases Like This."* Instill confidence in the client.

3. *Don't Ask the Client What the Fee Should Be.* This is one way to guarantee the client's using another lawyer.

4. *Distinguish Between Uncertainty in the Amount of the Fee and Uncertainty in the Manner of Setting the Fee.* When it is impossible because of the facts in the case to tell the client what the legal services will cost in total, you can still confidently set the method of computing the fee.

5. *Don't "Back Down."* If you quote "one-third" or "$135/hour" or "$750" for the matter, don't back down when the client suggests one-fourth or $60/hour or $500 for the matter. If you back down, the client will think you were deliberately attempting to overcharge. The same client will again try to get a discount as a precondition to letting you close the case. What you look upon as an accommodation will be taken as a symbol of overcharging or dishonesty.

6. *Don't Be Swayed by What the Client Says Another Lawyer Charges.* Usually there is no other lawyer, or if there is or was another lawyer, the client had no confidence in that person. Clients who really want to use another lawyer wouldn't be seeing you.

7. *Don't Be Tempted by the Client Who Wants You to Take a Case at a Reduced Fee with the Promise of More Cases Later at Rea-*

sonable Fees If You Do a Good Job on the First Case. Take my word for it that there will be no later cases. Simply tell this client that in your office every piece of work has to stand on its own and pay its own way. Say that high-quality work can't be handled at low-quality fees, and if price is a principal consideration, you're wasting each other's time.

Put yourself in the position of a patient getting a filling. You ask the price. The dentist says, "My standard fee is $65." You state that you'll pay $25. The dentists says, "O.K." Aren't you going to be concerned about the quality of the filling you'll get?

8. *Be Sure You Bring up Fees at Your First Meeting.* (Note I said meeting—not phone call or letter.) Tell the client that you wish to discuss fees and that the client should never be embarrassed or ashamed to discuss fees with you. Don't leave the client wondering if you use an Ouija board to set fees.

9. *Suggest When Appropriate that the Client Borrow the Fees from a Credit Union or Relative.* When the client says he or she doesn't want to go to relatives, watch out. That person may not want to go to relatives because there is no intent to pay.

10. *Suggest, When Appropriate, that the Client Give You Collateral or Security for Payment of the Fees.* This is extremely important when the client may be defunct, bankrupt, or jailed if the case is lost.

Remember, you can't have all the legal business in your state. Don't be overly concerned when a client goes to another lawyer for no other reason than cheaper fees. In these cases it is your gain and the other lawyer's loss. Be pleased that a client who was more interested in price than quality went elsewhere.

In summary, when discussing legal fees, you should exude confidence at every stage and be firm. Remember, if you can't properly represent your interests, the client will not think much of you.

When and How to Withdraw from a Nonpaying Matter

In this chapter, I am limiting my discussion to the aspects of withdrawal due to payment factors. I recommend very highly to you Model Rules 1.7, 1.8, 1.9, 1.10, and 1.16(a) which cover withdrawals for other reasons such as conflict of interests, the attorney's being a witness, etc.

To paraphrase a line from a popular play, "Poverty may not be a shame, but that doesn't mean it's necessarily a blessing." Don't let a client take you under, too. Get out when it is in the best interest of both you and the client.

Whether you call it "dropping the case" or "withdrawing from the matter," the end result is the same. The desired result is that you are no longer taking a financial bath and the client is free to make some other lawyer rich (or poor).

If you are unhappy with the economic arrangements for the case or the client, you are going to have difficulty psychologically observing the Model Rules that require you to *represent a client with zeal.* It should be obvious that if you like feeding your spouse and family, you may handle the paying cases and clients first, pushing the no-pay and poor-pay cases to the bottom of the pile where they may languish to the mutual detriment of both you and the client.

There are three possibilities with respect to withdrawing from a matter:

1. You cannot withdraw (you are stuck);
2. You must withdraw;
3. You should withdraw.

You Cannot Withdraw from a Matter

As a general rule, there are two instances when you cannot withdraw from a matter.

1. *The client has paid your agreed fee in full.* In this case, you have no recourse but to honor your fee agreement. You may not like the situation. If you erred in setting your fee, that's your problem. Chalk up your mistake as a learning experience. The next time a similar matter comes in, you'll have learned what a proper fee quotation should be.

You can sometimes get out of this mess by offering to refund 100 percent of the fees received. (Note: I said 100 percent—not some or part.) You should also offer to turn over your file to the client or to another lawyer.

Misunderstanding a fee arrangement is common with new lawyers because of their negligence in not putting the fee agreement in writing. I blame the lawyer, not the client, for misunderstandings. There is no excuse for misunderstandings.

2. *Your withdrawal would prejudice the client's case.* Although there are a few exceptions, you may not withdraw from a case unless you have taken appropriate steps to protect your client's rights. Oversimplified, you can't abandon your client on the courthouse steps a few hours before trial just because you haven't been paid. As above, if you allowed yourself to get stuck in this situation, you should grin and bear it. (See Disciplinary Rule 2–110(A)(2).)

You Must Withdraw

There are many times when you must withdraw from a case and these will be listed here. The problem from a financial point of view is whether or not you'll get paid for what you've done. As a very general oversimplification, you'll have a right to payment where the reason for the withdrawal is not your fault. If the reason for the withdrawal could have been, or should have been, foreseeable by you, then you probably won't get paid. In fact, DR 2–110(A)(3) may require you to refund what you've collected in fees.

The following is a "warning list" of situations where you may have to withdraw from the case after you've started working ("Forewarned is forearmed."):

1. *You intend to call yourself as a witness for your client's case.*

2. *You will have a financial interest adverse to your client.* To a certain extent, all fee agreements are to some degree financially adverse to the client. This "adverse financial interest" problem is overcome if the client understands the situation and consents to it. You

should protect yourself by getting the consent in writing when feasible.

3. *There is a conflict between two or more clients.* This problem can be solved by the client consenting to the continued employment.

4. *You know, or should know, you are not competent to handle the matter and will not associate with a competent lawyer.* Under the old Canons, competence was not considered an ethical matter. Under the Model Code and Model Rules, a lawyer must associate with a competent lawyer when he or she is not competent to handle a matter.

5. *The client's case has no merit whatsoever and is being maintained for some ulterior motive such as delay or harassment.*

6. *Your conduct in handling the case would either be illegal or prohibited under the Model Rules.*

7. *You are fired.* The most obvious situation where you should withdraw is when you've been discharged as the lawyer. This raises the question of fees. In fixed fee and hourly fee cases, you probably will be entitled to be paid in full for what you've done.

In cases where you've been paid in advance, you will have to refund some portion of the fee unless you and the client have agreed that the fee was a *minimum* retainer and that you earned it by accepting employment in the case.

In contingency cases, how much you're entitled to depends on the law in your jurisdiction. In some jurisdictions, you will be entitled only to *quantum meruit* recovery. In some jurisdictions, you'll be entitled to the contingency percentage on whatever offers you've already received on the case. In some jurisdictions, you'll be entitled to your contingency percentage on the final settlement obtained in the case, even though obtained by another lawyer or the client in "pro per."

Local Custom and Rules

In some jurisdictions and tribunals, you cannot be relieved as the attorney for a corporation unless there is another lawyer willing to accept the case. This situation is created because corporations cannot represent themselves but can only be represented by an attorney licensed to practice law. Keep this in mind when you undertake the representation of a corporation.

In some jurisdictions, you cannot be relieved in a criminal case once you have appeared. This is a throwback to the days before the extensive public defender system existed. In those days, private lawyers simply did work for free as a professional obligation that public defenders and other government-paid lawyers now do for salaries. Some judges, trying to avoid more work for overburdened public defenders, insist on a private lawyer continuing on the case for free. Fortunately, this practice is disappearing, and judges now let unpaid private lawyers "off the hook" and request the paid lawyers to take on the case.

Unfortunately, you are going to learn a lot of lessons the hard way. There are many areas of practice where you just can't get "off the hook" without your client's help. Divorce court, bankruptcy court, cases involving children or decedents or incompetents are typical situations. You will find that your client has disappeared, you haven't been paid and you can't get out of the case. It's a real nightmare that will happen to you sooner or later in spite of the warnings of this book.

You Should Withdraw

In my opinion, you should withdraw from a case as soon as clients give you the indications that they're not going to live up to their fee agreement. Model Rule 1.16(b)(4) specifically allows a lawyer to withdraw from a case when the client "fails substantially" to live up to an obligation to the lawyer, such as a fee agreement (provided the lawyer can mitigate the consequences to the client of his or her withdrawal).

It is a basic rule of money management reinforced by the famous "Prudent Person" dicta of your law school days that losses should be cut short and not allowed to roll on. It is better for you (and your bank account) to lose out on three months' work on a nonpaying client than to lose out on six months' work. Cut your losses short. Take the time you would have spent on the nonpaying client and devote it instead to your paying clients.

How to Withdraw from a Case

The best way to withdraw from a case is to do so cleanly, honestly, and with as much advance notice in writing to the client as possible. A series of letters would set the stage for your subsequent motion to be relieved or substituted out. The letter should contain language to the following effect:

Letter No. 1

Dear Client:

I cannot effectively represent a client when I have an overriding concern about being paid. In our written fee agreement, you promised to pay monthly as billed. My secretary has called twice to see if there is a problem or a mistake and you indicated that "a check is in the mail." You are now three months delinquent in paying your bill. Unless you pay the bill in full within the next ten days or make a new arrangement satisfactory to both of us, I shall have to terminate our professional relationship. I prefer to keep you as a client, but you will remember that when the case first arose, we discussed a fee agreement and put it in writing to make clear our arrangement. At that time, I was not willing to take the case on a contingency basis or on the basis of being paid at the end of the case. Nothing has happened to change that position. Please contact me within ten days.

Letter No. 2

Dear Client:

You have not responded to my letter of _____, a copy of which is enclosed. We no longer wish to be professionally responsible for your case and request you to seek other counsel. Please be assured that we will cooperate with your new attorney. Your trial date is about one year away, and you and your new attorney will have plenty of time to take reasonable measures to complete the trial preparation.

Letter No. 3

Dear Client:

We are enclosing a substitution-of-attorney form for you to sign where indicated by the red "X." We will file it with the court and will no longer be your attorneys in this matter. You will be your own attorney until you select another attorney. Upon receipt of the signed form, we will forward your files on to you.

Letter No. 4

Dear Client:

Enclosed is a copy of our motion to be relieved as attorneys in this matter. It will be heard _____, 19__, at 10:00 a.m. in room 123 of the Courthouse located at 5th and Elm. If our relief is granted, we will no longer be your attorneys, and you will be representing yourself until you select another attorney.

Letter No. 5

Dear Client:

Judge Jones granted our motion on_____. 19__. A copy of the order is enclosed. Effective immediately, we are not your attorneys in this matter. Your files have been sent under separate cover, "return receipt requested." We caution you to obtain new counsel as rapidly as possible to prepare your case for trial.

What Not to Do

Disciplinary Rule 2–110(C)(1)(f) specifically gives you the right to withdraw from the case where you are not paid. You *do not* have the right to keep the case and the client and refuse to do the work the case requires until you are paid. Therefore, you cannot, for example, refuse to proceed with a case until you are paid. You must either do what is required even though you are not being paid or you must withdraw from the case.

Part VI
Managing the Law Office

Management of the Law Office—General Comments

There are many gimmicks or tricks advocated by management experts for making the most effective use of your day. These suggestions run the gamut from that of training yourself to go to the toilet only during nonoffice hours to suggestions on how to dictate, where to place lighting, use of computers, etc.

Some of these suggestions are adaptable to law offices and some are not. I leave it to the reader to select his or her own management experts, books, consultants, etc.

The management suggestions I have made in this section and throughout this book are suggestions that I recommend to the new lawyer in practice based upon my experience.

Most of the suggestions are those that you will be able to use during your entire legal career, regardless of the size or nature of your practice or how long you've been in practice.

Overhead control and management of your office is to a great extent simply a matter of self-control and self-management in your first few years. Later you will have to control and manage others.

The difference between earning "a living" and earning "a good living" from the same practice will depend on how well you follow the lessons of this section on management.

Organizing Your Day
to Make More Money

The president of one of America's "Big Three" auto manufacturers supposedly comes into his office every morning and stares out the window for a few minutes. Then he turns around to his desk and begins a list of "Things to Do." He puts the most important thing at the top and the list continues with things of decreasing importance.

If he only does one thing all day, he does the first thing on the list. After days or weeks he may take that last thing off the list by either ignoring it or giving it to someone else to do. He may *never* get to the last item on the list.

I don't know if this story is true or false, but it makes sense.

In hospital emergency rooms, sometimes several people arrive at the same time. This often happens after a large accident such as a multiple auto accident, building collapse or train wreck. There often are only one or two doctors then on duty to handle a large number of emergencies. Decisions are made to rank the medical cases in order of priority. Red blankets are put on those who can be saved but require immediate attention, purple blankets are put on those who will be saved if they are taken care of later. White blankets are given to those who really don't need emergency medical care to begin with and also to those who are going to die anyway—or who require so much attention that many others would die if they were taken care of. These cases are quietly wheeled out of the emergency room and given pain killers and ignored until the red blanket and purple blanket cases are taken care of. (The blanket color code differs from hospital to hospital, but the principle is the same.) Just as the auto executive and the hospital emergency room have to organize their work load, you have to organize yours.

I recommend starting each morning with a list of "Things to Do."

Whether you use a plain legal pad or a commercially prepared pad is immaterial. The important thing is to discipline yourself to make a list and use it. The examples which follow this chapter, along with an explanatory note, should convey the idea. You might wish to review your list at fixed intervals such as lunch time, end of day, etc.

Things to do TODAY

DATE December 1

1	Call Bob Wilkins re program
2	Call Tom Peters re overdue bill
3	Answer attorney Smith letter re Sutherland
4	Have Mary call re stationery delivery
5	Start research on Jones case
6	Get accident reports in Jones case
7	Start research re Alaska statute
8	re transferee liability
9	Work on 9th circuit brief (due Feb 5)
10	Start research on Toy article for Bar Journal (due May 1)
11	Get contracts re auto damage in Owen case
12	
13	
14	
15	
16	
17	
18	
19	
20	

1. Beginning of day

Things to do TODAY

DATE December 1

		✓
1	Call Bob Wilkins re program	
2	Call Tom Peters re overdue bill	
3	Answer attorney Smith letter re Sutherland	
4	Have Mary call re stationery delivery	
5	Start research on Jones case	
6	Get accident reports in Jones case	
7	Start research re Alaska statute	
8	re transferee liability	
9	Work on 9th circuit brief (due Feb 5)	
10	Start research on Toy article for Bar Journal (due May 1)	
11	Get contracts re auto damage in Owen case	
12		
13	Saw someone re Mr. Peters	
14	Send fee letter to Mr. Ramos	
15	Get firm to help on Toy article	
16	Set deposition of Mr. Fiol	
17	Draft of release granted by new statute	
18		
19		
20		

2 and 3. During the day

Things to do TODAY

DATE December 2

	✓	☐
1	Get accident reports to Jones case		
2	Serve summons on Mr. Peters		
3	Send fee letter to Mr. Thomas		
4	Start research on Jones case		
5	Answer Attorney Smith's letter re Settlement		
6	Set deposition of Mr. Fish		
7	Decide if Peters engagement by new statute		
8	Work on 9th Circuit brief (due Feb 15)(Clarke by 1)		
9	Start research on Tax Article for Bar Journal		
10	Ask Tom to help on the Tax Article		
11			
12			
13			
14			
15			
16			
17			
18			
19			
20			

4. End of day

Explanation

1. Start with a list of things to do. Put the most important thing at the head of the list. This should be the one thing you want most to get done during the day. Continue the list in order of descending importance.

2 and 3. Cross off things as you do them. Add new things which came up during the day.

4. Rearrange the list for the next day.

Organizing Your Desk
to Make More Money

You will spend many hours at your desk. Your desk is not just a place to put ashtrays. It is the place where you will earn much of your living. You can make money at it.

1. Get a picture of your loved one(s) and place it on your desk facing *you,* not facing the client. Look at the photo whenever you feel awkward about charging fees. This photo will make it much easier to discuss fees, or to refer the client with no funds to legal aid. Update the photo when appropriate (e.g., when your children start to walk and then remind yourself that shoes cost money). Your family's growth will remind you of increased food needs. If you don't have a family, put up a picture of whatever is dependent on you, whether it be a boat or a plane or a pair of skis.

2. Put a clock on your desk facing you. A battery-operated, digital clock silently reminds you that time is a "wasting asset." (Use a battery-operated clock to avoid untidy electric wires all over your desk.) Put the clock squarely in front of you. Get in the habit of looking at it as soon as the phone rings, or the client comes in.

3. Put your telephone on the left side of your desk (if you are right-handed), so that you'll be able to dial or hold the phone with your nonwriting hand. Use a speaker phone so that you can use your hands to flip through a file when necessary.

4. Put your pen set on the right. Pick up your pen the moment you begin a telephone call or conference.

5. Your dictating microphone should be readily available on your desk.

6. Your time record book should be directly in front of you in the two o'clock position, in front of your pen so that you can jot down the client's name when you pick up the pen; and add the ser-

vices rendered when you put the pen back at the conclusion of the call or conference.

7. Keep a "Things to Do" pad. You can either buy a preprinted pad entitled "Things to Do," or just keep a list on any lined tablet. Every morning (or evening if you prefer), make a list of "Things to Do" and number them in order of importance. During the day, add the new things to the list as they come in and cross things off as they get done.

Prepare the list so that if you only did one thing all day, it would be the number one item. Don't be upset if it takes a long time to get to do the least important things, or if the least important things never get done (within limits of good sense and professional responsibility).

8. Files and papers neat on desk vs. cluttered desk:

This is another area where five lawyers have at least ten opinions. I have seen articles prepared by psychologists that indicate that a cluttered desk is psychologically debilitating to the lawyer, creating a subconscious dread and resistance to the amount of undone work. Supposedly, according to these articles, the client will feel that you are "too busy" to give personal attention, and will not hire you.

On the other hand, my desk looks like a rummage sale. Once a client refused to trust me with documents for fear they would get lost in the piles on my desk.

On some occasions, I have apologized to clients for my cluttered desk, and they have remarked that they want a lawyer who has lots of clients and work, and that they wouldn't want a lawyer who had very little work to do.

To me, a cluttered desk is a security blanket. When I see all the files, I don't worry that the phone won't ring that day.

This is an area where you should do whatever makes you feel comfortable.

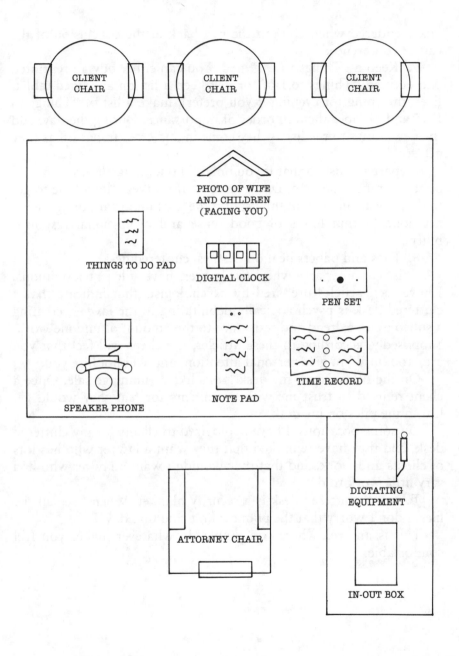

Organizing Your Desk to Make Money (Designed for a Right-Handed Lawyer)

How to Keep Time Records to Make More Money and to Preserve Evidence of Work Done

The famous Missouri Bar Survey shows that lawyers who keep time records earn 40 percent more than lawyers who don't. Recent studies indicate that lawyers who keep *good* time records earn 15 percent more than lawyers who keep poor time records.

If you are concerned enough about earning a decent living to read this book, you are probably already keeping time records.

Whatever system or method you use, whether manual or computerized, be sure you keep the time book or time slips on your desk in front of you as a constant reminder. There are many systems on the market. The Day-Timer System is adequate for most sole practitioners. When I first started out, I used the Day-Timer Junior book. After a few years, I "moved up" to the Day-Timer Senior Sample Sheets. (Illustrations follow this chapter.)

Time records are not just billing records; they are, or can be, evidence for a claim in the estate when your client dies.

Record All Services

Record *all* telephone calls and all correspondence. If you decide later not to bill for a telephone call or letter, you can consider the services rendered as your contribution to the client. If you do not immediately record the services rendered, you will not be able to remember later to charge. It's simply not possible to remember what you did at the end of the month or the end of the week or even the end of the day.

Allow No Exceptions

Record *all* services rendered. If you are selective, you will tend to err towards not recording enough.

Don't Wait

Pick up your pen with your right hand or make an entry on your PC when you pick up the phone with your left hand. Write the name of the client when you start the call or letter or conference and record the service the instant you hang up the phone or finish dictating the letter or returning from an out-of-office meeting or court appearance.

Time vs. Billing Records

You are keeping *time* records, not billing records. By recording all time, you will be able later to charge as appropriate, using hindsight. If you attempt to record only those services that at the time seem chargeable, you'll omit a lot of billable services. Remember, you are keeping time records, not billing records.

Review Your Time Records at the End of Each Day

Do not leave the office until you have added up your time for the day. If you come in at 9 a.m. and leave at 5:30 p.m. with an hour for lunch, you should have seven and one half hours of time recorded.

Time Records as Evidence

We keep time records for all work, including personal injury and worker's compensation. We have asked for and received fees based on time and services from various administrative agencies such as Worker's Compensation Boards, as well as from courts when submitting minors' cases for approval. Our time records have served as evidence in disciplinary proceedings brought against other lawyers; our records of telephone conversations with the other lawyers save them because their clients accused them of neglecting a case.

Time Records to Support Income Tax Deductions

You should record your out-of-pocket expenses immediately. Parking lot fees, public telephones, deductible meals and promotional expenses should be immediately recorded as the contemporaneous records required by the Internal Revenue Service.

21

APPOINTMENTS & SCHEDULED EVENTS

NAME	PLACE	IN RE:	HOURS
Mr. Ihm re 9th Circuit 8:30 a			8
			9
Conf John Cohen have @ 10 re Sweethead			10
			11
Conf + lunch with Mr. Busho - start here at noon lunch @ 12:30 at el Cholo			12
Barber appointment @ 2:00			1
			2
			3
Meeting at North Coast @ 4:00 p			4
			5
7:30 - UCLA Law School - Program			NIGHT HOURS

TO BE DONE TODAY (NUMBER EACH ITEM)

ITEM NO.

1

NOTES & MEMOS MADE TODAY

San Francisco by PSA for Thursday 20 bill	
Cab from airport	9.75
Cab from district court to 9th Circuit	2.00
Cab back to district court	7.00
Photo copies and certification fees	7.75
Airports back to airport	1.75
Parking LAX	3.00
	$26.25
21 Nov	
Parking lot El Ripoff tip	1.00
Fall to office for messages	15
Parking lot at Supervisor	3.00
Parking at UCLA	1.00
Lunch at the Ripoff	38.00

HOURS	File #	FOR Client	IN RE Parties	DESCRIPTION OF SERVICES Description of Services	HRS 1/10
8		CARA INC		Conference with client re filing of brief and stay with 9th Circuit in San Francisco a Thursday 20 November	3/4
9		Bala US Franchise Tax Board		Letter to client with explanation of regulation # 68-462 as applied to case	1/2
		Cara Inc		Telephone call with US atty re stay of execution	1/4
10		Sweetbread Inc		Telephone Conf with client re stay of execution	1/4
				Conf. John Cohen, CPA re depreciation possibilities for trucks	3/4
		Bangkok Properties		analysis of 30% withholding requirements on interest remitted	1/2
11		Sweetbread, Inc		Memorandum to file re possible application of IRC Sect 269	1/2
		Calif Bank us Thomas		Speed letter to client re renewing judgment	1/4
12		Client Relations		Lunch with Mr. Brooks at El Ripoff Restaurant re possible representation	1 1/2
1		Brazilian Trade Assoc.		Telephone call from Mr. Jones re proxies for meeting	1/4
		JGF Personal		Haircut at Barber Shop	1
2		Jones adv Smith		Telephone call from Mr. Jones with preliminary facts and to set up meeting in office on Monday	1/4 nc
		Sweetbread, Inc.		Conference at offices of Lena Northeast Co with Sam Peters and William Smith outside	
3				counsel for NE and Tom Jones House Counsel for NE and RH Samuels Controller for NG and William Arthur President of DE and Tom Goodguy President of Sweetbread	2
4				re possibility of arranging sale items to avoid avoidance of 269 problem	
				LM to client summarizing results of meeting	1/2
		Republic Pants adv. Pants	Schlock	Conference client re doing research and getting facts to determine liability	
5				Telephone call client at home Thursday night to set up meeting	1/4 n/c
		Bar Association		Telephone call from Tom Goodguy re my nomination for Trusteeship	1/4
NIGHT HOURS		Continuing Education		CEB program at UCLA on tax aspects of divorce and adoption	2
				TO RM	10 3/4

213

How to Interview a Client

The way you conduct your interview will have a profound effect on whether or not the client has confidence in you and whether or not you will be engaged. Often the interview is the only face-to-face contact you have with your client unless you go to court. In this age of good telephonic and postal communications, subsequent client contact is often not face to face.

In the Reception Room

1. Be sure there are some straight-back chairs. Injured or elderly clients can't get into or out of plush or overstuffed sofas and chairs.
2. If the client is early, have the receptionist offer the client coffee or a soft drink. As an international lawyer, I have met with clients and lawyers all over the world, in such places as Peking, Rio, Tokyo, Cairo, Nairobi, Hong Kong, Istanbul, Geneva and London, among other places. It is an international custom appreciated by clients to offer them something to drink to "wet the whistle." Your client will be put in a relaxed mood by the beverage.

Be Prompt

Don't be early or late. If you have a 10 a.m. appointment, go in to get the client at 10 a.m., not 9:55 or 10:05. The client may take tardiness as a sign of disrespect (I do), or earliness as a sign of nothing to do.

Greet the Client

Ask, "Ms. Smith?" Don't assume that the only person in the reception room is your client. Your client may have gone to the toilet or back to move the car. If the person says, "Yes," then introduce yourself. Offer your hand in a handshake and say, "I'm John Jones." Don't introduce yourself as Mr. Jones, or Attorney Jones, unless this is the custom in your community. Calling oneself "Mister" or "Ms." is often taken as a sign of lack of self-confidence. The client knows you're a lawyer or he or she wouldn't be there.

Help the Client

If the client has a purse or coat or envelopes or documents, take it upon yourself to help carry the burdens.

Take Command of the Situation

From this point on, you must take command of the situation. You must be firm in voice and mannerisms. The client wants to lean on you—not vice versa.

Give the Client Directions

Tell the client "Follow me, please" to direct the client from the reception room to your office. When you get to your office door (which you should have left open when you went to the reception room), stop at the door and say, "This is my office" (especially if there is more than one room that could be your office). "Please go in."

Tell the Client Where to Sit

Tell the client, "Please, sit down," indicating with a hand gesture the chair you wish the client to occupy. Help the client, if the client is injured or elderly. Ask the client if he or she is comfortable.

Close the Door and Sit Down Yourself

Insure Privacy

Call your secretary or the receptionist to tell her, "I'm in conference with Ms. Smith. No calls, please." Tell the client that when you're in conference you don't take calls, except for emergencies, because the client who is in your office is entitled to all your attention, and because you don't like to discuss one client's legal matters in front of another client.

Start Your Interview

Actually, the client started the interview with you when you came into the reception room. Now you are starting your interview of the client.

Ask Simple Questions

Start with simple questions such as name, home address, mailing address, home telephone, work telephone, etc. Establish the format immediately whereby you will ask the questions and the client will answer them.

Keep Control of the Situation

If the client is verbose and will not stop talking, tell the client that he or she must learn to answer questions and not to answer more than the question asked. Tell the client that each question and answer may have legal significance and that the client must listen carefully to the question and answer it carefully.

Make Tissues, Candy and an Ash Tray Available

If the client cries, offer tissues and ask if he or she would like a drink of water. Ask the client if he or she would rather finish the interview another time. (The client never says yes, but appreciates the offer.) Cigarettes may annoy you, but remember that tobacco is an addiction and it is easy to moralize about other people's addictions. Remember that the client may have a physical craving for the cigarette and he or she is paying you—not vice versa. Open a window if you have to, but don't ask the client not to smoke. On the other hand, you shouldn't smoke, without first asking the client's permission.

Limit Your Interview to Between One and One and a Half Hours

Interviews longer than this are physically and mentally exhausting and should be avoided if possible.

Discuss Fees at the End of the Interview

If the client tries to bring up fees at the beginning of the interview or before the end of the interview, tell the client that you don't want to discuss fees until you've gotten all the facts and have a better idea of what's involved. Tell the client that your first concern is to hear the facts, so you can tell the client what kind of help is needed. At the end of the interview, discuss the fees and then dictate the fee engagement letter in the presence of the client.

Always Ask the Client What He or She Wants to Add

Tell the client that sometimes in the interviewing process facts get overlooked. Say to the client, "Is there anything you want to tell me or ask me?" If you've done a good job with the interview there won't be anything else. You'd be surprised at some of the things clients ask you or want to tell you.

End the Interview

The client is dependent on you to say when the interview is over. The easiest way to end the interview is simply to stand up and walk over to the door. Tell the client when you want to see or talk to him or her again, or say that you'll begin work as soon as the fee engagement letter with the retainer fee is returned.

Walk the Client Back to the Reception Room

Don't assume the client knows the way out. Shake hands with the client and say you are happy to have met him or her and look forward to working on the case.

How to Maintain Bank Accounts

The day you open your office, you should open three checking accounts, as follows:

Personal Account

The checks, checkbook, and deposit slips should be printed "Personal Account." Use this account for nonoffice-related matters, such as food, clothing, etc. Your spouse may be a signator on the account to write checks if you desire.

Office Account

The checks, checkbook, and deposit slips should be printed "Office Account." This account should be used for all items which are, or which might be, related to the practice income and expenses. Your spouse or your secretary can sign on this account.

Trust Account

The checks, checkbook, and deposit slips should be printed "Trust Account." This account is for *client money.* You should *never* use it for your money. No person other than you should be able to sign on this account. You should *not* allow your spouse or a secretary or even another attorney to sign on this account. In some states the rules of trust account maintenance are set by the state bar in order to get the interest income. A more detailed discussion of the Trust Account will follow later.

Other Accounts

1. *Savings Accounts.* It is rare that you would have any use for a savings account insofar as your practice is concerned. Any interest income on trust accounts would belong to the client, not to you. (In some countries the attorney can keep the interest, but not in the U.S.) It is possible that where you will keep a large sum of client money for a significant time, that an interest-bearing account in your name, as trustee for the client, should be used, but this is an exceptional situation, and generally you should not keep trust account funds in an interest-bearing account.

2. *Payroll Account.* I recommend maintaining a separate checking account for payroll and payroll taxes, even though it is not required. As a practicing CPA, I learned to have a healthy respect for payroll taxes. When I hired my first secretary, I immediately opened a payroll account, and used the special payroll checks with appropriate spaces on the check and the stub to indicate the computation of the net pay. In some states, an employee is entitled by law to a statement of computation of the net pay, and the check with the computation will usually satisfy that requirement.

I also recommend transferring to the payroll account from the office account an amount equal to the *gross pay,* plus a flat percent allowance (10% to 12% is usually sufficient) to cover the employer share of the various payroll taxes, and worker's compensation, etc. In this manner, you set aside all payroll money as you go along, and don't have to worry about coming up with the payroll taxes monthly or quarterly.

It is foolish, in my opinion, to attempt to use or spend the difference between the employees' gross pay and the employees' net pay. This practice has led to serious problems for employers when they couldn't come up with the taxes withheld.

For example, assume a secretary is entitled to $100 gross pay, and the employer taxes are 6 percent Social Security, 1 percent Worker's Compensation Insurance, 3 percent Unemployment Insurance; assume 1 percent State Disability, and another 1 percent State Withholding and 20 percent Federal Withholding:

Gross Pay	$100.00

Employer Taxes:

Social Security	$6.00
Worker's Compensation	1.00
Unemployment	3.00
	10.00

Amount to be transferred from Office Account to Payroll Account:	$110.00
	$100.00

Gross Pay

Less Deduction:

State Disability	$ 1.00
State Withholding	1.00
Federal Withholding	20.00

Total Deductions:	22.00
Net to Secretary:	$ 78.00

It is very tempting to only set aside $78 and to hope to have the balance of $42 when the time comes to pay the taxes. It will give you great peace of mind to set aside the entire payroll cost at the time of paying the payroll, and then not have to be concerned about coming up with the balance.

Failure to make withholding deposits can be criminal.

"Laundering Money"

Be very careful when a client or prospective client asks you to deposit a check or cash to one of your accounts in exchange for one of your checks; or when you purchase a cashier's check for the client often payable to a third party. Banks shouldn't practice law, and lawyers shouldn't engage in banking. There is sometimes a valid reason for your handling a "secret" transaction for a client (such as sealed bids); however, be careful.

Picking a Bank or Banker

As a new attorney in practice, some banks or bankers will go out of their way to accommodate you. Others will not want your business until you are more firmly established. Normally the reason a bank wants your business is to get your trust account deposits. You may have anywhere from a few hundred dollars to hundreds of thousands in your trust account for days, weeks or months. Since your checking account doesn't draw interest, the bank will want these deposits. This may be modified by statute in those states where the state bar wants the interest income. Start with the bank or branch closest to your office (for convenience), and tell the manager that you are starting your practice and want to establish a banking relationship. Do the same thing with two or three banks. See which bank or banker seems more interested in you, and open your accounts with that bank or banker. A good relationship will give you access to loan funds as you need them for temporary cash flow problems, as well as equipment financing and other personal banking needs.

What to expect from the bank you select:
1. No service charges on any of your accounts;
2. Free check printing (within limits);
3. Lunch with the banker, at bank expense;
4. Wills and trusts form books;
5. Favored treatment on your banking needs.

Getting Business from Banks and Bankers

Banks and bankers are an excellent source of business for a lawyer. They are frequently asked to recommend a lawyer to a customer.

Unfortunately, the new lawyer will rarely get any of these referrals, which usually will go to the bank's general counsel, or to lawyers who give the bank a lot of business. The bank's general counsel is often represented on the board or key committees of the bank. A branch manager may not wish to place his or her own position at risk by referring business to lawyers.

Occasionally, a bank customer will specifically ask the bank manager to recommend a new lawyer, or a young lawyer, to handle a case that other lawyers have already declined to handle.

Look upon these referrals as a golden opportunity to demonstrate how hard you can work. Don't make unrealistic promises to the client. Be honest as to the merit or lack of merit of the case. If you handle it, work as hard as you can. The banker may learn of the customer's satisfaction from the customer, and you may get a referral on a good client or matter.

How to Maintain a Trust Account to Avoid Disbarment

When I read the disciplinary reports which say "and shall be disbarred effective January 1, 19___, and his/her name shall forever be removed from the roll of attorneys of the state," a chill goes through me. I think of the years of study gone to waste; I think of the shame and tears of parents, the dashed hopes of the spouse; the fears of wondering how to provide for children and of having to explain to the children years later about their disbarred parent. I think of the high degree of suicide among disbarred lawyers. Most of all, I think about the client or clients who may have gone under with the unfortunate lawyer.

There are many ways to get yourself disbarred. The surest, fastest way to lose your license is to ignore the rules for handling client funds.

If you are going to get involved with "close practices" with client funds, remember that in this game every rule in the book is written against you. The referees (your state disciplinary board) will not look for extenuating circumstances, and ignorance on your part is no defense.

If you ignore this section of my book, you are not only a fool, you are a damned fool. I cannot emphasize strongly enough the importance to you of understanding and applying the rules of Trust Funds.

Many attorneys are disciplined for various matters, ranging from failure to return telephone calls to fee disputes. Attorneys are sometimes thrown out of bar associations for violating ethical rules. However, most disbarments result from mishandling of client funds.

You can still practice law after being kicked out of the local bar associations. You can still practice law after your period of discipline is over. You can never, never practice law again if you are disbarred. With this background in mind, let's examine the basic rule and some practical examples of how to apply it in your everyday situations.

Model Rule 1.15 and Disciplinary Rule 9–102 are carry-forwards of ABA Canon 11 and will be found in the law of your state, either as part of the Rules of Court or codified in your Business and Professional Code or in your general laws. I recommend highly that you read the exact wording of the law in your state as well as some of the annotations to get a sense of how easy it is to get disbarred.

Opening a Trust Checking Account

1. Title the account "Trust Account" or a similar wording. Although the word "Trust" is not required *per se,* I recommend it.

2. Use a red checkbook cover. The color red obviously indicates "Danger."

3. Use checks of a color different from your office or payroll checks.

4. Yours should be the only authorized signature. Do not allow your spouse, secretary, or office manager to sign the checks.

5. Reconcile the account monthly.

Don't use savings accounts unless there are very exceptional circumstances. I am continually confronted by new lawyers who get the bright idea of putting trust funds into savings accounts to get interest on the "float." I have to deflate the egos of these financial wizards by pointing out two basic fallacies in the scheme:

1. The funds are the clients' and the interest on the clients' funds belongs to the clients whose money earned the interest.

2. DR 9–102(B)(1) and Model Rule 1.15(b) require the funds to be *promptly* paid to the client. Delaying the payment to the client in order to earn interest is not proper in any event, in my opinion, even if you did send the interest to the client.

I have been told, but have not independently verified, that attorneys in some countries can ethically and legally keep the interest earned on client funds. This may explain in part the delay I have experienced in getting client money from overseas lawyers.

In any event, if you have several clients' money in a savings account, you would have to bookkeep on a daily basis which client had earned the interest. The amount of work involved for the amount of interest involved for a particular client usually will not justify your going through all the work of computing the interest.

1. *Don't pay personal bills from the account.* If you have a fee in the trust account that you are entitled to, don't just spend the money from the trust account. Transfer the fee from the trust account to the office account, then transfer your draw from the office account to your personal account. Thus, you will have a clean record, and no explanations will be necessary at a later time.

2. *Don't make any disbursements without a client's written authorization.* Ordinarily, your fee agreement contains your written authorization to reimburse yourself any costs and fees you're entitled to.

3. *Suppose client Jim Jones whom you are representing on a good accident case has an unrelated problem such as a criminal or domestic relations matter. He wants you to work on the unrelated case with you getting your fee from his share of the proceeds of the accident case.*

   a. *Can you ethically do this?* Yes. A client may engage you on an unrelated matter and you may agree to defer the time of payment until the accident case closes.

   b. *Can you take the money from the trust account when the case closes?* Yes, providing you have the authorization to pay the fees in writing. You must understand that when you have client funds in your trust account, you are a fiduciary. When the client owes you a fee, you are a creditor. You must act as a fiduciary with the trust fund, even though your client acts as a debtor with the unpaid fee.

   c. *Suppose your client disputes part of your fee; can you take the undisputed portion out of the trust account?* Yes. You *must* withdraw from the trust account your funds and you *must* forward to the client his or her funds.

4. *Suppose your client engages you and gives you a retainer check of $725, representing a $250 minimum fee, $350 towards additional fees (if your fee exceeds $250) and $125 in costs. What do you do?*

   a. Deposit the check to your trust account.

   b. Wait three to five banking days for the check to clear (unless you want to take a chance on your client's credit).

   c. Withdraw your $250 minimum fee immediately because it is yours in any event and must be withdrawn (unless your fee agreement specifies otherwise).

d. Pay for costs out of the trust account as incurred. Stop when costs reach $125. At this point, either get more money from your client or advance costs from your office account. Do not use the "excess" fee funds. You may be obligated to return them if not used.

e. When you and the client have agreed in writing to your "excess fee," you may withdraw it from the trust account.

5. *Suppose client Jane Jones owes you $125 for a loan or for fees or costs on an unrelated matter. You then settle a case for her and have $35,000 in your trust account that belongs to her.*

a. *Can you simply send her a check for $34,875?* No. Again, you are a fiduciary with respect to the $35,000 and a creditor with respect to the $125. Therefore, you must send her the $35,000 and ask for your $125.

b. *Is there some way you can withhold the $125 from the trust funds?* Yes. Simply get her permission in writing to pay yourself the $125 from her trust funds.

6. *How do you get clients to agree in writing to your taking the fees from the trust funds?* The simplest way is to send a letter explaining what you wish to do and ask him or her to sign the carbon copy indicating permission and to send the signed copy back to you by mail. If you simply stick a piece of paper in front of the client and tell him or her to sign it, there may be a later claim that the letter wasn't understood when it was signed. By getting the letter mailed back to you, the client presumably had time to consider what was being agreed to.

7. *Is it required that the permission be given in writing?* There is nothing in the rules which require the permission to be in writing. However, you will be in a difficult situation two or three years later when the client simultaneously sues you, alleging a breach of fiduciary duty, and files a complaint with the state bar for unauthorized use of trust funds. Clients (and some lawyers) have a tendency to remember only what they want to remember, and it will be a matter of your word versus the client's word.

Insurance Needs of the New Lawyer

Insurance is an expense that new lawyers hate to pay since there is a cash disbursement with no probability of profit. However painful it might be, accept the fact that you are a complete and total fool if you are not adequately insured.

Malpractice Insurance

Accept two basic facts:

1. You are responsible for malpractice, even if you did someone "a favor," and did not charge or collect a fee;

2. At some time during your career, you will be sued for malpractice.

Whether you want to call it "errors and omissions" or "malpractice" or "professional negligence," it is the insurance that protects you, your clients, and third parties when you get sued. Often the costs of defense alone will be many, many times what you paid in premiums.

As a general rule, your local bar association will have gotten the best "deal" available for you. Sometimes a private agent or broker can get you a better "deal." Be careful. From time to time, insurance companies simply go out of the malpractice insurance business, and you may find yourself stranded without coverage. As a member of your local bar association, you will be part of a larger economic unit in a better bargaining position.

There is no substitute for working with a good insurance agent or broker who has your interests at heart. The purpose of this section is not to replace the broker, but rather to educate both you and the broker in the peculiarities of insurance as it affects a new lawyer in practice. Keep in mind that the terminology for insurance coverage changes from time to time and from place to place.

There are some points you should be careful about.

1. *"Gaps" in Coverage.* Some policies are "claims" policies and some are "occurrence" policies. The difference can best be illustrated by a hypothetical example. Suppose Company "A" insured you for 1992 on a "claim" basis, and Company "B" insures you on an "occurrence" basis in 1993. Suppose you commit a negligent act in 1992, and a claim is made against you in 1993. Company "A" will not cover you because the "claim" wasn't made during the policy period 1992, and Company "B" will not cover you because the "occurrence" didn't occur during its policy period, 1993. Therefore, even though you had policies in effect at all times, you have no coverage.

Another important thing to remember is that any time you change carriers, be sure that you don't have any gaps in your coverage.

2. *Settlement Approval.* If possible, try to get a policy that gives you the right to approve settlements being made. The problem here is to avoid the stigma or rating problem in the future when a settlement is made of a nonmeritorious claim.

3. *Deductible.* Many policies now provide for significant deductibility of $10,000 or more, *including costs of defense.* In other words, you must pay the first $10,000 of defense costs incurred.

4. *Exclusions.* There is a tendency for insurance companies to reduce risk by excluding certain areas of practice from coverage, such as securities. Be sure you read and understand your policy.

5. *Sufficient Coverage.* From time to time, you may have a very significant case matter, involving large amounts of money, and large exposure if you are negligent. Give consideration to buying more insurance to cover that matter, and don't be afraid to raise your fee so that you are adequately compensated, giving effect to the cost of the premium. Remember that insurance protects both you *and* your client.

Umbrella Coverage

"Umbrella" or excess coverage, in my opinion, is the best insurance value available, considering premium cost and coverage. Oversimplified, it picks up coverage where your underlying policies do not. For example, it normally would be cheaper for you to have a $300,000 malpractice policy and a $1,000,000 umbrella (in effect, a $1,300,000 policy with a $300,000 deductible), than to have a $1,000,000 malpractice policy. Additionally, the umbrella will often pick up the "excess" coverage in other areas of insurance besides malpractice. Any time your broker or agent quotes you rates for malpractice or other liability insurance, ask for quotes on rates for the same coverage using a smaller "underlying policy" with an umbrella coverage.

Non-owned Autos

Be sure you and your office help are covered if there is an auto accident when an employee is running an errand for you, such as going to the post office to mail that rush, rush letter.

Office Furniture, Etc.

Be sure that you are insured for "replacement value." In our inflationary times, insurance which pays claims based on cost less depreciation is close to having no insurance at all. Don't assume that just because the insurance company takes your premium based on present-day replacement costs that they will pay claims based on present-day replacement cost. Here again, either read your policy or get a good broker.

File Replacement and Cost of Insurance for Valuable Papers

For the first year or two, you will not have much concern over this problem, but ultimately, this type of coverage will be extremely important to you. This coverage includes the cost of replacing your files, rather than the value of the paper in the files. In the event of fire, it could cost you thousands of dollars to buy photocopies of documents, letters, etc., from the courts and clients and other attorneys to reconstruct your files.

Worker's Compensation

Remember to get this coverage when you hire your first secretary. That person may be real clumsy and push a typewriter off the desk onto a foot the first day of employment. Your first secretary's first task should be to call your broker to be sure of insurance coverage. If your state has a state fund or state policy, you should check their rates during your first year or two of coverage. With only one secretary or clerk you may fall within the "minimum premium" cost category. The minimum is often substantially lower with state-owned companies or funds than privately owned companies.

Office Block Insurance

This is a "package" available in some areas that combines several types of insurance which a law office needs into a single "block" or package. It is similar to the concept of "homeowners" package insurance. Here again, you need the help of a good broker.

Other Types of Insurance

The other types of insurance are not peculiar to new lawyers in practice and will be simply listed as a checklist here.

1. *Disability Insurance or Office Overhead Insurance.* Buy all you can afford. In my opinion, this type of insurance is more necessary than life insurance. Life insurance protects *others* if you die. Disability insurance protects *you* if you live. If you get sick or disabled and can't work, both your office overhead and your home overhead will continue. In some states, you are eligible for state coverage.

It is my opinion that, as a general rule, you should purchase this insurance through your bar association during your early years. It is not unknown for some insurance companies in this area to be very eager to accept premiums for coverage and later threaten you with cancellation and refusal to pay.

Unfortunately, when you need this coverage you need it badly and cannot afford the luxury of collecting your money with 7 percent interest three years later when you win your lawsuit against the insurance company. Possibly you will not be able to wait even the three to six months involved for the insurance company doctor to examine you and send a report to the insurance company. As part of the larger bar group, you and your claim will be in a better position to get faster payment of just claims. Insurance companies have been known to act rapidly when faced with the loss of hundreds or thousands of policies. On the other hand, if the insurance company drops the entire bar association (or vice versa), you'll have lost the bargaining position and might have been better off with your own broker.

Given all factors, I repeat my recommendation that you buy this coverage through your bar association for the first few years of your practice.

2. *Life Insurance.* Don't be pressured by arguments of how cheaply you can buy a six-figure policy "at your age." Remember that in your early years, cash flow and conservation are your biggest problems. Although premiums will be higher five years later, you'll be in a better position to pay for the higher coverage when you have the income. I suggest you investigate one-year renewable term insurance with your broker.

3. *Public Liability, Fire, Employee Bonding, ERISA, Health, Comprehensive, Medical, Notary Bond, etc.* These are general insurance problems not peculiar to new lawyers in practice and a competent broker or agent should be able to help you.

Checklist on Insurance Coverage

Contact or obtain an insurance broker or agent who is likely to refer you business (old family broker, if possible), or buy from different brokers:

1. Malpractice insurance (Errors & Omissions). Get occurrence rather than claims-made coverage, if possible.

2. General liability insurance for office.

3. Worker's Compensation.

4. Non-owned automobile insurance.

5. File replacement and valuable papers coverage.

6. Fire and theft (get replacement value).

7. Get "umbrella" coverage, if available.

8. Check with broker or bank for "premium financing" (monthly payments).

9. Check if "office block" policy is available.

Why You Need a Personnel Manual

As strange as it may seem, you should have a personnel manual *before* you hire your first employee. As a general rule, lawyers are soft-hearted and don't like to do unpleasant tasks, such as docking or firing employees who are habitually sick or late, or who abuse common rules of good office systems and decorum. Additionally, you, as a new lawyer, have had little or no experience or ability in personnel management. If you doubt this, figure out how you would handle the following factual situations:

1. For the third time in two weeks your clerk Jack calls in at 10:05 to say he's late because of car trouble.

2. Your 45-year-old secretary comes to work in Levis, T-shirt and no bra and torn tennis shoes. She calls you a male chauvinist pig for asking her to dress more conventionally and says she'll file a civil rights suit against you based on sex discrimination if you fire her or discipline her.

3. Your secretary is "into" Zen Buddhism and claims the right to a paid holiday for Buddha's birthday, equating it to Christmas for Christians and Rosh Hashana for Jews. Again, the threat of a civil rights suit.

4. Cigarette smoke annoys you, and your secretary insists on smoking on the job (or vice versa).

5. Your secretary takes home expensive legal pads for a spouse's night-school note-taking.

6. Your secretary claims time and one-half for dropping the mail into a mailbox on the way home.

7. After two months on the job, your clerk tells you a grandmother died, and he has to take one month off, and expects his job to be waiting for him.

Believe it or not, the above factual situations, and some even more bizarre, have happened to me over a period of years. It is not satisfactory to wait for problems to occur and then try to handle them on an *ad hoc* basis. You should have an employee office manual ready for *your first* employee. As a final step in the hiring process, you should hand the manual to the employee, getting a signed receipt in which it is acknowledged that it was read and understood and the employee agrees to be bound by it. Such things as tardiness, absences, sickness, holidays, overtime, dress, office supplies, etc., would ordinarily be covered in the office personnel manual.

Given that you now understand the need for a manual, where do you get one?

1. Create your own manual. The Fall 1975 issue of *Legal Economics* contains an excellent checklist for a complete manual. To obtain a copy, contact William S. Hein & Co., (800)828–7571. The Law Practice Management Section publishes a *Law Office Staff Manual* in both book and diskette formats; contact the ABA at (312)988–5555.

2. Copy another lawyer's personnel manual. This is one of those rare situations where a poor or mediocre solution is better than none. Use the other lawyer's manual until you can modify it for your particular purposes.

Subjects for Office Personnel Policy

Following is an alphabetical list of elements that should be considered for inclusion in an office personnel policy:

Absences	Decorum
Accidents	Deductions
Attitude	Disability insurance
Bonding of employees	Discounts
Bulletin boards	Discrimination
Cleanliness	Dismissal
Clothing	Dress
Coffee breaks	Economy
Complaints	Emergencies
Confidential nature of work	Emergency leave
Contracts	Employee addresses

Employee lounge
Employee personality
Employee-client relations
Employee roster
Fire
Funeral pay
Garnishments
Gossip
Grievances
Health insurance
Holidays
Housekeeping
Intoxication
Introduction
Jury duty
Labor laws
Leaves of absence
Liability & malpractice insurance
Loyalty
Lunches
Magazines
Marriage & pregnancy
Maternity
Meal schedules
Medical care
Meetings
Merit review
Military service
Misconduct
Moonlighting
New employees
Noise
Office supplies
Overtime
Parking
Pay day
Pay period

Pension plan
Personal mail
Personal phone calls
Personal visitors
Personnel counseling
Privileged communications
Privileged info
Probationary period
Professional ethics
Promotions
Re-employment
Resignations
Retirement
Safety
Salary
Salary calculation
Salary increases
Schedules
Sick leave
Smoking
Social security
Soliciting of employees
Suggestions
Supervisors
Tardiness
Telephone courtesy
Temporary employment
Terminal vacation
Termination of employment
Time cards
Trial period
Unemployment insurance
Vacations
Work evaluations
Work habits
Work periods
Worker's compensation
Working hours

Bookkeeping and Accounting Systems

Get a CPA.

Unless you have some accounting knowledge or bookkeeping experience, you really shouldn't try to maintain your own books or prepare your own income tax return. I am a Board Certified Specialist in Taxation and I am a Certified Public Accountant, but I don't maintain my own books or prepare my own tax returns. I am simply applying the old maxim, "The lawyer who represents himself has a fool for a client."

1. A CPA can be an excellent source of clients for a lawyer. CPAs normally are in periodic close contact with their clients. These clients frequently ask the CPA to recommend a lawyer for the problems of the business, and the employees of the business.

2. Try to select a CPA in a small- or medium-size CPA firm. A large firm rarely can refer anything to a new lawyer and may not have the same interest in you as a client as a small- or medium-size firm.

3. Unfortunately, you probably won't be able to send much business to the CPA. CPAs send many more clients to lawyers than vice versa. As a new lawyer, the kind of work you can generate for a CPA (other than your own accounting) is call "special engagement" work, such as looking for assets in marital cases.

In any event you need some simple accounting procedures and systems for your day-to-day financial transactions.

Keep It Simple

You won't have many transactions your first year or two, so you really don't need a national CPA firm with an IBM mainframe. A

234

simple checkbook for your office expense checks should be adequate. If you want to use a four-part snapout checkbook for client costs, you can.

Your accountant will probably recommend a "write-it-once" system for you.

Read the chapter on bank accounts and the simplified "chart of accounts" that follows this chapter. Note that the trust account does not appear on your statements since the money in that account is not yours. Your accountant may wish to show the account with a *"contra"* or offset. This is an area of theoretical debate among accountants. The important thing is that you do not include the trust account on your financial statements.

Leave Tracks

An accountant can easily reconstruct transactions if you leave tracks. Put explanations on your duplicate bank deposit slips and explain in detail what you are writing checks for.

Use Cash Basis Books

For income tax purposes you'll want to be on the cash basis. After you're in practice a few years you can get sophisticated with accounts receivable and accruals, but not at the beginning.

Buy the ABA Monographs

The American Bar Association Section of Law Practice Management (750 N. Lake Shore Drive, Chicago, Illinois 60611) publishes several monographs on law office accounting. You should buy one of each that is available and keep it as part of your permanent library for your CPA to use. Let your CPA firm buy their own set. Don't let them remove yours from your office. I contributed to several of the monographs in various capacities and recommend them highly.

Chart of Accounts for the New Lawyer

Assets	*Expenses*
Cash in Bank—Office	Accounting
Cash in Bank—Payroll	Associate Fees

Assets (cont'd)
Client Costs Receivable
Deposits—Lease, Utilities, etc.
Deposit Account—Sheriff and
   Marshal
Prepaid Expenses
Desks and Chairs (accumulated
   depreciation)
Typewriters (accumulated depre-
   ciation)
Dictating Equipment (accumu-
   lated depreciation)
Other Office Equipment (accu-
   mulated depreciation)
Library (accumulated deprecia-
   tion)
Lease Hold Improvements (ac-
   cumulated depreciation)

Liabilities
Withheld Payroll Taxes Payable
Equipment Contracts Payable
Bank Loans Payable
Other Liabilities

Capital
John Lawyer Capital
John Lawyer Draw (Nondeduc-
   tible)
John Lawyer Draw (Deductible)

Income
Fees Received—
   Personal Injury
   Domestic Relations
   Criminal
   Business
   Probate
   Other

Expenses (cont'd)
Attorney Service
Auto
Bank Charges
Business Promotion
Continuing Education
Depreciation
Dues, Professional
Employee Meals and Incentives
Employee Procurement
Equipment Rental
Insurance
Interest
Investigation, Investigators
   (non-receivable)
Medical Insurance
Meetings and Seminars
Office Supplies
Outside Secretarial
Payroll Taxes
Postage
Postage Equipment Rental
Professional Periodicals
Rent—Office
Rent—Parking
Repairs and Maintenance
Salaries—Secretaries
Salaries—Office
Salaries—Clerks
Stationery and Printing
Taxes and Licenses
Telephone
Travel and Conventions
Photocopier Rental and Supplies

The Office Cash Flow Survival Budget

You must have a positive cash flow if your practice is to survive. The incoming cash must equal or exceed the outgoing cash or you soon will be out of business. Do not confuse a cash flow budget with profit and loss since the latter involves depreciation, amortization, accruals, and other noncash items.

By budgeting your cash income and your cash outgo, you will be able to prioritize where you do and do not spend your funds. The budgeting process will force you to think about what it will cost to run your practice. Monthly, you should compare your actual cash in and cash out to the cash flow budget to take stock of where you are. Revise your estimates monthly so you will be prepared for cash-poor periods.

Monthly revisions will enable you to change directions and to be prepared to meet your anticipated needs when events do not occur exactly as you anticipated.

Learning to make budgets both on a cash-flow basis and on a profit-and-loss basis will help you set goals and targets during your entire professional career. If you do not have the foggiest idea of what your operating costs or income will be, than ask a CPA, another lawyer, or an office manager to help you with your first budget. Subsequent budgets will be much easier to prepare and revise.

Making and monitoring your cash-flow budget can make the difference between success and failure. It takes effort to make your first and subsequent cash-flow budgets, but it is a wise investment of time and effort in starting and maintaining your practice.

The following categories of cash in and out may help you accumulate your figures and estimates.

Anticipated Cash Requirements for New Lawyer for First 12 Months of Practice

	Budgeted	Actual
Income: Fees from clients; overflow work from other lawyers; working spouse; parent loans; other loans to your business, etc.	$_____	$_____
Total Income	$_____	$_____

Expenditures:

	Budgeted	Actual
Occupancy: Rent, parking, landlord "pass throughs," security deposit.	$_____	$_____
Payroll: Secretary, paralegal, receptionist, word processor, law clerks, others (add 20 percent for payroll taxes).	$_____	$_____
Taxes and Professional Associations: City license fee, state bar dues, fees for admission to courts and for certificates of admission, sales tax permit, bar association dues (American, state, county, city), law specialty associations.	$_____	$_____
Insurance: Malpractice, auto, general liability, fire, workers' compensation, medical insurance health plan, disability, valuable papers, EDP for computer and software, umbrella, other.	$_____	$_____
Court Service: Messengers.	$_____	$_____
Communications Equipment: Deposit, telephone equipment, yellow and white pages, monthly service charge, E-mail, fax, telex, postage.	$_____	$_____
Periodicals: Legal journals, specialty journals, periodicals for reception room.	$_____	$_____

Furniture: Down payment and monthly payments for attorney, staff, and reception furniture—down payment and monthly payments for other furniture. $_____ $_____

Office Equipment: Down payment and monthly payments for computer and printer, word processor, dictating equipment, fax machine, photocopy machine, postage meter, file cabinets or filing shelves and book shelves. $_____ $_____

Library: Purchase and installment payments on books not available to you from lawyers' libraries (electronic libraries through WESTLAW or LEXIS are more economical than hard copy libraries if you are proficient). $_____ $_____

Stationery: Letterhead, second sheets, envelopes, professional cards, pleading paper, photocopy paper, computer paper. $_____ $_____

Promotion: Tickets for athletic and cultural events, business lunches, seasonal greeting cards, announcements, firm newsletter or brochures, dues for service organizations. $_____ $_____

Automobile: Monthly payments, gas, oil, repairs. $_____ $_____

Travel: State bar, American bar or specialty bar meetings and conventions. $_____ $_____

Client Costs: Medical reports, depositions, filing fees, investigators' fees, etc. $_____ $_____

Accountant: Bookkeeping and payroll and income tax return fees. $_____ $_____

Banks: Check printing, safe deposit box, bank charges. $_____ $_____

Loan Payments: Student loans, parents, banks, etc. $_____ $_____

Office Supplies: Small office equipment, pens, pencils, paper clips, staplers, legal and note pads, scissors, rubber stamps, postage, insurance, etc. $_____ $_____

Other: $_____ $_____

Total Cash Expenditures $_____ $_____

**Estimated Total Cash Surplus or Shortage for First Year
(Income Less Expenditures)** $_____ $_____

Simple Filing Systems
for the New Lawyer

File Cabinets

If a well-meaning relative bought you an old-fashioned two- or four-drawer file cabinet, throw it out or give it to charity; but don't use it. Use vertical files. (See sample on exhibit following this chapter.)

Using vertical files, you can store two and a half times as many files in the same space or, to put it another way, your rental cost for floor space when using vertical files is 25 percent that when using horizontal files.

A file cabinet will usually occupy about six square feet (including drawer pull-out space). At 50 cents per month per square foot (a nominal rent), you'll pay $3 per month or $36 per year for that file cabinet. The cost per file is four times the cost of using vertical files. Use low-cost shelving instead.

Ask your stationery store for samples of each type.

Organizing the File

Keep it simple. There are dozens of systems for organizing files. Some are good for personal injury plaintiff, some are good for personal injury defendant, some are good for probate, some are good for wills and estate planning. Some systems appear to have been invented by geniuses, some appear to have been invented by idiots. My advice to the new lawyer is to ignore all these fancy file folder systems until you are somewhat established and can appreciate and understand what you actually need in a filing system. I suggest a simple file folder as illustrated in the exhibit at the end of this chapter.

Keep everything in chronological order. Don't open multiple files for the same matter. After a couple of years, this system will probably become inadequate for you. At that time you can make changes depending upon your specific needs.

Use a Numerical Filing System

The simplest and best system for you is to use a year-matter system. Each year start a new series. For example, 90–1, 90–2, 90–3, etc., then 91–1, 91–2, 91–3, etc. If you are embarrassed over the small number of files you have, then cheat on the numbering system. About February 1 of each year simply add 200 or 300 to the last number so that in February your numbering system would start with 90–202, 90–203, etc. Other lawyers will think you're doing a lot of business.

Make an alphabetical cross-index system, putting the client names on index cards cross-referenced to the file number.

When and How to Open and Close Files

1. *Opening files.* Open a file when you have a client and a case and are professionally responsible for the matter. Until then, keep the copies of the documents, letters, etc., in 26 alphabetical, miscellaneous files, each in chronological order. When you open the file, remove the documents from the miscellaneous file and put them in the separate numerical file for the client matter. If you never open a file, simply leave the documents in the miscellaneous file for that alphabetical letter.

2. *Open a new file for each matter.* Believe me, it will make your life much easier to keep each matter in a totally different file with its own file number.

3. *Closing files.* After you've been in practice a few years you can get involved with microfilming. Until then, stick with my simple system.

    a. Fill out a closed file sheet. It will replace the bulky file and become the basis of future work. This closed file sheet can be kept in a three-ring notebook in your office. The filling out of this form will serve as a "last chance" to clean up any loose ends or errors you spot. A sample closed file information sheet follows this chapter.

    b. Remove duplicate copies of documents that you know will

never be needed. (Remember pleadings can always be obtained from the court.)

    c. Send valuable original documents back to the client with a cover letter (unless you enjoy being a bailee-insurer of the item).

    d. Get the file folder out of your high-rent office to a low-rent or no-rent storage area and file it in numerical order.

    e. Remove the alpha-numeric cross-index card from the active index and put it in the closed file card index.

    4. *When to close a file.* Close the file when there is nothing more for you to do on the case and when you've informed the client in writing that you are doing nothing further and are closing your file.

    5. *When to destroy a file.* I'm a coward and have never destroyed files. Other more courageous lawyers than I close them after three-year or five-year intervals. I don't recommend file destruction. Microfilm them before destruction.

Color Filing to Prevent Lost and Misplaced Files

During your first year or two, lost or misplaced or misfiled files will not be a problem. As time goes on and you accumulate a large number of folders, misplaced files can be a serious problem. I invented a color filing system that virtually eliminates misfiled files. Simply get your file folders in different colors. When I last counted, 13 different colors were commercially available. *Change colors* every 100 files or every letter. For example, all file folders for matter 91–1 through 91–99 are blue; from 91–100 through 91–199 red; from 91–200 through 91–299 green; from 92–1 through 92–99 orange, etc. Or use "A's," "B's," "C's," etc., and have a different color folder.

The theory is simple. You can misfile a red folder in the section with the other red folders, but you can't misfile it in the green folder section or the brown folder section. Believe me, the system works.

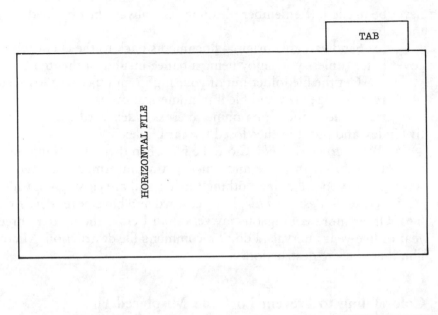

HORIZONTAL FILE

TAB

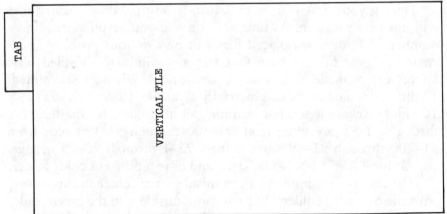

TAB

VERTICAL FILE

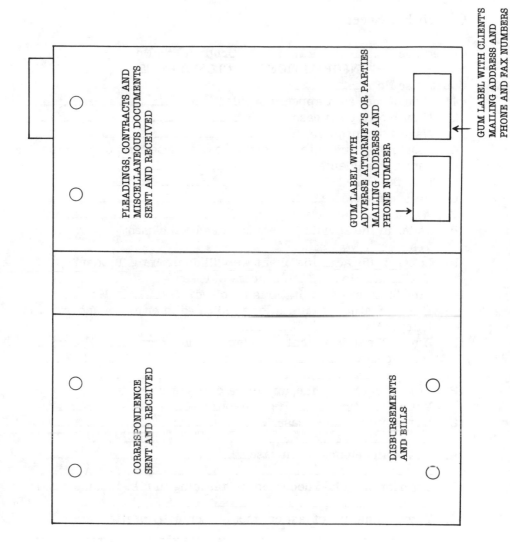

PLEADINGS, CONTRACTS AND MISCELLANEOUS DOCUMENTS SENT AND RECEIVED

GUM LABEL WITH ADVERSE ATTORNEY'S OR PARTIES MAILING ADDRESS AND PHONE NUMBER

GUM LABEL WITH CLIENT'S MAILING ADDRESS AND PHONE AND FAX NUMBERS

CORRESPONDENCE SENT AND RECEIVED

DISBURSEMENTS AND BILLS

245

Closed File Sheet

Closed File No._____   Original File No._____
INFORMATION FOR CLOSED FILES
Court Case No._____

1. Title of case as it appears on file_____
2. Nature or type of case_____
3. Names of our clients_____
4. Last known business and residence addresses and phone numbers of our clients_____
5. Date file closed_____
6. Reason file closed_____
7. Who authorized closing of file?_____
8. Letter in file advising client file has been closed?
   Yes_____ No_____
9. Letter in file advising client we will do nothing further?
   Yes_____ No_____If so, date of letter_____
10. Any Statutes of Limitations involved? Yes_____ No_____
    If so, is Statute of Limitations indicated in either of above letters? Yes_____ No_____
11. Any original documents of client in file? Yes_____ No_____
    If so, specify_____
    _____
12. At time of closing file, any unpaid fees or costs due?
    Yes_____ No_____ If so, amount: $_____
13. List all plaintiffs in case_____
    _____
14. List of all defendants in case_____
    _____
15. Description of last document or pleading in file (include date)
    _____
16. Date and nature of last contact (letter, call, meeting, etc.)_____
    _____
17. Number of file folders and estimated thickness in inches
    No._____ Thickness_____
18. Is party a minor? Yes_____ No_____ If yes, date of birth and indicated activity required upon majority_____
    _____

    Has client been advised as to what must be done upon majority?
    Yes_____ No_____

19. Dismissals filed? Yes_____ No_____ If yes, against whom?

_____

With prejudice_____ Without prejudice_____
20. Abstract of Judgment in file? Yes_____ No_____ If yes, recorded?_____ Date of recording_____
Released?_____ Date of release_____
21. Satisfaction of Judgment in file? Yes_____ No_____ If yes, recorded? _____ Date of recording _____ Amount of Satisfaction _____ If Partial Satisfaction, indicate amount, date, if recorded_____
22. Date judgment entered_____
23. What is there to do in the future?
   A. Review judgment after 10 years_____
   B. Disburse money (to whom?)_____
   C. Need renewal or notice because of lease_____
   D. Need renewal or notice because of provision in contract
   E. Trust involved?_____ If so, need to notify client when trust terminates or other reason for notifying client? Yes_____ No_____
24. Anything requiring us to notify client in the future? Yes_____ No_____ If so, what?_____

_____

When?_____
25. Has there been a request made on the 20-year calendar? Yes_ No_____ If so, nature of request_____

_____

How to Build a Good Form File

Your form file will be one of your most valuable assets. During the first few years you'll be doing a lot of things for the first time. You'll be copying from form books, from other lawyers, and you'll be doing a lot of drafting of forms. If you are like most lawyers, you'll want to copy prior work whenever possible, changing the names and adding or subtracting a few paragraphs. This practice is to be commended, provided you know what you are doing. Blindly copying pages of "boiler plate" language that is neither intelligible nor applicable will eventually get you or your client into trouble. Remember that many forms appear in form books because the intent of the drafter was upheld, defeated, or left uncertain in litigation over the wording of the form.

Keep in mind that during your first few years, the work of other more experienced lawyers is likely to be somewhat better than yours. Therefore it makes good sense to take the work of another lawyer *as a starting point* and improve from there.

In the final analysis there are only two things you need for a good form file. These two things are: (1) Good Forms, and (2) A Good Index to the Forms.

Good Forms

The best way to get good forms is to start with form books. Keep a healthy respect for the copyright laws, but don't forget the doctrine of "Fair Use" which allows you to copy most forms that are not copyrighted, and to a certain extent some that are copyrighted. Normally, form books and pleadings are copyable for your own use without difficulty.

Save and hard copy everything that you feel is or may be useful to you. Put it into a permanent form file. Get the forms bound by a commercial bookbinder with your name engraved in gold on the outside. *Don't* use loose-leaf files, as over a period of time the best forms tend to disappear as you remove them and forget to replace them. The theory underscoring saving *everything* is that the latest form on a subject should be the best and you can put several together to develop what you need.

A Good Index to the Forms

You can either invent your own subject matter index starting from scratch, which is a gross waste of time, or you can use a system developed by experts at a cost of millions of dollars. The West Key Number System is a good one. A copy of the basic index form follows this chapter.

If your state has another index system which you feel is superior, then use it, but don't try to create your own (subject to a penchant for masochism on your part).

I recommend that you index everything that goes into your form file along the following classifications:

1. Subject matter (using the commercial index developed by someone else);
2. Client's name;
3. Adverse party's name;
4. Statutes involved;
5. Court or tribunal in which you appeared;
6. Judge or administrative person who heard the matter;
7. Adverse attorney involved.

You cannot over-index a document; you can only underindex it. Using this index system (which I invented and which you can copy), you'll be able to recall almost anything you've done or seen if it's in your form file. Admittedly, this form file will be of more value to you the longer you're in practice, but start it with the first document or pleading you prepare.

The above system will more than service your needs for the first few years of your practice. Eventually you should read *Retrieval Systems for Lawyers,* published by the Section of Law Practice Management of the ABA (American Bar Association, Order Fulfillment, 750 N. Lake Shore Drive, Chicago, IL 60611).

You may also use forms prepared by opposing counsel, using OCR (optical character recognition) equipment to copy other lawyers' hard copy into your word-processing system.

WEST KEY NUMBERS AND TOPICS

1	Abandoned and Lost Property	74	Champerty and Maintenance	148A	Employers' Liability
2	Abatement and Revival	75	Charities	149	Entry, Writ of
3	Abduction	76	Chattel Mortgages	150	Equity
4	Abortion and Birth Control	76A	Chemical Dependents	151	Escape
5	Absentees	77	Citizens	152	Escheat
6	Abstracts of Title	78	Civil Rights	154	Estates in Property
7	Accession	79	Clerks of Courts	156	Estoppel
8	Accord and Satisfaction	80	Clubs	157	Evidence
9	Account	81	Colleges and Universities	158	Exceptions, Bill of
10	Account, Action on	82	Collision	159	Exchange of Property
11	Account Stated	83	Commerce	160	Exchanges
11A	Accountants	84	Common Lands	161	Execution
12	Acknowledgment	85	Common Law	162	Executors and Aministrators
13	Action	86	Common Scold	163	Exemptions
14	Action on the Case	88	Compounding Offenses	164	Explosives
15	Adjoining Landowners	89	Compromise and Settlement	165	Extortion and Threats
15A	Administrative Law and Procedure	89A	Condominium	166	Extradition and Detainers
16	Admiralty	90	Confusion of Goods	167	Factors
17	Adoption	91	Conspiracy	168	False Imprisonment
18	Adulteration	92	Constitutional Law	169	False Personation
19	Adultery	92B	Consumer Credit	170	False Pretenses
20	Adverse Possession	92H	Consumer Protection	170A	Federal Civil Procedure
21	Affidavits	93	Contempt	170B	Federal Courts
22	Affray	95	Contracts	171	Fences
23	Agriculture	96	Contribution	172	Ferries
24	Aliens	97	Conversion	174	Fines
25	Alteration of Instruments	98	Convicts	175	Fires
26	Ambassadors and Consuls	99	Copyrights and Intellectual Property	176	Fish
27	Amicus Curiae	100	Coroners	177	Fixtures
28	Animals	101	Corporations	178	Food
29	Annuities	102	Costs	179	Forcible Entry and Detainer
30	Appeal and Error	103	Counterfeiting	180	Forfeitures
31	Appearance	104	Counties	181	Forgery
33	Arbitration	105	Court Commissioners	182	Fornication
34	Armed Services	106	Courts	183	Franchises
35	Arrest	107	Covenant, Action of	184	Fraud
36	Arson	108	Covenants	185	Frauds, Statute of
37	Assault and Battery	108A	Credit Reporting Agencies	186	Fraudulent Conveyances
38	Assignments	110	Criminal Law	187	Game
40	Assistance, Writ of	111	Crops	188	Gaming
41	Associations	113	Customs and Usages	189	Garnishment
42	Assumpsit, Action of	114	Customs Duties	190	Gas
43	Asylums	115	Damages	191	Gifts
44	Attachment	116	Dead Bodies	192	Good Will
45	Attorney and Client	117	Death	193	Grand Jury
46	Attorney General	117G	Debt, Action of	195	Guaranty
47	Auctions and Auctioneers	117T	Debtor and Creditor	196	Guardian and Ward
48	Audita Querela	118A	Declaratory Judgment	197	Habeas Corpus
48A	Automobiles	119	Dedication	198	Hawkers and Peddlers
48B	Aviation	120	Deeds	199	Health and Environment
49	Bail	122A	Deposits and Escrows	200	Highways
50	Bailment	123	Deposits in Court	201	Holidays
51	Bankruptcy	124	Descent and Distribution	202	Homestead
52	Banks and Banking	125	Detectives	203	Homicide
54	Beneficial Associations	126	Detinue	204	Hospitals
55	Bigamy	129	Disorderly Conduct	205	Husband and Wife
56	Bills and Notes	130	Disorderly House	205A	Illegitimate Children
57	Blasphemy	131	District and Prosecuting Attorneys	205H	Implied and Constructive Contracts
58	Bonds	132	District of Columbia	206	Improvements
59	Boundaries	133	Disturbance of Public Assemblage	207	Incest
60	Bounties	134	Divorce	208	Indemnity
61	Breach of Marriage Promise	135	Domicile	209	Indians
62	Breach of the Peace	136	Dower and Curtesy	210	Indictment and Information
63	Bribery	137	Drains	211	Infants
64	Bridges	138	Drugs and Narcotics	212	Injunction
65	Brokers	140	Dueling	213	Innkeepers
66	Building and Loan Associations	141	Easements	216	Inspection
67	Burglary	142	Ejectment	217	Insurance
68	Canals	143	Election of Remedies	218	Insurrection and Sedition
69	Cancellation of Instruments	144	Elections	219	Interest
70	Carriers	145	Electricity	220	Internal Revenue
71	Cemeteries	146	Embezzlement	221	International Law
72	Census	147	Embracery	222	Interpleader
73	Certiorari	148	Eminent Domain	223	Intoxicating Liquors

Beware of the Library Trap

I have devoted a large portion of this book to the subject of library because this is the single largest waste of money by new lawyers. For reasons that I don't understand, new lawyers rush out to buy books and periodicals that they don't need and can't afford.

Library expenses can be a bottomless pit. The gradual growth of your library and the corresponding increase in monthly payments can deprive you of cash when you need it most. Before ordering a book, put the order form in your desk drawer for 24 hours; then take it out and examine it again. Put it back in the desk drawer for another 24 hours and if you still feel you need the book, then sign the order form.

Free and Low-Cost Publications

These books are usually available from two sources: government and commercial.

Compose a form letter which you can have printed along the following lines:

Dear _____:

    I am a newly admitted lawyer about to open my own practice. I anticipate that I may have contact with your agency in the near future.

    I would appreciate being placed on your mailing list for publications and forms which you make available to attorneys. If there is a charge for the publication or forms either on a periodic or other basis, I would appreciate your informing me by return mail of the cost.

Thank you for your courtesy and cooperation.

Very truly yours,

J. Novice

Government Sources

Many government agencies distribute materials free or at nominal cost (less than a few dollars). Don't worry about getting or buying useless information. Any library contains some information that will never be used. The cost is so low that you can afford to make a few mistakes.

There is an element of surprise or grab bag involved. You'll be surprised to find which agencies administer which laws. In California the corporation checklist with invaluable information for forming corporations comes from the Secretary of State rather than the Department of Corporations. I got an adoption manual from the Department of Social Welfare for about $2. Within a few weeks I had my first adoption matter and every form and procedure was spelled out in detail. I also got a free subscription for all Security and Exchange Releases. After 20 years I'm still waiting for my first Security and Exchange case.

You should get the local phone books (from the phone company or public library) for your state capital, the largest commercial city in the state, and your home town. Write to *every* agency listed under the state, county, city, and federal governments. If you are really ambitious you can get the Washington, D.C. phone book and write to every federal agency listed.

In the first few years get everything free and everything that is available at nominal cost. After a few years you can cancel the unnecessary subscriptions if you don't want them.

The forms you will receive are exceptionally valuable, particularly those that you receive from courts and administrative agencies. You will soon learn that when an agency or court makes a form available you'll be acting at your peril to use a different form or to make up your own form. Some civil service clerks are very definite in their opinion that there are two ways to do things, their way and the

wrong way. In most cases you'll end up using their forms and recommended procedures, so you might just as well start that way and
save yourself and your clients delay, expense, aggravation and embarrassment.

Commercial Sources

Free books, publications and forms are usually available from
banks, insurance companies, title or escrow companies, trust companies, form printing companies, etc. Not only will you get free publications but you will also get some free lunches when the business
development or sales representative calls on you to deliver the forms
and books and wants to take you to lunch. As a new lawyer with 40
or 50 years of practice ahead of you, you are a very important potential source of business for these companies. The representatives know
that as a new lawyer you can't send much business to them so there
won't be any "hard sell." As you might expect, the banks' and trust
companies' form books contain Will Forms and Trust Forms naming
the sponsoring bank or trust companies as executor and trustees in
the wills.

The life insurance companies' form books contain business buy/
sell agreements for partnerships and corporations (funded with life
insurance), pension and profit-sharing and retirement plans (also
funded with life insurance), and question-and-answer questions
about insurance taxation.

The title insurance companies and escrow companies have good
forms for deeds and mortgages as well as good publications with
highlights of real estate law.

The form printing companies will usually send a "sample kit" of
forms available from them. Some of the companies charge for these
sample kits.

More Expensive Books

When in doubt—don't. Law books are very expensive as is the
maintenance. You should not buy one book that costs more than a
few dollars during your first few years unless you know exactly what
you are getting and unless you have a need for it. Use the law libraries of the courthouses, the law schools and other lawyers whenever
you can.

The materials available vary from state to state. Depending on your state, and recognizing that lawyers differ as to what is best, I recommended obtaining your books in the following sequence:

1. Law dictionary;
2. Unannotated codes or statutes (most recent edition);
3. Annotated codes or statutes;
4. Legal encyclopedia (if available in your state);
5. Digest;
6. Reporters;
7. Specialized works
   a. Continuing education
   b. Pleading books
   c. Tax services
   d. Bankruptcy services
   e. Etc.

Use the Resources of Other Law Libraries

During your first few years of practice you'll have the time to go to the nearby law libraries including the libraries of nearby established law firms. These nearby firms will gladly make their libraries available when you explain that you are a new lawyer. In my opinion a good library is essential to doing complete, thorough, professional legal work. Most if not all lawyers with good law libraries feel the same way and will respect you for trying to do a thorough job. Using their library will enhance your reputation in the community—but *don't abuse your privileges.*

Follow these simple rules:

1. Never "drop in" to do research. Call first to ask if it's all right to come over "for a few minutes" (libraries are often in use as conference rooms, collating rooms, evidence rooms, etc.).

2. Be unobtrusive; remember you are a guest.

3. Don't interfere with other attorneys doing research. Be polite. Exchange a few pleasantries (introducing yourself to whoever is using the library at the same time). Ask if that person can suggest one or more works in the library which may help you, but don't let him or her do your research and don't let a friendly lawyer spend more than a few moments with you. Remember that person is being compensated by a client to do the client's work, not to do your work. It won't do you or the associate any good if a senior partner who has

clients in the office and who is waiting for the research comes into the library and finds you and the associates in a "bull session" discussing college football teams.

4. Copying and photographing of books. If you must get a form or case or statute photocopied, offer to pay for the cost. If there is a reluctance to accept your money, ask the reproduction operator to take the money and to use it for the employees' coffee room. If the firm doesn't want the funds, offer to pay at the same rate charged by the local library. Your few dollars won't be needed by a firm which has a six-figure monthly overhead, but your desire not to be even a slight burden on your host will make a favorable impression and keep the doors open to you.

5. Clean up your mess before you leave. Put all books back. Clean out the ashtrays (whether or not you filled them) and straighten the chairs.

Subscriptions

In my opinion money spent on subscriptions to periodicals during your first few years of practice is a better investment than money spent on hardbound books. Generally speaking, such works fall into three categories:
1. What's new in the law;
2. How-to-do-it articles;
3. Scholarly research and writing.

1. *What's New in the Law.* These are the most important periodicals for you.

a. In law school you learned general legal theories, sometimes using cases 300 years old as teaching guides. You now must apply the principles to a specific factual situation in a modern context. Reading these periodicals will give you a good feeling for what is happening currently.

b. Clients and potential clients will be very impressed when you tell them about new laws and new cases which apply to them. They will be grateful that you are thinking of them.

c. Several of my cases in my early years were cases where another lawyer had told the clients that their case had no merit. In some of these cases the first attorney simply didn't know the current state of the law. By being aware of recent changes, I helped the clients and got devoted clients who many years later still brag to their friends and anyone who will listen about the "miracle attorney" who helped them when the other attorneys said the case was hopeless. This kind of client will send you new clients as long as you live. (Wouldn't you if you were the client?)

      d. You have no choice. If you don't keep up, you will soon be skilled in what the law used to be.

      2. *How-To-Do-It Articles.* These articles are usually valuable to you for the forms and procedures they contain. If you have a problem in any area covered by the article you will save valuable time. Use of these articles is on a hit-and-miss basis. The best article on zoning won't be of much help if you never get a zoning matter. Unless you have a particular interest in a particular field it is my opinion that this type of publication should be deferred until you have been in practice two or three years.

      3. *Scholarly Research and Writing.* If you have an interest in keeping up with the law reviews or journals of your particular law school and you want to subscribe and continue your subscription, then do so. Absent this motivation, I recommend against these types of periodicals. The cost simply isn't warranted in view of the probable uselessness early in a law career. This type of publication can be of great value in appellate briefs, but you probably won't have many cases going to appeal in your first few years. After you are established three or four years and can afford the luxury, you can subscribe to all those you care to, for example, textbooks with annual supplements.

Specific Types of Periodicals

      1. *What's New in the Law.* The local legal newspaper for your community is a must. Advance sheets are also excellent. Bar journals of the American, state and local bar associations also contain excellent critiques on what is new in the law. If you wish to keep current in specific areas such as taxation, there are innumerable journals available such as the *Journal of Taxation.* Both Prentice-Hall and Commerce Clearing House have excellent weekly reports. Other areas of the law have similar journals.

      2. *How-To-Do-It Articles.* Here again, bar journals and legal newspapers are excellent investments.

3. *Special Prices.* Most legal newspapers and bar associations have free or reduced prices for new admittees or for a trial period.

4. *Section Publications of the American Bar Association.* Bar Association Sections have excellent publications; however, they often are of limited value to a new practitioner with a "local" rather than national type of practice. It is difficult to generalize on these publications; the new attorney should carefully consider, however, which sections are likely to be of any use early in a career.

How to Buy Law Books

Book salesmen are sometimes less than candid in telling you how much law books cost. Keep in mind that most law books have three elements of cost:

1. Initial cost;

2. Annual or more frequent upkeep for pocket parts or supplements;

3. New volumes.

1. *Initial Cost.* When you ask a book sales representative how much a set of books cost, you may hear double talk about "monthly payments" being small. Be insistent on knowing what the set costs.

2. *Annual Upkeep.* Insist on knowing what the annual cost of pocket parts or supplements is, based upon the most recent year's cost. Don't be put off by the sales rep answering your question by referring to the fact that this is "free" for one or two years. Remember, it won't be free after the first year or two.

3. *New Volumes.* Book publishers periodically replace old volumes with new volumes. They often do this when the pocket parts become too thick. Sometimes you'll still be paying off the old volumes when the new volumes get added to the bill. Perhaps you remember one or more instances in college of not being able to sell a used book at the end of the course due to a "new edition" (often with nondetectable changes except for the edition year); this is similar to new volume problems. Here again, the sales rep wants to talk about "low monthly payments." Try to negotiate a written guarantee that if a volume is replaced within a certain number of years, then you won't have to pay for the replacement volume.

How to Save Money Buying Used Law Books

1. *Law Schools and Law Libraries.* Let the librarian know you are interested in buying law books. These institutions are frequently

the beneficiaries of inter vivos and testamentary gifts from lawyers or their widows. Often the set is a duplicate or triplicate of a set the law library already has. The library may be willing to sell you a set to use the cash for other purposes.

2. *Widows.* The estate of a deceased lawyer will usually want to sell the library.

3. *Mergers and Dissolutions.* When you receive notice or read about two firms getting together, you can call to see if there is an extra library for sale.

How Much to Pay for Used Books

You should be able to buy used books for 50 percent to 60 percent of the equivalent new book price. Obviously you may be willing to pay more or less depending upon the condition of the books and the urgency to sell or buy. Before buying be sure to check the age of the pocket parts, especially if the books have been around awhile. If you're not careful, the cost of your "bargain" and the cost of bringing the books up to date may be more than the cost of buying a new set.

Financing the Purchase

Although the book companies claim to sell you the books "interest free," you might do better borrowing money from the bank to buy the used books. Ask how much the cash price is to determine whether to use bank or publisher financing.

The Cost of a Library

A very modest one- or two-lawyer library for an established firm costs between $6,000 and $10,000 per year and therefore should not be purchased by the new lawyer.

How to Avoid Library Costs

1. Try to avoid library costs totally by affiliating with lawyers where there is already an existing library.

2. Courthouse law libraries. Judges have libraries and usually share with local lawyers.

How to Buy Law Books

The Federal Trade Commission issued its "Guide for the Law Book Industry" on August 18, 1975, because of abuses in the law book industry. An excellent in-depth article on the subject was written by Raymond M. Taylor and appears in the November 1975 issue of the *American Bar Association Journal.*

Before spending your hard-to-come-by dollars on a law book which you think you do need or will need, ask the following questions at a minimum:

1. *When was the book originally published and when was it last revised?* Is the book a 1990 reprint of a 1963 book with no updating? Be careful about books with copyrights from several years ago. It is difficult, if not impossible, to ascertain if the book is really current or is just the 1980 original with a few chapters modified to allow the publisher to claim it is a 1990 edition.

2. *Does the publisher plan a substantial revision* or replacement within a year or so, and if so, will you get some credit or refund for your nearly obsolete book?

3. *Does the title really reflect the contents?* Often titles are chosen with a view in mind to selling the book rather than describing the contents.

4. *Are supplements intended, and if so, what will they cost?* Be careful when a publisher won't commit to a maximum price on supplements in progress.

5. *What is the total price?*
   a. For cash.
   b. For installments.

Don't waste your time with a book company that won't give you an honest answer to an honest question. When the advertisement or the sales rep insists on talking about monthly payments instead of total price, you can assume they have something to hide.

6. *Are you sure you ordered or received the book?* You'll be surprised at how many bills you will receive for books you never ordered or never received. I suppose there is a thin line between "bookkeeping mistakes" and attempting to obtain money under false pretenses in some instances. Be very careful about paying for books.

7. *Do you understand the bill?* As you expand your library and incur a lot of monthly payments (it's unbelievable how fast they add up), your monthly bill will become very complex. The opportunities for "bookkeeping mistakes" are immense with large companies and their complex internal computer systems. If you don't understand the bill, don't pay it until you get a satisfactory explanation. Be sure that the bill conforms to your "deal" with the sales rep.

Saving Money on Postage

You may think that postage expense is beyond your control. This is not so. There are several things you can do to reduce postage expense.

Eliminate Postage Stamps

Postage stamps are commonly lost or stolen by employees, cleaning crews, etc.

1. *Outgoing mail.* Get the cheapest postage meter available. The meter will save you money. Postage meters can be rented on a monthly basis.

2. *Incoming mail.* Get a reply permit from the post office. (See details on following page.)

Get a Small Postage Scale

If you put too much postage on a letter, you'll waste the excess. On the other hand, if you don't put enough on, you may waste whatever you've used, if the recipient refuses to pay postage due and the letter is returned. Governmental agencies such as courts and sheriffs' departments ordinarily won't pay postage due. The delay in getting the mail back to you and out again may be detrimental and even fatal to your client's case and your malpractice liability.

You'll have many occasions to send out packages of documents. It is easy to waste money on excess and insufficient postage. Break the package into segments that can be weighed individually with the totals added together for the total cost of the package.

1. Go in person to the post office to fill out a form for Permit No.

2. Have envelopes printed (post office will give you samples).

3. For two or three months letter carrier will collect postage due when mail is delivered.

4. Your cost is regular postage plus five cents per item delivered to you (you pay 25 cents for 20 cents postage due).

5. After two or three months you can open a "Postage Due Account" with the post office and the postage due will be charged to your account without daily collection by letter carrier.

The principal advantage to this system is that you only pay for postage actually used. You don't spend money on stamps which clients never use and you don't risk employee theft or loss of postage. Although this seems expensive, it actually will save you money. Also your clients can immediately return their documents or payment checks to you.

Squeezing Extra Hours into the Day to Make More Money

If you can squeeze an extra 15 minutes a day into your billable day, this would translate into one and a fourth hours per week or about 60 hours per year, allowing for vacations, etc. At $100 per hour, this multiplies out to $6,000 per year at 15 minutes per day, or $12,000 per year at 30 minutes a day.

Here are some "tips" for squeezing extra time into the day.

1. *Keep a portable tape recorder in your car, in your home and in your brief case.* Whenever you get a "brilliant" idea concerning a case or a client, dictate it immediately and enter it into your time records when you get back to the office.

2. *Keep small note pads near your home telephone.* When a client calls you at home, make a note of the call on the pad, and enter the call on your time records when you get to the office. People sometimes call you at home, hoping to get free legal advice. When they see "telephone conference at home on Sunday re: mechanic's liens" on the bill, they will respect you for accuracy of your records. These notes may also protect you in a malpractice claim.

3. *Live as close as possible to your office.* In my entire professional career, I have never lived further than 15 minutes from my office. The difference between a 15-minute commute and a 45-minute commute is obviously five hours of chargeable time a week. In my early years, I frequently went home for dinner to see my children, and then returned to the office for an hour or two to work or for a meeting with clients.

4. *Don't waste your commuting time.* If you commute by public transportation, use the time for reading advance sheets and journals or listening to continuing education tapes.

Should You Hire a Secretary or Use a Secretarial Service?

Having a secretary on either a full-time or a part-time basis immediately available for your work is a luxury that you will not need initially. If you are in a suite with other lawyers, you may be able to borrow or buy a small amount of secretarial time from one of the lawyers who does not use a secretary's time fully.

I strongly recommend, however, that the new lawyer in practice contact the various secretarial services in the immediate neighborhood. You will find that these secretarial services will offer to the lawyer one or more of the following features:

1. Dictating equipment;
2. Daily pick-up and delivery of finished work;
3. A reasonable, minimum cost;
4. A cost per word, or per line, over and above the minimum, based on actual usage;
5. General familiarity with legal terminology.

Basically, the concept of a legal secretarial service is that you give the secretarial service a supply of your stationery. You then dictate all of your work into a tape recorder. (You could hand-write, if you wish, but this is not a good habit to get into.) The secretarial service will pick up your tapes at the end of the day. The next morning your dictated material has been typed and is ready for you.

For the first several months of your practice, when you have very little need for secretarial service, this is probably the most efficient and economical way for you to generate and handle secretarial work. Depending upon the particular secretarial service, you may be able to walk over there for a rush-rush emergency, and have them do it while you wait.

An additional side benefit of the use of secretarial service is the self-disciplining and good dictating habits which can be formed early in your career.

Due to the fact that you do not know who will be typing your particular work at the time, you must develop the habit of giving full and complete instructions when you dictate. In other words, you will not simply be able to say, "Send a letter to Mr. Jones." You will have to give specific instructions as to Mr. Jones' name, address, how many carbon copies or photocopies have to be made, etc. This giving of complete instructions for the secretarial service will be of invaluable assistance to you later in your professional career, when you dictate letters and documents for your own secretary, or for a secretarial pool.

I am not aware of any outside secretarial service using word processors or microcomputers with software packages. If you personally have the ability, you may be wise to use a microcomputer as a word processor instead of the traditional typewriter.

Dictating Equipment

Don't make any investment in dictating equipment until you have to. Use the dictating equipment supplied free by your outside secretarial service. Don't buy used dictating equipment unless it's been under warranty or maintenance contract. After you buy equipment, be sure to keep it under maintenance contract. Use only equipment that has a thumb-operated stop, dictate and reverse on the microphone handle. When you open your doors, get cheap portables for your car and briefcase. Get them cheap enough so that you can throw them away after a year or two and not feel badly. Footage meters are not necessary. Don't dictate tapes of more than five minutes' duration if you can help it. Secretaries get psychologically depressed by a 20- or 30-minute tape, but don't seem to mind 5- or 6-minute tapes.

Checklist for When You Start Secretarial and Nonlawyer Hiring

1. Get personnel manual—copy from *Lawyer's Handbook*.
2. Check with local high schools, junior colleges, business colleges and universities for trainee secretarial and clerical help who will

work for free or low pay to get work training credits. Excellent source of trainees with intelligence.

3. Get "Secretarial Hiring Kits," to test basic skills from Wonderlic of Northfield, Illinois; Minnesota Clerical Test; or Law Research Institute, Salt Lake City, Utah.

4. Get Leo Eisenstatt's *A Style Manual for the Law Office,* and plagiarize it. Available from American Bar Association, Order Fulfillment, 750 N. Lake Shore Drive, Chicago, IL 60611.

5. Allow three weeks for advertising and interviewing of applicants, and an additional two weeks notice which the successful candidate will have to give his or her present employer.

Should You Use a Telephone Receptionist, Telephone Exchange, or Mechanical Answering Device?

Obviously, having your own secretary and/or telephone receptionist is nice. However, it may be a luxury that you can easily do without for the first several months. It is not likely that your phone is going to ring off the hook the first day, or even the first week, or possibly even the first month. After a couple of months, however, you can reasonably anticipate that you will have some telephone volume.

If you have an office in a suite with other lawyers, the receptionist is normally included in the cost of the suite.

As between using a telephone exchange with live operators, or a mechanical answering device, I strongly recommend the exchange. Try to find an exchange that services doctors and lawyers. These exchanges are experienced in handling emergency situations. They often are very well trained in calming the nervous or hysterical client until you can be contacted. From time to time, you should call your own number, to see what kind of service the exchange is giving your clients.

There is an expression which goes, "I needed you, I tried to get hold of you, I couldn't get hold of you, I don't need you anymore." This is self-explanatory as to the necessity of having a good telephone exchange to handle your calls when you are at lunch, or during nights and weekends.

Currently, there is a trend for executives and professionals to answer their own telephone. I personally do not feel that this should be done in a law office. If you are with a client, you should not have to interrupt your interview or conference to answer a telephone. When I call a lawyer, and the lawyer answers the phone, I do not assume that the lawyer is following a modern trend. I assume the lawyer cannot afford someone to answer the phone. Therefore, I recommend against this practice. The problem with this type of telephone answering becomes obvious: You would have to tell one client to hold on so you can answer the other ringing telephone. Therefore, do not answer your own phones if you can possibly avoid it. Even if you have to bring in your spouse or a friend to answer the phones for you, in my opinion, this is preferable to your answering your own telephones.

How to Answer the Phone

Volumes have been written on how to answer the phones. I recommend that the phone be answered as follows: "Good morning, Carolyn Jones' office. This is Mary Moore speaking. Can I help you?" We use this method and get many compliments from clients.

Why You Should Use Investigators

As soon as possible after opening your office, ask several lawyers for recommendations for investigators. Meet with a few of them and choose one who really seems to want your business.

Investigators cost money, but they cost relatively little compared to what they will earn for you and your client or save you and your client.

When you tell your client that his or her case requires investigators and that investigators cost money, the client will be more than willing to pay you money "up front." The client will also be impressed by your professionalism. There will be a confidence that the case is being handled properly.

Investigators have the proper photographic equipment and recording equipment. They seem to have "friends" in place where you can only get a closed door. They know how to interview witnesses and to follow up leads. I've often gotten good settlements on cases by showing the insurance adjuster my investigator's reports and asking to see theirs.

As a new lawyer you'll need the investigator's help in evaluating the case. They've seen hundreds of cases and are more skilled than you in most of the areas in which they work.

Within limits, investigators will work with you on payment, sometimes deferring part or all of their fee until the case settles. Never let an investigator or any other witness testify who is owed money by you or your client. Their testimony may be weakened due to a suspicion that their compensation is predicated on the results of the case.

Part VII
Ethics and
Professional
Responsibility

Professional Responsibility and Practice Management

Words such as "professionalism," "ethical," and "responsibility" are vague words that must be defined in light of how and where they are used.

Professional responsibility does not mean just memorizing a list of dos and don'ts based upon ethical concepts that have lasted 500 years as modified by a recent court decision.

Professional responsibility involves understanding the role and responsibility of the legal profession in our society and then further understanding the lawyer's individual role and responsibilities within the profession.

We in America have a legal system that gives Americans more political, religious, economic and social freedoms than any system has provided to its citizens in the history of the world.

Our system of freedom and liberty for the rich and the poor, the weak and the strong, the individual and the multinational corporation is based upon the legal rights and responsibilities found in our Constitution.

Our Constitution was created by a committee of 55 men, 33 of whom were lawyers. Our constitutional system is put into action daily in the courts by lawyers representing plaintiffs and defendants, the government, and the accused. The system is applied by lawyers sitting as judges and by other lawyers sitting as appellate judges. About two-thirds of the presidents of the United States were trained as lawyers. About one-half of all local and national legislators have been lawyers. We lawyers can take the credit for creating and maintaining the greatest system of constitutional freedoms in the history of the world.

Our Constitution is a living document that changes in application and interpretation to meet the changing needs of a dynamic America. Some changes are made by amendment and some by interpretation, and from time to time we discard obsolete sections. Similarly, our professional responsibility is a changing responsibility that adapts our role to meet the needs of our society. The predecessor Canons of Ethics, adopted by the American Bar Association in 1908, were increased from 32 at origin with 15 amendments. The Model Code of Professional Responsibility was adopted in 1969. The present Model Rules of Professional Conduct were adopted in 1983.

We lawyers are accorded an elevated position within our society in recognition of the important function we perform in helping people manage the relationship between themselves and government. We are highly compensated as a profession. We receive great respect from the public, which adds titles such as "attorney" or "esquire" before or after our names. In a manner, it is similar to the respect given to physicians and ministers. We have access to the powers of the court and to the decision-makers in our society.

As part of the *quid pro quo* for occupying this respected position in our society, we have a professional responsibility to our society that arises because we are lawyers. If we were not lawyers, we would not have that responsibility. I have known lawyers who left the legal profession so they could conduct their profit-seeking ventures without the constraints of professional responsibility.

The American Bar Association's Model Rules of Professional Conduct is more than a list of ethical dos and don'ts. It is a strategic plan that addresses our relationship with our clients, the courts, the government, and other lawyers. Included within this relationship is competence, which itself includes the perception by our clients and the public of our professional competence, individually and collectively.

If we as lawyers are perceived not to be competent or if we are perceived not to be helping people, then we shall lose both our ability to maintain our American system of constitutional rights and responsibilities and our ability to be accorded a high level of respect by our society.

Good office procedures and good client relations help us to deliver legal services competently, and help us in maintaining client and public confidence that we are in fact delivering competent legal services. It does little good for a lawyer to deliver technically competent legal services in a manner which alienates the client to the point where the client perceives the services to be incompetent, even though they are in fact competent.

A court system that causes parties two to three years of waiting for an available courtroom or judge, or that requires parties to pay for lawyers to come to the courthouse three or four times to be told there are no courtrooms available, will affect the clients' perception of the competence of the legal system. The clients will not blame the State or County for not voting money for courtrooms and judges. The client will blame the lawyers and will lose confidence in the legal system.

Competent and efficient delivery of legal services not only benefits the clients who receive it, but also our society as a whole; because as we lawyers become more competent in delivering legal services, more members of the public will have access to our services and to the system.

Fifty Ways to Win or Avoid the Ethics War

This chapter is based on my experience of more than a quarter century of practicing law and advising both new and experienced lawyers on ethical problems and matters of professional responsibility that arise in the day-to-day practice of law.

The purpose of this chapter is to help a lawyer recognize common ethical or professional problems in the real world of practicing law. In some cases, I've made editorial comments based on my experiences, while in others I've suggested solutions. I've emphasized the applications to civil cases, although most of the rules relating to how you practice law apply to both civil and criminal practice.

We lawyers are granted certain rights and privileges and access to the power of the legal system. In exchange for these rights and powers, there are rules as to how we can practice. These rules may be voluntarily self-imposed or may be imposed by others. These rules have various names and may be called rules of conduct or rules of ethics, or may bear other designations.

There are various bodies promulgating rules which will affect how you must practice law. It is important that you learn what rules exist and whether you are governed by them, either directly or indirectly. You may be subject to rules issued by one or more of the following types of organizations:

1. State supreme court
2. State legislature
3. State voluntary bar association
4. Mandatory or unified state bar organization
5. County and local bar associations
6. American Bar Association
7. Various national and specialty bar associations

8. Individual local courts

9. Various federal, state, and local administrative bodies which promulgate and maintain their own rules

10. Various federal, state, and local courts which promulgate and maintain their own rules. (Some of these courts are technically administrative bodies.)

Some of the bodies which issue rules create their own rules independently, and some simply refer to the rules of other bodies. One of the more common sets of rules referred to by other groups are those rules promulgated by the American Bar Association over the years. At various times these have been called the Canons of Professional Ethics, the Model Code of Professional Responsibility, and the Model Rules of Professional Conduct.

It was my original intent to append the current ABA Model Rules to this book in order to provide a guide for young lawyers, law students and those lawyers who wanted continuing education. Unfortunately, the ABA's Center for Professional Responsibility demanded royalties for the right to repeat the rules. The Center would not allow reprinting, on a nonroyalty basis, of the rules as a whole in this book. The Center also refused to allow printing of the rules without the copious comments.

The cost of the royalties and the additional printing costs involved would have placed the price of the book beyond the reach of lawyers starting a practice. This chapter deals with practical problems faced in everyday law practice. If you want the Rules and Comments for your reference library, the Center for Professional Responsibility will sell them to you.

I have deliberately avoided making reference to any specific rules of professional responsibility, professional conduct, or ethics in this chapter because of the large number of these sets of rules currently in effect. I leave it to you the reader (or to your professor) to identify the rules in your jurisdiction(s) which are applicable to the situations described.

Avoid the Ethics War

As my main point, I repeat here something which I've said elsewhere in this book and in the many articles and seminars I've authored in the last twenty-five-plus years. THE IMPORTANT THING IS NOT TO WIN THE ETHICS WAR, THE IMPORTANT

THING IS TO AVOID THE ETHICS WAR. Fighting an ethics war is a lose-lose proposition. Even when a lawyer is totally and completely exonerated of any wrongdoing, an ethics complaint puts a permanent blot on his or her reputation. After that, the common misconception that where there's smoke there's fire will apply. The lawyer is forced to spend time and money and attorney's fees to dig out old files and try to reconstruct records long after the event. The client has in most cases lost faith in the legal system. This disgruntled client will bad-mouth the lawyer and the legal system even though the lawyer is totally innocent. The client (and often the press) will treat the exoneration of the innocent lawyer as a cover-up or a whitewash.

According to a recent article in *The Wall Street Journal,* there has been a dramatic increase in the trend toward investigating lawyers for real and imagined complaints. In California during 1989, 19,767 complaints were processed against the 101,226 lawyers in the state. This amounts to one complaint for every 5.12 lawyers. In Florida the figure was one complaint for every 6.16 lawyers; in Texas it was one complaint for every 7.15 lawyers; in Illinois it was one complaint for every 9.42 lawyers.

I repeat: *The important thing is not to win the ethics war. The important thing is to* avoid *the ethics war.*

Fifty Problems and How to Avoid Them

Keeping in mind that your goal is to avoid ethics wars by recognizing and solving ethics problems, let's proceed to examine fifty of the most common problems you are likely to encounter in the real world. These fifty problems are not necessarily presented in the order that you will encounter them, nor necessarily in the order of their importance in your jurisdiction. In many cases these situations will apply to your adversary rather than to you. Being aware of unethical conduct on the part of your adversary can, in some cases, give your client's case an important negotiating or litigating position to the benefit of your client.

1. *Amount of Your Fee.* In some jurisdictions the amount of your fee must be "reasonable." In some jurisdictions the amount must not be "unreasonable." In some jurisdictions it must not be "unconscionable." In some jurisdictions, the fee is purely a matter of contract subject to the same rules as any civil contract. Most jurisdictions

have some sort of a list of factors to be applied in determining how to classify a fee. Unfortunately for you as a practicing lawyer, everybody else can look at the amount of your fees with hindsight. Only you have the burden of needing foresight.

When you enter into an unusual situation, it's often a good practice to pick up the phone and call a couple of other lawyers with experience in the area of law involved to get their input. Be sure to take notes and document these calls in your time records. By getting input from other lawyers, you will simultaneously create an appropriate fee arrangement with the client and prepare a defense should a complaint later be made by an unhappy client.

You should also consider calling the bar ethics hotline or committee of bar discipline personnel. Making these calls and considering the advice given may help demonstrate that you are an ethical lawyer trying to do the right thing in an unusual situation.

2. *Disclosure of Your Fee Agreement to Third Parties.* In some situations your fee agreement must either be disclosed to, or approved by, a third party. Failure to make the disclosure or get the approval may violate an ethical rule. And your failure may be deemed an indication of cover-up rather than ignorance. Depending on the forum or your jurisdiction, you may be required to make disclosure or get approval in the following types of cases. (This list is not intended to be all-inclusive.)

a. Cases involving minors as clients.

b. Probates (even though the fee is not related to probate assets).

c. Family law matters such as adoptions, conservatorships, guardianships, and divorces.

d. Insolvencies and bankruptcies. In some cases, trustees will try to recover fees paid to you prior to the proceeding.

e. Criminal cases. Disgruntled clients are quick to file complaints from prison. Prosecutors may try to separate the client and the attorney by attacking the attorney to seize fees paid or to be paid.

f. Contingency fees. Some administrative bodies require disclosure and occasionally approval of contingent fee agreements as part of their administrative rules of practice.

g. Cash fees. The law is unclear as to the extent, if at all, various government agencies are entitled to know the details of your fee agreements with clients when the fees are paid in currency. Although contingent fees in criminal cases are normally unethical, the practical effect of these invasions of government into the attorney-client relationship may in fact be to make criminal cases contingent. That is, if your client is acquitted you can keep or get the fee, but if your client is found or pleads guilty, you may not get paid or you may have to refund what has been paid. Various courts would provide a back-up arrangement wherein the attorney would get paid what attorneys on the conflicts or indigent panels get paid. This would ensure that only the amount of the fee would be contingent.

h. Any fee where a complaint is made. Whether or not your fee agreement requires prior approval or disclosure to be effective, it will be reviewed by one or more authorities when a complaint is made by an unhappy client, and you'll have to prove your fee agreement meets all requirements.

In short, always keep in mind when you make a fee agreement that some unfriendly or skeptical third person may be reviewing it at a later time, at which point you'll have to defend it.

It is my experience, both as an arbitrator of fee disputes and after representing clients and attorneys in fee dispute litigation, that the most common reason attorneys lose their cases for fees is their failure to obtain a written fee agreement that spells out what is expected of the client and of the lawyer. This lack of a clear agreement as to the scope of representation, coupled with poor time records, results in lawyers losing their cases for fees, in whole or in part, 64 percent of the time.

3. *Fee Splitting.* In some jurisdictions fee splitting with lawyers is permitted where the lawyers share both work AND responsibility. In some jurisdictions, fee splitting is permitted where the lawyers share work OR responsibility. In some jurisdictions the lawyers do NOT have to share either work or responsibility if the fee is a forwarding fee.

In most if not all jurisdictions, the client must be informed in writing that there is a fee-splitting agreement and the total amount of the fee to the client cannot be more than if there were no fee-splitting agreement. In some jurisdictions the client must consent in writing to the fee-splitting agreement.

A nonlawyer cannot receive any part of a fee. In a small firm, giving part of a fee to a nonlawyer for bringing in business or a particular matter would probably be considered unethical "capping." In a large firm, giving the same money to a nonlawyer might be permitted if the nonlawyer held some managerial or executive position, such as marketing director, and was entitled to the payment as a year-end or incentive bonus.

Fee splitting with nonlawyers outside the firm is theoretically always prohibited. If your firm were economically strong enough to have nonlegal subsidiaries doing various forms of ancillary work such as consulting, if the fee splitting were indirect enough, and if the payment by the client were diverted from the law firm to the consulting firm, dividing the fees with the nonlawyer subsidiary or affiliate would probably not be questioned, even though you would in net effect be splitting fees with nonlawyers.

4. *Fees with Out-of-State Clients and Lawyers.* In many jurisdictions, an out-of-state or nonlicensed lawyer is considered a nonlawyer. Accordingly, you may ethically be unable to pay or receive fees from that lawyer. You may need two fee contracts with the client, with a separate fee agreement for each lawyer in each jurisdiction.

If your client is an out-of-state client, you may find that you are illegally or unethically practicing law in the state where your client is located.

If you or your adversary are in a large firm with offices in more than one state, your local bar will probably either ignore the application of these rules or will find or create an exception.

5. *Fees Paid by Third Parties.* Your first duty is to your client, no matter who in fact is paying your fees. Often the legal fees are paid by a third party such as an insurance company, employer, union or trade association, or another organization which seeks to advance its own interests through the medium of the client's case. Before accepting such a case you should make clear in writing, preferably both to the client and the payer, that your professional duty will be to the client should there be a conflict. These conflicts frequently arise as the case progresses. A common example is that the insured, your client, wants the case settled to be able to devote his or her time and energies to ordinary pursuits, while the insurance company, who is paying the fee, wants to drag the case out even to trial and appeals in order to suit its own economic interests. Another common example is that of an employee who is "taking a fall" for the employer who is paying the fees. A union, trade association, or activist organization may want to push or drop a case for its own interests or the

interests of a larger group of parties. Any time a lawyer is looking to someone other than the client for payment of fees, the lawyer should check the rules and be careful.

A similar though not identical dilemma arises when the client is a corporate officer, director, shareholder, or employee and wants personal legal services billed to the business. The most the lawyer can do in such a case is to send bills to the individual at the business address and leave it to the client and the corporation's bookkeepers and auditors to make the appropriate bookkeeping allocations. Again, reread your local rules.

6. *Dropping a Client or Case for Failure to Pay Fees.* Typically you can only drop a client for failure to pay fees if you have a written fee agreement which spells out that you have the right to discontinue working if the client does not pay. In some types of cases (criminal and divorce, for example), you will not be allowed to withdraw for unpaid fees regardless of what your fee agreement says. You will never be allowed to withdraw from a case if your withdrawal would severely prejudice the client's case. These problems can, of course, often be obviated by applying "Foonberg's Rule," which is: "Cash up front."

7. *False Billing Practices.* False billing practices are normally not grounds for disciplinary proceedings (with one exception). Firms sometimes lie to a client about the number of hours worked on a case (reputed to be a major problem with associates who are under pressure to record chargeable time). Firms also misstate who did the work, billing paralegal time as attorney time and billing associate time as partner time. It is my personal opinion that this type of false billing is not only a breach of the fiduciary and confidential relationship between a client and an attorney, but is also grand theft and embezzlement. Fortunately (or unfortunately) this type of false billing is usually treated as a civil fee dispute rather than an ethics matter.

A common situation where an attorney can be disciplined for false billing practices is when the attorney accepts payment in advance to do work, does not do the work, and also refuses to refund the fee paid. This type of disciplinary proceeding can normally be avoided by the attorney making prompt refund to the client of the unearned fee.

8. *Depositing Fees Paid in Advance.* When a client pays cash up front for fees and costs for the case, the attorney should put all the

funds into a trust account until the fees are earned or the costs incurred. Most lawyers ignore this rule without consequence. The amount of the minimum or nonrefundable fee can be put directly into the general account, but the balance belongs in the trust account. Lawyers are particularly remiss in depositing money for future costs (rather than money for reimbursement for past costs incurred) into the trust account where it belongs.

9. *Suing Clients for Fees*. There is normally no ethical prohibition against suing a client for earned and unpaid reasonable fees. Some codes caution that a lawyer should only sue a client for a fee in "exceptional situations."

As a practical matter, you can expect an often nonmeritorious cross-complaint for malpractice. You should not sue a client for fees unless your conduct has been exemplary and there is nothing in the file that you would feel awkward about explaining. In some jurisdictions you must offer arbitration as a condition precedent to suing. Be sure to read all the applicable local rules before suing a client for fees. Be sure you have complete and accurate time records and that there is some evidence that the client understood the terms of the engagement, including what the maximum fee was likely to be.

10. *Written Fee Agreements*. For more than twenty-five years I have been a voice in the wilderness, advocating written fee agreements for the mutual protection of the client and the attorney. I have written about what to put in a fee agreement in this and other books. Some professional rules now make a written fee agreement or a written fee memorandum mandatory. At a bare minimum, the agreement should cover what the lawyer is being hired to do, what the lawyer is not being hired to do, what the fees will be and/or how they will be calculated and charged, and when fees are payable. The right of the lawyer to stop working under specific circumstances and the right of the client to fire the lawyer under specific circumstances should also be covered. A letter to the client or a memo to the file is not as good or sufficient as a fee agreement but is better than nothing.

11. *Settlement Offers*. In some jurisdictions it is mandatory for a lawyer to communicate settlement offers to a client. In all jurisdictions it is good lawyering to communicate settlement offers to a client. You are perfectly free to recommend to a client that the settlement be accepted or rejected but you are not free to hide the offer from the client. You might wish to enclose an extra copy of the letter containing the offer for transmission to the client when you send an

offer for the adverse client to consider. You should be careful not to omit any of the terms of the offer if you paraphrase or summarize it. In most cases, the letter containing the offer will contain self-serving opinions of the merits (or lack of merit) of the other side's case, and for this reason, I don't recommend forwarding a letter from the other lawyer to your client. It is adequate to accurately summarize the other lawyer's offer to settle in your letter to your client.

12. *Keeping Your Client Informed.* You have a professional obligation to keep your clients informed of the developments (or lack of developments) on their cases. Unfortunately (in my opinion) this may not be the law in your jurisdiction. Failure to keep your client informed is, in theory, grounds for disciplinary action, although I've never heard of a disciplinary proceeding for failure to keep a client informed unless the failure to communicate was considered evidence of abandonment or cover-up. Frankly, I think that failing to keep a client informed of everything happening on a case is bad lawyering, and is certainly just plain stupid from a client-relations point of view.

The best way to keep your clients informed is to bombard them with paper via mail and fax. Legal services are intangible, and lots of paper makes tangible the intangible.

13. *Calling Yourself "Judge."* It is not uncommon for a lawyer, even a new lawyer, to serve as a pro tem or volunteer judge, often in small-claims court. It is also not uncommon for a lawyer to serve as a full-time judge for a period of time and then return to private practice. In some jurisdictions, if you are a former judge you may not use the title "Judge" when the phone is answered, nor can you indicate on your professional cards or letterhead the fact that you are or were a judge. There appears to be concern that you would be intimating that your status as a judge or former judge would enable you to get special treatment for your clients in litigation. If this situation applies to you or someone in your firm or another lawyer, you should check the rules to see if the conduct is permitted or prohibited. The public should never feel that their chances of winning or losing a case might be affected by a judge on the bench favoring a former judge.

14. *Listing Organizational Memberships on Stationery.* In most cases you probably can list your membership in professional or non-professional organizations, provided the information is truthful. You will need to be careful, though, if your jurisdiction prohibits specialty listings. If you feel that it is important to let people know on

your stationery that you belong to the National Aardvark Association, such a listing would probably be permitted if there is no claim on your part that this membership makes you a specialist in some area of law. The law in this area is currently in a state of flux.

15. *Listing Titles, Degrees, and Qualifications on Stationery.* Many of the same questions are also found in the area of listing organizational memberships. Some licensing authorities take the position that if you say anything more than "Attorney at Law," you are indicating that you have some specialty area and accordingly cannot do so in those jurisdictions which prohibit or regulate specialty designations. Since there is no fixed pre-law-school major in college and since many lawyers become lawyers after they have attained distinction in some field other than law, lawyers frequently have titles, degrees, and certificates other than a law degree and admission to practice as lawyers. (Interestingly enough, some lawyers have neither a baccalaureate or law degree from any university.)

I predict in time that the listing of these degrees and certificates will be permitted so long as the information is truthful. Clients and potential clients will have the right to know their prospective lawyer's qualifications and the lawyer will have the right to tell the client or prospective client who wants to know. Whether or not to provide this information (assuming it is truthful) will become a marketing question and not an ethics issue. You are, of course, cautioned to check your local rules.

16. *Restricting Practice by Not Representing Other Clients with Similar Claims.* If you have done a good job in representing a client, the opposition may want to include in a settlement that you as a lawyer will not represent other clients with similar claims against that party or against other parties in the same industry. In most if not all jurisdictions you may not make such an agreement even if you and your client are both willing. You may not ask opposing counsel to be party to such an agreement.

17. *Competence.* Competence is now included in the rules of professional conduct of most jurisdictions. This is relatively new and signifies one of the differences between ethics and professional responsibility. In the past, one could be both ethical and incompetent. Under most current rules you can be disciplined for undertaking or prosecuting work for which you or your firm are not competent. Your State (or whatever agency is involved in licensing or granting

permission to practice) said that you were competent when you were admitted to practice. Lack of experience may be deemed lack of competence.

With the ever-increasing public demand for specialization (or whatever name you wish to call it), the differences between competence and incompetence become even more fuzzy and difficult to define or identify.

My solution to the problem is to get help. When you truly don't feel comfortable that you know what you are doing, call another lawyer for his or her opinion on what you should be doing.

It's possible that you should associate with another lawyer or law firm to work behind or alongside you to give you ongoing help with the case. The choice of whether the other firm will work with you or alongside you may be determined by your relationship with your client and whether the other firm wants to accept professional responsibility to the client. If you are in over your head, it may be in everyone's best interest for you to simply tell the client that since additional facts and research have come to your attention, it now appears that the client's interests would best be served by calling in specialists, and that you will remain in the case to serve as liaison to the specialist. This will normally please most clients, and the truth is that you will feel better and breathe easier knowing that the client has the right lawyer for the problem.

Many, if not most, bar associations maintain a lawyer-to-lawyer directory listing lawyers available to help other lawyers. Even if your bar association does not have such a directory, you can network other lawyers through the bar committees to find the right lawyer to help out. I have never been turned down in my entire career when I've asked other lawyers for help, and no lawyer will turn you down when you ask for a few minutes of their time by telephone. A truly caring lawyer will not want any fee for giving you a few tips to get you and the client down the right road. (Obviously there are limits to what any lawyer should ask another lawyer to do without compensation.)

18. *Media Advertising.* Media advertising, for purposes of this section, will be defined as advertising by radio, television, newspaper, magazine, or other print media; that is, advertising which is cleanly bought and paid for as advertising, as opposed to that advertising which is indirectly bought and paid for through a public relations

firm or other third party, whom you have paid to obtain free or indirect advertising disguised as news or public interest information.

In general, media advertising has to meet the "three Ts" Test. It must be Truthful, Tasteful, and Tentative. It must be truthful in that it cannot contain lies. It must be tasteful in that it doesn't offend the person who decides whether it is tasteful or offensive. It must be tentative in that you can't guarantee results. You may or may not be required to deposit a copy of your ad with a bar committee before or after using it. Read your local rules. Decide whether to comply, try to change the system, or forget about using direct media advertising and stick to indirect media advertising. (See next section.)

My personal feelings are clear and have never been subtle. I believe that all people and institutions should have access to the legal system and that we as individual lawyers and the legal profession as a group have a responsibility to help people and institutions with meritorious legal needs find the lawyer or firm for their needs by whatever means that get the job done.

It is far beyond the scope of this book or this chapter to repeat in detail all of the evidence which clearly demonstrates that media advertising does not create the need for legal services. The need for legal services exists or does not exist independently of media advertising. Media advertising does not stir up litigation. Clients do not contact a lawyer until after they need a lawyer. Most if not all of the firms and individuals who obtain lawyers through media advertising would not utilize media ads to find a lawyer if they could access the legal system by contacting a lawyer they knew or to whom they could be recommended.

Most of the complaints about legal advertising come from lawyers, not from clients. Most of the complaints deal with taste, not with whether the advertising helps the American public find the lawyer they need.

As mentioned, the current requirements for professional, paid-for media advertising for legal services is that it must be truthful, tasteful, and tentative. What constitutes truthful, tasteful, and tentative is, of course, a matter of both fact and opinion. Some attorneys would gladly abolish all media advertising. These attorneys normally have no problem with advertising which is bought and paid for through third-party sources, so long as it's disguised as information. In many cases, the person accused of violating the applicable rules is going to have an unfriendly judge or jury deciding whether the particular ad involved is truthful and tasteful.

If you are going to go heavily into paid-for media advertising you should include in your budget funds to have your materials reviewed by a lawyer who has experience in disciplinary proceedings and/or first-amendment law. In some jurisdictions, you may be required to deposit a copy of the materials with some committee or board before using the materials.

In summary, before you spend any significant amount of time or money on paid-for media advertising, be sure you know the current rules and understand that no matter what you do, you may have to invest time and money getting some sort of prior approval. The alternative is to take the risk of sailing through uncharted waters, which could cost you a lot of time and energy.

19. *Indirect Media Advertising.* I have heard statistics saying that more than 80 percent of all space in a newspaper is paid-for advertising or information planted by groups advocating their own economic interests through the guise of news. Less than 20 percent is true news such as current events, sports, and weather. Indirect media advertising is that type of paid advertising which finds its way into the media disguised as being newsworthy or as being some sort of public service. Rather than buy advertising space or time as such, you or any law firm can buy "high visibility." Rather than making a self-proclaimed statement of expertise in an advertisement clearly bought and paid for, the law firm can pay for and get a third party such as a newspaper reporter to claim that the lawyer or law firm are experts, when in fact the lawyer or firm may know little or nothing about the area of law involved. A public relations firm can set up individuals in your firm as experts to give an opinion on cases or laws in the news. Public relations firms are paid significant sums of money to keep a lawyer or firm in the public media. They have their own methods of getting information into the media by creating a newsworthy event out of the lawyer or law firm.

The line between publicity for the benefit of the client and publicity for the benefit of the lawyer is further blurred when litigants can hire public relations firms to flood TV, radio, and newspapers with coverage during a trial in an effort to influence the judge or jury. In major cases, the litigants who have enough money to spend or who have an important enough political motive to advance spend unbelievable amounts of money on the theory that judges and jurors, who may sincerely try to judge the case only by the evidence presented in the courtroom, still won't forget what they hear and see on TV and in the newspapers.

While you as a new lawyer may not have the resources to wage a second front in the newspapers, you should keep in mind that your client may have the resources, and the apparent state of affairs currently is that news coverage is not only ethical, but an important part of case management.

20. *Direct Mail Solicitation.* The subject of direct mail solicitation is a very heated one. As with other areas of advertising, the complaints come from lawyers, not from clients. The major problem with direct mail solicitation is that the mail may be reaching someone who is already represented by counsel. A letter counseling a person to do or not to do something may be contrary to the advice given by the current counsel. The mail could also be interfering with an existing attorney-client relationship in that it might be giving legal advice to someone represented by counsel. Both of these activities are usually proscribed by the various rules. Targeted direct mail should include a statement to the following effect:

> If you are already represented by counsel, it is not our intention to interfere with your relationship with your attorney, and we ask that you seek appropriate advice from your attorney. If you are not represented by counsel we would be pleased to discuss the possibility of our representing you.

The rules of your jurisdiction might require some sort of notice or warning in or on the letter that the letter consists of legal advertising. (See next section dealing with nonsolicitation mailings.)

21. *Nonsolicitation Mailings.* Nonsolicitation mailings, such as firm announcements, newsletters, bulletins, alerts, brochures, Christmas cards, seminar announcements, public relations mailings concerning published articles and firm activities, and a large variety of other mailings, may or may not have to carry a warning on or in the mailing. The warning usually must say something like "Legal Advertising Enclosed" in big letters on the outside of the envelope. In some jurisdictions the warning must be printed in the contents. I believe one lawyer closes off the mailing by stating that the preceding message was legal advertising. You will have to check your current rules.

22. *No Recovery—No Fee.* In contingency cases, attorneys often

quote "no recovery, no fee" to a client. I believe that the problem with this type of fee quotation is that it often may be false and deceptive advertising, or may simply be lying to a client. Some attorneys fail to disclose that in the event the case is lost there may be a bill of taxable costs to be levied against the client. Clients have had to go bankrupt because of taxed costs. Lawyers often file a notice of appeal upon losing the case and then negotiate dropping the appeal for a waiver of costs. Obviously an attorney should discuss the possibility of a bill for costs if the case is lost.

Attorneys rarely, if ever, discuss the possibility of losing a contingency case. I've never heard of a lawyer getting into trouble over filing a notice of appeal as an inducement to waiving costs. My problem is whether or not the client truly understands what is happening. There used to be an absolute prohibition against a lawyer advancing costs on a contingency case without such costs being considered a loan to be paid back by the client when the case was over, even when the case was lost. Many professional rules now allow an attorney to openly advance costs on a contingency case with repayment to come only out of the recovery, if at all.

23. *Firm Name.* Unless you are going to call yourself JOHN DOE, ATTORNEY AT LAW, you'll have to find out what is or is not permitted in your jurisdiction. In some jurisdictions you cannot practice under a fictitious name; in other jurisdictions you can. In some jurisdictions, using the names of dead lawyers unknown to any human being alive is considered to be using a fictitious name. In other jurisdictions, it's not. In some jurisdictions you can use any name you wish to use. It is not uncommon in these jurisdictions to practice under names like "AAAA and AAAA, Attorneys at Law" in an attempt to be the first name in the telephone book. In some jurisdictions you can practice under a name like "American Institute for the Defense of Drunk Driving Charges" (a name I created for this example.) You can be disciplined for false advertising if you call yourself "Jones and Smith, Attorneys at Law" if Mr. Jones is not in fact a general partner, but an associate. The rules pertaining to firm name often are arbitrary and are not evenly applied to big and small firms.

24. *Buying or Selling a Law Practice.* In many states it is unethical to sell or buy a law practice if you are a sole practitioner. One has to use the guise of forming a partnership with the purchaser and then selling the goodwill connected with the partnership interest. Many states are now changing the rules to conform to what is happening

in the real world. It is incumbent on the buyer and seller to carefully apply the existing rules to the transaction. In other words, it is theoretically prohibited to buy and sell practices, but it can be done in such a way as to comply with the rules.

25. *Coaching Your Client to Lie.* There are no jurisdictions of which I am aware that advocate a lawyer instructing a client to lie. Most if not all jurisdictions have express rules dictating that a lawyer may not counsel a client to lie. Some jurisdictions even want the lawyer to withdraw from the case and "turn in" the client to a judge or prosecutor if the lawyer knows the client is lying.

Some lawyers avoid this situation by prefacing important questions with a statement along the following lines: "The answer to the next question is critical. If you tell me the answer is 'yes,' you may win your case. If you tell me the answer is 'no,' you will definitely lose your case. Now—what is the answer to this question?"

26. *Turning Over Files When You Are Discharged.* You must return to the client anything that is the property of the client. You must also turn over whatever the next lawyer will reasonably need to effectively represent the client. You cannot hold onto records because of an unpaid bill. You clearly *do* have the right to photocopy what you turn over in order to protect yourself for malpractice and tax purposes. You certainly can agree with your client beforehand (in your fee agreement) that the client must pay for these photocopy charges.

A file may contain misfiled items which belong to other clients. You must protect the confidences of the other clients whose documents are erroneously filed by removing them before you turn over the file. Accordingly, it is necessary to review or screen the contents of a file before divulging the contents to a client or another lawyer or during discovery. Rules regarding turning over work product vary from jurisdiction to jurisdiction.

27. *Destroying Files.* The destruction of files is covered by professional rules due to the fact that the file may contain items which belong to the client or to others. There may be special rules concerning files on criminal cases. Some firms simply send everything off to the cheapest warehouse they can find, often hundreds of miles away, believing this to be the most economical thing to do. Some firms simply throw files away and cross their fingers that nothing will go wrong. Most firms seem to pick an arbitrary deadline of five or ten years, and then throw the file away, hoping that they won't ever need

the files in the future. Putting files onto microfilm or other electronic media, such as CD-ROM, may provide economical solutions to the problem of the seemingly perpetual costs of file storage. As a new lawyer, you should plan to move files into storage as soon as possible to save rent costs, but don't destroy files until much later in your career. The subject of file destruction is of ethical concern because of the ethical mandate to protect property which belongs to the client.

28. *Going Out of Practice.* Your jurisdiction may have special rules on file preservation if you decide to leave the practice of law on either a short-term or long-term basis. You may be required to make some sort of arrangement with another lawyer to take over your files.

29. *Turning Your Files Over to Third Parties Pursuant to Court Order.* There is an increasing tendency on the part of lawyers to attack other lawyers. Often a government agency will obtain some sort of court order such as a search warrant or a civil subpoena to seek the contents of a client's files. Some overly aggressive lawyers are quick to sue both the adversary client and the adversary's lawyers, hoping to get access to the lawyer's files through the guise of doing discovery on the lawyer. In these cases I would recommend simply refusing to comply by asserting attorney-client privilege, work product, etc., as reasons for not complying and respectfully requesting that the other side get a court order after giving the client an opportunity to assert all appropriate claims in court. As in other situations, you have to review and screen files beforehand to be sure you don't inadvertently turn over misfiled information concerning other clients.

30. *Inadvertent Violations of Attorney-Client Confidences.* Lawyers rarely violate attorney-client confidences deliberately. You must read the rules carefully to get a feeling of what information outside of the legal issues themselves are included and what practices constitute violations of attorney-client confidences. While you may not get disciplined for accidentally violating confidences, your reputation will suffer and you'll have a difficult time collecting on the unpaid balance of your fee.

31. *Sending Client Mail to the Wrong Address.* You should always ask clients where to send mail concerning their legal matters. Some clients don't want their employees to know their legal problems and some don't want members of their families to know what's happening on their case. It's not too smart to send a strategy letter on a divorce case to the client's home where the spouse can get the letter

and read it. Similarly, you don't want to send a letter concerning the company's high earnings to a place where the employee's union representative can see it.

32. *Sending Copies of Mail to the Wrong Person.* I enjoy receiving copies of confidential letters sent by a lawyer to a client when the lawyer's mailroom erroneously sends me copies of *all* correspondence just because I'm on the mailing list to receive copies of pleadings filed with the court.

33. *Sending the Wrong Enclosures in the Mail.* I've often received the last page of a letter showing who gets the blind copies of correspondence. I've learned the identities of other clients and lawyers and law firms, which were meant to be confidential. I've also gotten original letters intended for the other lawyer's client. I suppose the other lawyer's client got the pleading I was supposed to get.

34. *Failing to Put "Personal and Confidential" or "To Be Opened by Addressee Only" on the Mail Envelope or the Fax.* Failure to use these words or similar wording such as "privileged and confidential information enclosed" on the outside of the envelope may make your mail fair game for whoever can get to it first. This problem is compounded by the now widespread use of Fax transmissions. For reasons that I do not understand, many law firms do not indicate that a fax communication is from a law firm on their cover sheet or in their sender ID code which appears at the top of each page of the document transmitted.

35. *Not Protecting the Identity of Clients.* The identity of a client is as much a confidence as the nature of the legal work for which you are consulted. You won't get disbarred, but it won't help your reputation or the firm's when a client is upset because you've been using their name in public without their permission. Lawyers and nonlawyers in the firm have a tendency to want to advertise or brag about who their clients are. The identity of your client can be just as important to the client's case as the case itself. Accordingly, you should keep that identity confidential.

You can understand that clients or the value of their companies' shares could be prejudiced if it were known that they had just become clients of a firm specializing in bankruptcy, or tax fraud, or divorce, or whatever. Individuals normally don't want anyone knowing they have legal problems.

36. *Failure to Teach Client Confidentiality to Family Members.* A lawyer should teach and reinforce client confidentiality to family

members. You need to instruct your children or spouse not to repeat outside the house what they overhear on the phone or see in a document. Your family members did not take a course in professional responsibility, and unless you teach them what not to do, you run a serious risk that they will do just that.

37. *Failure to Teach Client Confidentiality to Independent Contractors.* A lawyer has to supervise and be responsible for what marketing directors, public relations firms, and other nonlawyers do for the firm. Most of these people have no knowledge about law or legal matters, except in how to sell their services to and for lawyers. Some of these people may simply be loose cannons rolling around on the deck who will eventually get the firm or a particular lawyer into deep trouble with a client or the bar or the public, simply because they didn't know that they were doing something unethical. You should at least tell them to buy a copy of the Model Rules of Professional Conduct from the American Bar Association—or buy them a set yourself.

38. *Failure to Teach Confidentiality to Office Staff.* You will be responsible if members of your staff commit a blatant violation of the rules, and defend themselves by truthfully stating that they didn't know they were doing anything wrong. Your staff manual and the package you hand to new employees, both professional and non-professional, should include a copy of the rules of conduct applicable to your firm. It wouldn't hurt to have a once-a-year luncheon where the most common problems are taught or reinforced to the staff. You can buy or rent a videotape on this subject to show once a year and to every new hire.

39. *Trust Accounts.* Putting client money that belongs in a trust account into your personal or office account is an easy way to get disbarred, especially if you use the money for personal purposes and don't give it back to the client. The usual pattern is for a desperate lawyer to put money that should have gone into the trust account, such as a client's settlement money or unearned fees received from the client, into some account other than the trust account. Typically, the client is told that the case has not yet been settled or that the work has been done. Falling into this classic pattern is the simplest and fastest way I know of to get disbarred. The trust account should be clearly labeled as such and only the lawyer should have the power to write checks on the account.

Some lawyers who are in financial trouble put their own personal funds into the trust account and pay their personal bills from that account. They typically do this to hide money from creditors or spouses. It is clearly wrong to put your personal money in the trust account, but I've never heard of a lawyer being disbarred or disciplined for doing so, since no client suffers from the conduct.

40. *Going into Business Deals with Clients.* An undercapitalized client may offer you a "piece of the action" in lieu of a fee or as part of a reduced fee. You may have visions of simultaneously doing the client a favor by conserving the client's cash flow and possibly getting rich on the investment. These deals rarely produce anything but aggravation for the lawyer. If the deal turns out well, the client may want to renege on the basis that you were overreaching. If you are tempted to take a piece of the action, be sure to send the client to another lawyer before finalizing the agreement. At the very least, put into writing your advice to the client that they have the right to see another lawyer before agreeing and that you recommend they do so. Get the client to sign a copy of the letter where you give this advice. If *you* suggest the possibility of taking a piece of the deal, you'll be in even worse shape when the client simultaneously files a lawsuit and an ethics complaint.

Historically, contingency fee agreements are excluded from the application of these rules. In some areas of law, such as entertainment law, lawyers get a piece of the deal in addition to a cash fee. I would assume this is allowed because the clients are presumed to be sophisticated and able to protect their own interests.

41. *Alternative Billing Methods.* Many lawyers try to raise their effective hourly rate through ingenious alternative billing methods. These methods are frequently just a contingency plus an hourly rate. They are sometimes called "results-oriented" rates or "performance reevaluations." I've heard one client refer to them as begging for tips. In any event, if you are going to go for some exotic alternative billing method, you may face the identical problems as you would face if you were to go into a business deal with your client. Be careful when you get innovative.

42. *Representing a Client with Zeal.* Many lawyers take this rule to be a blank check to be hostile and unnecessarily aggressive. If it were up to me, I would limit application of this rule to serious criminal cases or abolish it altogether. This rule may be a good rule in terms of helping a single client on a single case, but it may be doing the legal system more harm than good. I am seeing considerable ov-

erkill in civil litigation and in the "Rambo" atmosphere of hostility among lawyers. The public is lowering its opinion of lawyers and the legal system as they are asked to pay for this legal excess and as they witness the legal system and the courts becoming the instruments of those who have the resources to pay for this overkill. This rule can be a convenient safe harbor for you or your firm when you are accused of overkill or running up a bill with unnecessary work unlikely to add anything to the outcome of the case.

In serious criminal cases where human life is involved and in most serious criminal cases (you'll have to define "serious"), the rule may be a good one in theory but prove hard to apply. If every defendant pled not guilty and demanded a jury trial, our criminal justice system would probably come to a complete halt or reach the point where only the most serious cases were tried, leaving criminals free to attack society without punishment.

In applying this rule the lawyer will have to balance duty to the client, duty to the legal system, and duty to society. No matter what balance the lawyer reaches from a personal point of view, the lawyer will be forced to prove, after the fact, that the client was represented with zeal.

About the only advice I can give for this situation is to make sure that the client is aware of how much work you could do on a case and then let the client limit the amount of work to be done based on the client's view of the importance of the matter, relative to how much the client wants done or is willing to pay for.

43. *Prosecuting Nonmeritorious Cases.* You may not prosecute a case which you know to be nonmeritorious or to assert defenses based on knowingly false information. You may be subject to personal sanctions applied to you as an individual or to your firm, and you will face disciplinary proceedings when the court refers the matter for investigation and prosecution. This is one of the few areas where judges take the initiative in instituting disciplinary proceedings. They probably do so because they are eyewitnesses to the transgression and are angry about the waste of their time and the waste of court facilities that could have been made available to clients with meritorious cases. If you feel or know that the case is nonmeritorious, get the opinion of a second lawyer (protecting the client's name), then tell the client that the case is *over* as far as you are concerned and that the client should substitute *in propria per-*

sona or you'll make a motion to be relieved, thereby entering into the court record your opinion that the case is nonmeritorious, which might later hurt the client's case if the client is determined to prosecute.

44. *Moral Turpitude.* In many jurisdictions, one can be disciplined for "moral turpitude" or "conduct unbecoming a lawyer" or similarly vague transgressions. Typically, these transgressions are unrelated to the practice of law. The range of transgressions is unlimited. In some jurisdictions one will not be allowed to take the bar exam if one is in default on a student loan. In some jurisdictions, conviction of or pleading *nolo* to a felony means automatic disbarment, even though the felony is totally unrelated to the practice of law. In some jurisdictions, conviction of a felony is not grounds for disciplinary procedure unless the felon is related to the practice of law or deals with some particularly serious matter. I've heard of a lawyer being disbarred for moral turpitude for pleading guilty to a misdemeanor charge or having sex with a prostitute.

I can only suggest that if you are in trouble, you should consider whether the resolution of the matter will affect your license to practice law. An expedient or practical solution to the nonprofessional problem may create an unanticipated professional problem with the bar.

45. *Communicating with an Adverse Party Represented by Counsel.* It's basic that a lawyer cannot communicate with an adverse party who is represented by counsel. To do so will result in discipline. One cannot use the guise of communicating with the attorney with a copy to the attorney's client or vice versa. A serious problem arises when you want to do investigation either directly or through an investigator. Depending upon the jurisdiction you may be prohibited from contacting family members, employees, co-workers, expert witnesses, and a large variety of other people who have some special relationship to the adverse party. You will simply have to read the rules and the case law under the rules to decide each situation as it arises. One can communicate directly with an adverse person represented by counsel only if you have the attorney's permission. Based on my experiences with overzealous attorneys who interpret their mandate to represent a client zealously to include lying and who have thus lied about obtaining permission, you should confirm the permission in writing by mail or fax before contact. If the represented

person calls you by telephone, hang up until you can confirm your right to contact the client. If the scope of what you can discuss is unlimited, the letter should so reflect.

Some attorneys let the adverse person tell everything before asking if the person is represented by counsel. This is a dangerous technique and can backfire if the person claims later that they disclosed up front the fact that they were represented by counsel.

46. *Suppressing Evidence.* I personally do not hide discoverable evidence in discovery proceedings, nor do I counsel clients to do so. It appears that I'm in a small minority. Many lawyers tell me that they have their clients screen evidence before turning it in to the attorney for transmission to the other side. Apparently, the attorney also screens the evidence. I get the impression that the only discovery that's worthwhile is when the other party and their attorneys accidentally leave something important in what was turned over, or when the source of the documents is from a third party. I totally disapprove of this conduct, but it's done and I'm not aware of any serious disciplinary proceedings resulting therefrom. If you can prove that opposing counsel has suppressed evidence, I ask you to make it a point to file a complaint. When a lawyer tells a client to suppress evidence, the client is justified in inferring that all lawyers suppress evidence.

47. *Turning In Other Attorneys for Violating the Rules.* Different jurisdictions have different rules governing an attorney's obligation to turn in other attorneys for violations of the rules. In many jurisdictions, the authorities simply disregard complaints filed by attorneys, believing that there is a game going on and deciding that they don't want to be in the middle of a dispute between lawyers. (There's an old expression that it's the grass that gets trampled when elephants fight.) The same complaint will receive more serious attention if it is filed by your client rather than being filed by you as the attorney.

48. *Preventing Your Client from Committing a Crime.* In some jurisdictions you are supposed to turn in a client who is planning to commit a crime. Where adopted, this rule is sometimes referred to as the "Squeal Rule."

49. *Counseling Your Client to Commit a Crime.* You can never counsel a client to commit a crime. Such counseling can get you named as a co-conspirator in a criminal proceeding. No exceptions exist for those people who want to commit a crime through civil

disobedience in order to get free publicity and attention for their cause. If you counsel a client to commit a crime to draw attention to a clearly unjust law or practice, you may find yourself in trouble with the bar as well as the criminal authorities, despite your good intentions. Only you as an individual can decide the price you are willing to pay to help a client make a point. There are some narrow exceptions and limitations in the area of challenging improper laws. Read the rules carefully.

50. *Getting Copies of All Applicable Rules for Your Personal Library.* Ethics is statutory. The rules change from time to time in an attempt to be responsive to the society we serve. The rules differ from body to body and jurisdiction to jurisdiction. You owe it to the public, yourself, your family, your clients, others in your firm, and most importantly to the legal system to practice ethically and professionally. You can't follow the rules or change the rules if you don't know the current rules. What you learned in law school may have been accurate when you were in law school, but may not reflect the current rules issued by those courts and administrative bodies where you will be representing your client.

What Are the Consequences of "Violating" the Canons of Professional Ethics, the Code of Professional Responsibility, or the Model Rules of Professional Conduct?

This is a difficult question to answer. The answer depends on the particular "violation" and upon your licensing laws.

A brief review of some basic definitions will be helpful.

Bar association usually means a *voluntary* group of lawyers. Associations are normally organized on a geographic basis and may be on an international, national, state, county, city or neighborhood basis. A state or local bar association may have its own "canons" or "code," or it may adopt *in toto* or by reference the canons or codes of another association. In some states, the bar association can "recommend" a license proceeding against a lawyer.

State bar usually means a mandatory bar group that you must belong to to practice law in the state. This type of bar is often called an "integrated bar" (having nothing to do with civil rights) or a "uniform bar." "State bars" can sometimes do more or less than "bar associations."

Canons of Professional Ethics are the pronouncements of the American Bar Association adopted in 1908 which remained in effect until 1970.

Code of Professional Responsibility. The Code contained nine Canons (general statements) that were subdivided into 128 Ethical Considerations and 39 Disciplinary Rules. The Code was adopted in 1970.

Model Rules of Professional Conduct. The Model Rules were adopted in 1983, superseding the Code of Professional Responsibility. They consist of 52 rules on seven broad topics (see my chapter on "The Model Code of Professional Responsibility and the Model

Rules of Professional Conduct"). Copies are sold by the American Bar Association's Center for Professional Responsibility.

State Rules of Professional Conduct. These are rules promulgated by licensing bodies such as the supreme court or legislature of a state.

With some of the definitions in mind, we can go back to the basic question of the effect of violation of accepted standards of ethics.

The Code and the Model Rules, in my opinion, represent the sincere efforts of well-meaning experts to develop standards of conduct for lawyers on the highest level for the benefit of the public. Some of the rules may not be practical or enforceable and there are other objections. Notwithstanding all of the criticisms of the rules, on balance, it is a good work and deserving of respect and following.

The new lawyer should not be frightened or awed by the rules. Violations of some of the provisions will cost you your license. Violations of other provisions could result in disciplinary proceedings such as a reprimand or being expelled from the association.

Is unethical conduct *per se* also illegal? Some unethical conduct can be illegal, such as trust fund violations or fee splitting with the laity, and could result in criminal prosecution as well as disciplinary proceedings. Some unethical conduct could result in disciplinary proceedings only, such as telephone book advertising violations. Some violations probably have absolutely no effect in some states, such as fee splitting.

In summary, "violating" the Code of Professional Responsibility or Model Rules of Professional Conduct can have either serious consequences or lesser consequences, depending upon whether the rules are or are not part of your disciplinary system and upon the powers of your state bar or bar association.

As a new lawyer, you do not have enough sophistication or experience to decide selectively not to observe portions of the rules. You should initially observe the rules in their entirety, both in letter and in spirit. When you are an established attorney and better understand the needs of the public, you can and should attempt to modify the local application of the rules to meet the local needs of the public.

Remember that, even if you do not lose your license to practice law, expulsion from a bar association can leave an ugly stain on your career and can cost you money by loss of referrals.

I must strongly advise that you thoroughly understand exactly what the situation is in your state or community *before* you begin your practice. If you're in sole practice there is no one to review your work and you may be inadvertently doing something unethical, without realizing it. Somewhere in your legal education you were taught or exposed to legal ethics. Be sure you understand the interrelation of ethics and licensing.

Ten Rules for Avoiding Disciplinary Complaints

It is estimated that every year about one disciplinary complaint is filed for every 10 lawyers. Very few of these complaints result in any discipline against the lawyer, either because the nature of the complaint is not covered by the disciplinary system or because the lawyer is innocent of any wrongdoing. But the complaints are made. Most complaints are made by clients, some are made by attorneys, and a few by judges.

The important thing with disciplinary complaints is not to win the war, but rather to avoid the battle. A nonmeritorious complaint against you can hurt you no matter how innocent you are of any wrongdoing.

There is a very basic defect in almost all disciplinary systems in that the file on the lawyer which contains nonmeritorious complaints stays open forever, or at least as long as the lawyer lives. Assume, for example, that a totally nonmeritorious complaint is made against you. Assume that a full investigation is made and that you did absolutely nothing wrong. Assume it turns out that the client is mentally disturbed or unhappy about a divorce and in a moment of anger files a complaint that is a "pack of lies." Assume you are completely and totally innocent of any wrongdoing—legally, morally, ethically, or otherwise—and that you are totally exonerated.

That nonmeritorious complaint may stay in your file forever. It is possible that additional complaints will be made over the 30 to 40 or more years you are in practice. These complaints may also be nonmeritorious, but they will be cumulative files of prior complaints and there may be a "where there's smoke, there's fire" mentality on the person or committee investigating the complaint. You may be prejudiced by prior nonmeritorious complaints.

A convicted felon who pleads guilty and goes to jail may have a right to expunge his record, but an innocent lawyer has no right to expunge any records. This is the system in many, if not almost all, states. I think it is grossly unfair, but it is the system. Accordingly, the important thing for you to do is to avoid the complaint, not to win the war with the complaining client.

Although what follows may be duplicated in other parts of this book, it is worthwhile to repeat them here in this most vital chapter.

To avoid many, if not most complaints, you should:

1. Discuss fees and expectations with clients so that they have an opportunity to understand clearly what you can and cannot do for them, what it will cost, and how long it should take. Use estimates, if necessary.

2. Have a written fee agreement clearly stating what you will do, what you will not do, what is or is not covered by the fees, and any other factors you feel are important to you and to the clients as outlined in Rule 1.

3. Bombard your clients with paper keeping them informed of what is happening, including letters explaining why nothing is happening. The client's file should almost duplicate your file.

4. Return all telephone calls or have someone take them and return them for you, but never ignore them. If you are unable to make telephone contact with the party, send a postcard or form letter indicating that you tried to return the call.

5. Be honest and open when a case is lost. Tell the client as rapidly as possible after you find out.

6. Be "holier than thou" when handling a client's money. To quote an old proverb (which I just created), "It is better to see your kids without new clothes than to touch the client's trust money."

7. Cooperate fully with the next lawyer and the client if you are discharged.

8. Respond immediately to communications from disciplinary boards or investigators. Offer immediate access to yourself and to your files. It is possible that if you respond rapidly enough, a file will not be opened on the complaint.

9. Keep accurate time records detailing what you did and when you did it. Retain old records, including notes of telephone calls and conferences until the statute of limitations for malpractice expires.

10. Read, reread, and remember the Model Rules of Professional Conduct as adopted by your state.

The Model Code of Professional Responsibility and the Model Rules of Professional Conduct

When you start your own law practice, you must know the Model Rules of Professional Conduct to protect your clients and to avoid claims of unprofessional conduct, suspension, or, worse, disbarment.

I am justifiably proud of the role of *How to Start and Build a Law Practice* in making lawyers understand they have a professional responsibility. In earlier editions of this book, I refer to the ABA Model Code of Professional Responsibility and the Model Rules of Professional Conduct. Many young lawyers ask questions about problems they face in their everyday practice of law. A large percentage of the questions they ask are answered at least preliminarily in the Model Rules of Professional Conduct. I use the word "preliminarily" because the "final" authority is, of course, the rules of their own state licensing authority.

On the one hand, I am proud that my readers recognize the problem areas as they arise. On the other hand, I am concerned that these lawyers frequently don't have a copy of the Model Code or of the Model Rules in their offices.

I recommend that you read the section on Professional Responsibility *after* you read the other sections of the book. You then will have a clearer understanding of how and why following the suggestions of this book will help you practice law within the limits set forth in the Model Code and the Model Rules.

You may wish to observe the rules out of a sense of obligation to our profession and our society or out of fear of being disciplined or disbarred for violating the rules. In either case, you must know the rules so you can observe them. Naturally, the rules may be modified in your state or jurisdiction. You must take it upon yourself to learn the interrelation of the Model Rules and the rules of your jurisdiction.

As you go through the rules, you will see that many areas are covered or at least touched upon in this book. Such areas as competence, scope of representation, diligence, communications with clients, fees, procedures to preserve confidentiality, conflict of interest between your clients, conflict of interest with your clients, conflicts with former clients, clients under disability, safeguarding property through trust accounts, declining representation, withdrawing from a case, and many others that appear in the Model Rules are covered in this book.

New lawyers (and, indeed, older lawyers) are sometimes confused by references to "ethics" or "Codes" or "Rules." Although this chapter contains overgeneralizations, I hope it will clear the air a bit.

The original Canons of Ethics of the American Bar Associations were adopted in 1908. (I leave you to your law school professional responsibility class notes as to what happened in England and America prior to 1908.) The Canons set forth high ethical conduct. Some would say they were goals rather than standards of actual law practice. If you "violated" the Canons you could be kicked out of the voluntary bar associations you belonged to, but you rarely, if ever, got disbarred or disciplined for violating the Canons unless trust funds were involved. The number of lawyers in America was relatively small both in absolute numbers and in proportion to the general population. Law firms were small. Almost all lawyers went to court on occasion, even in the big cities, and the lawyers and judges pretty well knew one another. If they did not actually know one another, in fact, they knew of one another by reputation. If a lawyer did something "unethical," the other lawyers and judges quickly knew about it and the resulting ostracism and damage to reputation were probably more effective in disciplining the lawyer than any formal proceedings, which in some cases were designed simply to give the lawyer a chance to present his side of what happened or did not happen in an attempt to clear his name and reputation.

The "judges" of the lawyers were volunteer members of the association who were practicing lawyers and who understood the practical day-to-day problems that arise in a law office. These lawyers preferred a "quiet" type of discipline without publicity that might undermine public confidence in the bar or the legal system. When lawyers were disciplined, they simply were referred to as "Lawyer A" or "Lawyer B," using no real names. Expulsion from the voluntary bar association was often tantamount to being disbarred. This system worked reasonably well to protect both the bar and the public in an America that was rural and where everyone in the legal profession knew one another, either in fact or by reputation. Some bar associations or licensing authorities still have a Canon of Ethics.

By the 1960s the number of lawyers had increased greatly, the lawyers and judges still knew one another but not very well, and lawyers began specializing so that some did not go to court. Firms began getting bigger and anonymity could protect an errant lawyer from the peer pressure of other lawyers and judges. The Canons simply no longer did the job of protecting both the bar and the public. A series of court decisions began eroding seriously the ability of the bar to protect itself or the public through the Canons.

In 1969, the ABA adopted the Model Code of Professional Responsibility to replace the Canons of Ethics. The Model Code contained canons worded in broad statements. It also contained disciplinary rules, violations of which could lead to lawyer discipline, and lofty ethical goals like the old Canons. By the 1970s many states had adopted a mandatory bar (sometimes called "unified" or "integrated").

The mandatory bar by definition is not optional. You cannot practice law without belonging to it and paying "dues," which, in fact, are license fees.

The mandatory bars exist alongside voluntary bar associations, but the mandatory bars have the power directly on their own, or indirectly through the court system, to discipline and disbar lawyers. A lawyer or judge could not escape discipline simply by resigning from a voluntary bar association.

By 1983, the number of lawyers in America had exploded both in regard to the absolute number of lawyers and relative to the population of the country. Law firms had mushroomed in size and numbers of offices to the point that the lawyers in a community did not know one another, and often, even the lawyers in a firm did not know one another. Additionally, by this time, many lawyers never expected to go to court during their entire careers. The ability of the legal profession to police itself through peer pressure, judicial pressure, or general reputation clearly had collapsed.

Lawyers who specialized either never knew why some of the rules existed or, if they had once known, forgot through lack of contact with the area of law or client relations involved in the rules.

Peer pressure and a sense of *noblesse oblige* could no longer protect others, the rights of clients, or the role of the bar within our society.

Accordingly, by 1983, it became necessary for the ABA to adopt the Model Rules of Professional Conduct. These Model Rules are intended to lead to disciplinary action when violated.

Allegations of violations of the Model Rules often are investigated by nonlawyers and administered by referees or judges who may have become judges without ever having had a fee-paying (or nonfee-paying) private client in their entire lives. They may come from government service where they neither considered nor dealt with the rules they are now applying to other lawyers.

This is not to suggest they are not serious or competent. This is to warn you that, unlike the judges in the disciplinary hearings of bar associations under the Canons, your judge under the Model Rules may never have had the problems you have. They may have no experience, feeling, or understanding of why you did or did not do what you are accused of. They may never have had to deal with a weeping spouse or parent begging you to help by doing something or not doing something that at the time seemed the human thing to do but which, upon cool, detached study with good hindsight, appears possibly to have violated a disciplinary rule. A practicing lawyer might have compassion and be forgiving, but your judge might not. The body that applies disciplinary conduct may be under pressure, like a district attorney's office, to administer discipline, prosecute a large number of lawyers, and get a high percentage of disbarments to justify the funds being spent on the office and staff.

The Model Rules of Professional Conduct are intended to be the minimal standards that must be followed to avoid disbarment or discipline. Most states have adopted, or will adopt, some form of these Model Rules. Accordingly, the new lawyer must know them.

Again, I recommend most strongly that you read and periodically reread the Model Rules of Professional Conduct. Unfortunately, as of this third edition, you cannot get a set of the Model Rules for free. You can, however, contact the ABA Center for Professional Responsibility, which will sell you a set.

Part VIII
Resources and
Advice

Where to Go for Help

Most lawyers reading this will have almost no knowledge of how to manage a law practice. Therefore, you should increase your knowledge immensely just by reading this one publication.

This publication should go a long way towards getting you started in the creation and building of your law practice.

This book is only intended to get you started. You will soon find that you need more resources than are available here.

When I first decided to write this book I spent several hours in a university law library looking for sources of materials for new lawyers. I then had one of my law clerks spend weeks going through the sources that I had found, plus finding additional sources I had missed.

Shortly after spending a lot of time and effort, I discovered Robert P. Bigelow's list, which is the best I've ever seen and far better than mine for both new and established lawyers.

Mr. Bigelow's article is contained in the Fall 1975 issue of *Legal Economics,* which can be obtained from William S. Hein & Co., (800) 828–7571. This issue also contained an excellent article on preparing your staff manual.

Join the American Bar Association's Section of Law Practice Management and receive *Law Practice Management;* consult back issues, which you can identify by using LOIS (Law Office Information Service). On balance, *Law Practice Management* will be an investment, not an expense.

There are many good publications available. As with the law library, it's a question of balancing the value of the publication to a new lawyer against the expenditure of cash, which is in short supply to the new lawyer.

This book is intended to teach basics, which do not ordinarily change radically in a short time. However, law office management and administration is now mushrooming as a profession, and there are major changes occurring due to technological advances in word processing, computers, communication, document reproduction, etc.

Therefore, until you are established, as a general rule, you should stay away from hard-bound publications that may become rapidly obsolete and dated; and as a general rule, you should concentrate on periodicals during your first few years.

The following are recommended to you in the first years. Prices are approximate.

1. *Law Practice Management*. American Bar Association. 750 N. Lake Shore Drive, Chicago, Illinois 60611 (bimonthly/via membership in the Section of Law Practice Management, ABA, which includes a subscription).

2. *The Practical Lawyer*. 4025 Chestnut Street, Philadelphia, Pennsylvania 19104 (eight times per year/$15 per year).

3. *Barrister*. Publication of Young Lawyers Division, American Bar Association, 750 N. Lake Shore Drive, Chicago, Illinois 60611 (quarterly/via membership in the Young Lawyers Division, ABA, which includes a subscription).

Thus, for a fairly nominal sum, you can get some "upgrading" of what is in this book.

When you have been in practice a few years and your practice is booming, you and/or your office manager can get more deeply into what is then current with one or more of the following:

1. *Law Office Economics and Management*. Callaghan and Company, 155 Pfingsten Road, Deerfield, IL 60015 (monthly).

2. *The Business of Law: A Handbook on How to Manage Law Firms*. Prentice-Hall Law & Business, 270 Sylvan Avenue, Englewood Cliffs, NJ 07632 (binder format with periodic supplements).

3. *How to Manage Your Law Office*. Matthew Bender & Company, 11 Penn Plaza, New York, NY 10001.

Books, Pamphlets, etc.

I hesitate to recommend a book today that may be obsolete or out of print by the time you need it; however, I strongly recommend that you keep current on those materials available through the publications of the American Bar Association Section of Law Practice

Management. For relatively few dollars you can have a library that is up to date, with systems that in most cases are easily adaptable to your office.

Courses, Conferences, Etc.

It should be kept in mind that there are many opportunities during the year to attend programs and workshops put on by various organizations. Some of these have a service to the profession aspect. A little careful planning will enable you to combine these programs with your vacations, getting at least a partial income tax deduction for the travel expenses involved. (See chapter on "The Importance of Continuing Education.")

The Importance of
Continuing Education

If on January 1 of a given year you know all the law there is to know in any typical area of law, and if for one year you make no attempt to "keep current," at the end of the year you will be an expert on what the law used to be. You went to law school to learn legal principles and to spot legal issues. If you learned well, your legal education will probably last you about five years. You must keep up with the law.

The First Two or Three Years of Your Practice

There are many courses and seminars offered by universities and various institutes. In the main, these courses are too expensive for the new lawyer and are not suited to your needs. The costs run as much as several hundred dollars. The basic courses are too far below your level of experience, and the sophisticated courses are too far above your level of experience. In some states, the state university with the state bar puts on low-cost programs with excellent textbooks. Fees of $50 to $75 for a two- or three-hour program, including the book, are reasonable and worth the price. Therefore, although continuing education is important, getting it cheaply can be difficult. In my opinion, the cheapest and easiest ways to keep current are as follows:

1. *Daily Legal Newspaper.* These papers are often free or low cost your first three to six months. They normally contain cases of interest to practicing lawyers.

2. *Bar Association Committee Luncheons and Programs.* You can get the benefits of experienced attorneys' views and help for the price of a luncheon or an hour or two out of the office.

314

3. *Bar Association Journals.* The state and local bar journals are excellent low-cost sources of new legislation and major cases as well as "How-to-Do-It" articles.

4. *Audio Tapes.* Audio tapes run anywhere from a few dollars to $20 or $30 for a one-hour tape. The advantage to audio tapes, in my opinion, is that you can listen to them in places where it's not practical to read, such as your automobile on the freeway.

Unfortunately, some tape performances are dull and boring. The panelists or speakers often read prepared papers into a microphone with all the emotion and feeling of a log. The tapes sometimes constitute a traffic hazard by putting you to sleep on the freeway. I suggest that you try a few and form your own opinion.

The audio tapes are normally available from or through various state bar associations as well as through other commercial sources. The bar journals will usually contain information on the availability of the tapes.

5. *Video Tapes.* Excellent video tapes are available from varied sources on varied subjects. The commercial tapes are normally best because they use speakers who are interesting as well as informative. The American Bar Association Section of Law Practice Management video tapes, for example, use only entertaining speakers.

University tapes and local bar association tapes are often a waste of time and money because you can't stay awake for the dull, boring speaker.

You could make your own video tapes for training lawyers and secretaries, and for informing clients. Additionally, you can "write off" or deduct for income tax purposes video equipment that you use in your practice.

After Two or Three Years

1. *Non-Practice Areas.* After you have been out of school two or three years, you will have started your downhill decline in those areas in which you haven't had any practice. Therefore, some of the institutes and seminars that would have been below you right out of law school are no longer below you and are worth the expense if you want to keep some familiarity with the area.

2. *Practice Areas.* If you are, in fact, doing some work in the subject area of the seminar or institute, then these courses are worth their weight in gold. You *must,* however, undertake the courses with

the proper perspective. In most courses, you should already know 85% to 95% of the material *before* you attend. Your purpose in attending should be to pick up a few "pointers" or tips. I've never yet attended a seminar where I didn't pick up one or two tips or techniques.

I've traveled thousands of miles and spent thousands of dollars to attend seminars and institutes that lasted from one to five days. I've never been disappointed because I maintained the proper perspective. To put it another way, if you don't know 85 percent to 95 percent of what you'll hear before you get there, then perhaps you're not as sharp as you think you are.

Follow the Leaders

If you don't believe that continuing education is important, look about you when you go to a program. You'll see the "specialists" and lead lawyers in the big law firms. They know the importance and value of continuing education.

Getting Maximum Tax Dollar
From Your Educational Expenses

Amounts spent to maintain your skills as a lawyer are deductible for income tax purposes, including transportation, meals and lodging away from home as well as the tuition charges.

With a little careful planning, you can combine your educational expenses with a rest away from your office. Courses today are offered on cruise ships and resorts as well as in hotels and classrooms. Another advantage in attending courses away from home is the opportunity to meet lawyers from other areas of the state or country who can give you new or different approaches or perspectives in areas you deal with. From time to time, you may get some referral business from these lawyers, but this should be a minor factor in attending the program.

The Wheel Has Been Invented

At several places in this book I have emphasized that as far as the new lawyer is concerned, the basic principles of starting and building a law practice remain constant over the years. I spent a lot of time and money and made a lot of mistakes learning the lessons I've tried to teach you in this book. This book simply attempts to put the things a new lawyer in practice has to know into one place.

This book has been written over a period of more than a year, and updated over a period of 17 years. I've written parts of it on airplanes and in hotel rooms on five continents. On one trip to Morocco and Kenya, I met John P. Clark, a lawyer from Winslow, Arizona. John was interested in this book and told me about an incident that occurred in 1932. An itinerant bookseller approached John in 1932 and offered to show him how to increase his income for a $5 fee. Things were bad during the depression and Winslow, Arizona, was no exception, so John paid the $5.

The sales rep printed up some forms and gave them to John for the $5 fee, telling him to fill out the form at the end of the interview and to give it to the client with the charge filled in. A copy of the form was placed in the client file. (A copy of the form follows this chapter.)

In 1975, I spent six months and $25,000 to program a $40,000 in-house computer for billing. In 1990, a $1,500 PC clone and a $199 billing package would be adequate. The Missouri Bar Survey was made in 1964. The American Bar Survey was done in 1980. On reflection I'm not sure that my computer or the Missouri Survey or the American Bar Survey has given us much new information that wasn't sold for $5 by the itinerant bookseller in Winslow, Arizona, in 1932.

LAW OFFICES
JOHN P. CLARK
ATTORNEY AT LAW
WINSLOW, ARIZONA

CLIENT'S LEGAL ADVICE MEMO

CLIENT—

FACTS BY CLIENT—

DATE—

ARRIVAL—

DEPARTURE—

FEE—

LAW AS READ—
   SEE _____

OPINION BY ATTY.—

Handwritten original is given to client at end of interview, two copies kept by lawyer, one for accounts receivable, one for client file.

How to Manage and Collect Accounts Receivable

Effective management and collection of your accounts receivable is critical for a lawyer, but especially for the new lawyer.

What Is an Account Receivable?

Very simply, an account receivable is money people owe you for work done or costs advanced *after* you have sent them a bill. Until you send a bill, you don't have an account receivable. You have work in process or, if you wish to be fancy, you can call it deferred time, or unrelieved time, or any other number of fancy titles, but it is not an account receivable until after you send a bill.

Professional credit managers have written volumes of information on this subject. In this chapter I'll try to convey what a lawyer, especially a new lawyer without formal training in accounts receivable collection or management, has to know. Although this chapter may appear lengthy, it contains only the bare minimum of what you have to know.

Reasons for Accounts Receivable Management

1. *Your own cash flow.* You can't pay bills at home or in the office with warm feelings and professional satisfaction. You need cash. Landlords, secretaries, booksellers, supermarkets, auto repair shops, stationery supply stores, credit card companies, etc., all will insist on cash for payment. The best source of cash is "cash up front." The second best source is your accounts receivable.

2. *To recognize the danger signs at the earliest possible point for those cases who are or may become problem cases for any number*

of reasons. Sometimes people don't pay because they can't, or think they can't. Sometimes they don't pay because they don't want to pay. In either case, you may have a problem that can only get worse as time goes on. Your client may be dissatisfied with you or with the way the case is being handled. In either case, you had better find out as soon as possible.

Sometimes a client simply ignores the bill rather than telling you of his or her dissatisfaction. You must find out what is wrong.

3. *To have facts upon which to decide to terminate the professional relationship when the client refuses to pay the bill.* It is better to say: "Mr. Jones, you now owe $775. You still need $2,500 more work. You haven't paid anything since March when you paid $50 and before that, December, when you paid $100. I'm asking if possibly we should make an arrangement or terminate the case," than it is to say: "Mr. Jones, your bill is overdue. And if you don't pay, I can't work."

4. *To keep your bad receivable losses as low as possible.* Every business and profession has some bad accounts receivable. You can't avoid them (unless you only work for cash up front). The secret is to keep them as low as possible and to prevent small losses from becoming big losses.

5. *Because every dollar of accounts receivable is 100 percent profit or loss.* Collecting an account receivable is 100 percent profit and not collecting it is 100 percent loss. It is right on the bottom line. Your income as a lawyer is heavily dependent on your not having bad accounts receivable.

I have practiced as a CPA and as a lawyer for a quarter of a century. I've lost more money on uncollected receivables for good work done than I've lost because a contingency case was lost or because the case was a bad case.

Definitions

1. *Bill.* The bill is the document you send wherein you first inform the client that you did the work or advanced the costs and that you expect payment *now!* The bill is the *first* communication asking for money for work previously done. The bill might be for a period of time (monthly, etc.), or for a quantity of work done (stages in a proceeding), or work to be done in the future.

2. *Billing.* Billing is the *process* of preparing and sending the bill.

3. *Statement.* A statement is the document you send *after* you send the first bill and you are still owed all or part of what you asked for on the first bill. In some cases there will be an overlapping or combining of the statement where you ask for money for work previously billed and a new bill where you ask for money for the first time for new work or costs.

4. *Account Receivable.* What the client owes you after you have sent a bill.

5. *Work in Progress.* A case or matter that is not completed and not ready for billing (probate, contingency case, etc.).

6. *Deferred Time.* The work is done. You could bill the client, but you don't want to just yet. (The case will be over next month and you'll send a final bill, or the client is temporarily upset with the bill and it's better to wait, etc.)

7. *Delinquent.* It is easier for me to give an example than to explain. The time sequence is as follows:

    a. Send Bill no. 1 for work done or to be done (at this point not delinquent).

    b. Send Bill no. 2 for additional or different work or to be done along with statement for first bill unpaid (at this point still not delinquent).

    c. Send Bill no. 3 for new or additional work done or to be done along with statement for first bill unpaid in whole or in part. *You now have a delinquent account receivable that demands immediate attention.*

Note that I have defined "delinquent" in terms of the number of times you have told the client you wish payment rather than in terms of days, weeks, or months.

8. *Accounts Receivable Listing.* A list of all accounts receivable, normally in alphabetical order.

9. *Accounts Receivable Aging.* A list of all accounts receivable normally showing a "spread" of amounts due by time periods (often combined with a listing).

10. *Priority Accounts Receivable List.* These are the 10 or 15 largest receivables and must be reviewed weekly. These are important clients who must be monitored continually as to whether they are current or delinquent.

11. *Delinquent Accounts Receivable.* This is a case where you and the client have a problem that must be faced. (See definition of "delinquent.")

How to Analyze and Use Account Receivable Information

1. Get the information on *all* accounts receivable *monthly* so you can, in a timely manner, recognize the problems that are developing and have developed. Normally, you get this information when you do billings.

2. Get the information on your *ten* most serious problems (if you have that many) *weekly* so you don't forget about them or lose sight of their importance.

3. Always get your accounts receivable information in terms of dollar size, not in terms of alphabetical listing. Pay the most attention to the "biggest," whether or not it is delinquent. Always be aware of whom your major debtors are so you can respond accordingly.

4. Define what a "delinquent" account is for your purposes. I have my own definition which I consider a "softie" approach, but which works. (See definition no. 11 above.)

5. Decide whether or not you can continue working on the case without payment and, if you can, under what arrangement.

6. Contact client. (See "How to Collect Accounts Receivable" section below.)

    a. First contact: short note from secretary, bookkeeper, or office manager;

    b. Second contact: telephone call from you to client;

    c. Third contact: letter from you to client setting forth telephone call summary.

7. Decide whether this would be an appropriate time to allow client to make some other lawyer rich before you get in deeper.

8. Consider refunding all money paid by a client as fees to get out of a bad case before it becomes a serious case. It is better to refund $750 and not collect $1,500 more than it is to do $3,000 more of work you'll never get paid for because the client can't or won't pay.

9. *Never forget* you are your client's lawyer, not the client's partner. You have no obligation, moral or legal, to go under financially just because your client is going under or can't or won't pay for services. Legal aid does exist. There is nothing wrong with your budgeting a percentage of your time for *pro bono* work, but you, and not the client, must decide when you can do *pro bono* work.

How to Manage Accounts Receivable

You manage accounts receivable by getting the proper information and then *acting* on that information. Simply knowing about your accounts receivable isn't adequate if you don't *do* something about them. Obviously, you can't do something about them if you don't have the information. Collecting the accounts receivable is 100% profit, since you already have invested the time and money to earn the accounts receivable.

Information Needed

To maintain a simple, effective account receivable management system, you must have the following information *before* contacting a client:

1. How much all of your clients owe you.
2. How much a client owes on this matter.
3. How much a client owes on other matters.
4. How much work (in dollars) has been done.
5. How much work (in dollars) remains to be done and over what period of time.
6. History of payments made (especially dates and amounts of last two payments).
7. When you last discussed fees with the client and what the client said and what you said (you should have a memo to the file on this).
8. What your fee agreement (preferably in writing) requires the client to do and whether or not the client is in default on the agreement.
9. Other factors (client sent you a $25,000 case, or is the brother-in-law of the president of your best corporate client), etc.
10. The priority accounts receivable list. These are the biggest accounts receivable you have (typically 10 to 15) and warrant review at least once a week.
11. The delinquent accounts receivable list. These are accounts receivable that are delinquent.
12. The action accounts receivable list. These are the delinquent receivables that require immediate action. (Don't waste time on a $300 receivable when someone is delinquent $2,200.)

How to Collect Accounts Receivable (Accounts Receivable Collection Technique in Chronological Sequence)

1. Have the bookkeeper sign and send a short note included with the bill but not typed on the bill to the effect, "It has come to our attention that your account is overdue. If there is a problem, please call me."

2. Have the secretary or bookkeeper call client's bookkeeper or accounts payable person. Be helpful, not threatening: "We notice that your May account of $_____ has not been paid and I'd like to know what to tell Mr. Foonberg." Write down the response.

3. Always send the bill to both a company name and a person's name. People don't like seeing their own name on an unpaid bill.

4. The attorney should call the client and say something to the following effect: "Joe, I'm very concerned that our bill is being ignored and we're wondering if there is a problem with you. You owe $_____. Nothing has been paid since _____ and there's more work to be done and we want to know what you want to do."

Say nothing more. No matter how long the silence, no matter how awkward the silence, say nothing more. The next move is up to the client.

5. Get a commitment. "I'll send you $_____ by _____ and $_____ every week thereafter."

6. Send a letter to the client confirming the new arrangement to be sure there is no misunderstanding.

7. If the client refuses to make a commitment, begin the process of dropping the client.

8. Try to match the client's payment to you with the client's income (pay days, contract closing, etc.).

9. If you have a loser, face up to the fact as soon as possible and begin to devote your energies more to the clients who honor their agreements.

10. Remember "Foonberg's Rule"—it is better not doing the work and not getting paid than doing the work and not getting paid.

11. Every lawyer should do some *pro bono* work, but the lawyer, not the clients, should decide which clients don't pay.

12. The *billing* is the *process* of preparing and sending the bill.

13. A *statement* is the *document* where you ask for money after you have sent the first bill. In some cases you will be overlapping.

    a. Send bill—*not* delinquent.

    b. Send statement following the month with first bill unpaid—*be aware* that a problem may be developing.

    c. Send statement the following month with first bill unpaid. You have a problem that demands immediate attention.

14. Decide whether or not you can continue working on the case without payment and, if you can, under what arrangement.

15. Contact client.

Where to Get Cost-Effective Help to Build and Expand Your Practice

As far as I'm aware, *How to Start and Build a Law Practice* was the first book devoted to building a law practice. In 1968, when I began doing programs on starting and building a law practice, the subject was considered to be unethical. There was objection to using law school facilities for such programs and we held them in the basement of a savings and loan. The county bar association refused to announce the availability of the programs to new admittees because they thought it was unethical. I had to print the first copies of the first edition of this book at my own expense because its subject matter was considered controversial and possibly unethical.

Today the world has changed. Bar associations, law schools and national and international organizations now invite me to speak and lead workshops on practice development. *How to Start and Build a Law Practice* is the all-time best seller of the American Bar Association and is deemed a classic. I was told that the Law School Library Association has classified this book as the title most stolen from law school libraries in the U.S.A.

Law firms of every size, including the largest and most prestigious law firms in the world, now have marketing directors as part of the administrative staff and marketing committees. These marketing directors are organized into a group called the National Association of Law Firm Marketing Administrators (NALFMA). I am regularly invited to teach basic marketing skills to prestigious law firms throughout the United States.

There are now many experts on practice development. There are now also other books on the subject. Some of these books have some value. There are also "consultants" who will help you design a firm brochure, TV advertising or other media advertising. Public relations experts will get your photo on the society pages. Other experts will tell you how to dress, what artwork to hang in your office, etc. There are other experts, besides myself, who will lead "in-house" marketing seminars or workshops for your firm. There are universities that provide seminars and lectures on lawyer marketing; there also are periodicals on lawyer marketing.

I list the foregoing sources not to recommend them, but to advise you that they exist in the event you wish to use them. In the main, I advise great caution in using them for the following reasons:

1. They are normally directed toward the larger firm that has an established practice and lots of time and money to invest. They often are not responsive to smaller firms and sole practitioners. Those techniques that work for a small firm or sole practitioner are normally applicable to larger firms, but not vice versa.

2. They require a large cash outlay *now* and promise long-term cash results *later*. New lawyers, sole practitioners and small firms can't afford the impact on cash flow.

3. They are excellent in helping you self-inventory your problems and self-define your goals, but they don't help you solve your problems or give you the techniques and tools you need to actually get results. (It has been said that a consultant borrows your watch to tell you what time it is and breaks your watch in the process.) They often stir up ambition and desire but leave you unfulfilled in terms of the end product needed.

At the risk of being immodest, I am recommending to you a book I have written which took more than five years to complete because of the rapid changes in defining permissible and non-permissible practice development methods. First published in 1988, the book is now in its second edition. It is cost-effective and immediately usable for every lawyer in America, especially the sole practitioner and small firms that have limited cash but need immediate results.

This book is based on four sources:

1. What I have learned from other lawyers in doing more than 300 programs and workshops for tens of thousands of practicing lawyers (as well as doctors, architects, dentists, small businesses, etc.) in every state of the Union and many foreign countries over a period of two decades. Most of these programs were done at bar association conventions where I got input from lawyers from all over the United States or from specific states. My input is literally from every possible size and type of law practice.

2. Those things that I have applied in my own practice and are successful.

3. Those things that I have advised others to do, which have worked in their practices as reported by their unsolicited reports to me over the years.

4. Those things that are found to be immediately feasible and successful, based on my consulting for law firms and their feedback to me.

The book I am recommending is entitled *How to Get and Keep Good Clients,* subtitled "Practice Development and Lawyer Marketing Techniques for the Sole Practitioner and Small Law Firm."

How to Get and Keep Good Clients assumes an existing practice and deals only with marketing and getting paid for work done. This book, *How to Start and Build a Law Practice,* devotes itself to both management and entry-level practice development. It assumes a starting point of zero experience. Most of the work, then, has to be done by the lawyer and indeed can be done by the lawyer prior to opening his doors. This book also provides a master plan where all of the actualities are integrated. The basic concepts and lessons of *How to Start and Build a Law Practice* would apply to any lawyer in America.

Much of the work detailed in *How to Get and Keep Good Clients* can be done and indeed should be done by either lawyers or nonlawyers. *How to Get and Keep Good Clients* uses some of the same fundamental concepts as *How to Start and Build a Law Practice,* but recognizes that the existing law practice has the demands of clients, staff members and family members co-existing with the desire to get and keep better clients. Each of the techniques in *How to Get and Keep Good Clients* can be applied one at a time in any sequence that the particular lawyer wishes to implement. Many of the techniques can be used or not used by an individual lawyer, depending on whether or not he or she feels comfortable with the technique. There is no need for every lawyer in the firm to do the same thing at the same time. Those who are comfortable utilizing the most number of techniques will become the better "client-getters." Others may still remain good technicians, who can just "get along" with existing clients, as their success or failure may not be dependent on client-getting abilities. *How to Get and Keep Good Clients* also assumes a practice/experience frame of reference so that the individual lawyer can understand why some prior activities were successful and some were not.

Although there is a small amount of common ground in the two books, I recommend that every lawyer have both books and that they periodically re-read each one.

How to Get and Keep Good Clients is the most cost-effective practice development investment you can make. My agreement with the publishers (Lawyers Alert Press, Boston, Mass.) provides a 100% refund to any purchaser who is not happy with the book for any reason. Lawyers Alert Press publishes *Lawyers Alert,* a national publication, and seven state legal newspapers.

How to Get and Keep Good Clients is a runaway best seller because it works and lawyers recommend it to each other. If you are interested, contact Lawyers Alert Press, 30 Court Square, Boston, Mass. (800) 444-LAWS. The book is also available in an audiotape version.

I guarantee it will help you make more money with very little effort.

Foonberg's Short Course in
Good Client Relations

If this chapter looks familiar to you, it may be because it has been reprinted in many bar journals both within and outside the U.S.

This chapter is intended to give you a five-minute course in good client relations. It also is intended to be a teaser to entice you to buy my book *How to Get and Keep Good Clients* when you can afford it.

Each of the 51 tips here on what to do or not do is expanded, in my other book, into a two- to five-page chapter on *how* to do it.

How to Get and Keep Good Clients, subtitled "Fundamental Techniques of Lawyer Marketing for Solo Practitioners and Small Law Firms," contains more than 200 different techniques with *how-to-do-it* checklists and forms. I sincerely recommend to you this compendium of techniques for busy lawyers. I insisted, as a condition of my contract with the publishers, that it be sold with a money-back guarantee. If you would like a copy of the book, contact Lawyers Alert Press, 30 Court Square, Boston, Massachusetts 02108; (800) 444-LAWS.

The list below was developed during my 20 years of doing more than 300 programs for bar associations and private law firms in every state of the U.S. and several foreign countries. The number 51 simply represents the 50 states and the District of Columbia.

I recommend that you add your own rules to the list.

1. Always carry high-quality professional cards.

2. Always offer clients and other visitors coffee or a soft drink while they wait in the reception area.

3. Be sure your reception area contains periodicals indicative of the kind of practice you want people to think you have.

4. Be careful when you answer the question, "What kind of law do you practice?" Don't limit yourself or your firm.

5. Always send thank-you letters when someone refers you a client.

6. Always send thank-you letters to the witnesses who testify for your side.

7. Either return all telephone calls yourself or be sure someone returns them for you.

8. Always send clients copies of all "correspondence in" and "correspondence out," relating to their cases.

9. Dress the way you would expect your lawyer to dress if you were a client paying a fee.

10. Always get as much cash up front as possible from new clients. This is known as Foonberg's Rule and is a modification of Lincoln's statement that when a client has paid cash up front, the client knows he has a lawyer and the lawyer knows he has a client.

11. Always be sure your fee agreement is in writing.

12. Always send your clients Christmas cards or "Season's Greetings" cards.

13. Remember that your invoices are a factor in your clients' opinion of you.

14. Dump the "dogs." Get rid of the "bad news" cases and clients before they really give you problems.

15. Learn how to convert "social consultations" at weddings, etc., into paying clients by being attentive, letting these acquaintances know they may have a serious problem, and suggesting they come into your office where you have the facilities to helping them.

16. Remind the nonlawyers in the firm that they can refer their friends' legal matters to the firm.

17. Remember that availability or nonavailability is the single most important factor in your being selected or not being selected after you are recommended.

18. Always send a tax newsletter in November reminding your clients of new tax laws that might affect them. Be sure to remind them that cash-basis taxpayers can deduct legal fees only if they pay them before December 31.

19. Send clients "no-activity" letters when a case is inactive for 90 days or more.

20. Always discuss fees and payment schedules at the first meeting.

21. Always remind the client that the firm has a good reputation in the community.

22. Always reassure the client that you have handled similar cases to theirs (if true). Clients don't like being used for educational purposes.

23. Calendar ahead and remind clients of the need for annual minutes of shareholders' or directors' meetings, lease renewals, judgment renewals, etc.

24. Always show clients how your bill can be tax-deductible, if possible.

25. Recognize and appreciate that clients have a high anxiety level when they go to see a lawyer. Try to put them at ease.

26. If you adjust a bill downward, be careful that the client doesn't think you deliberately were overcharging in the first place.

27. Be sure that you, and not the clients, decide which clients are going to get free legal work.

28. When collecting fees, try to match clients' payments to you with the clients' receipt of money.

29. Always be firm and in control with clients when discussing the case or fees. If you act wishy-washy or wimpy, your clients quickly will lose confidence in you, stop using you, and stop recommending you.

30. Don't complain about how hard you're working.

31. Have sample letters prepared to explain conflicts of interest and to obtain waivers of the conflicts.

32. Always use high-quality legal stationery with your address clearly legible.

33. Always have some firm, hard-backed chairs in the reception room for injured or elderly clients.

34. Always introduce your clients to your secretary.

35. Always introduce your clients to paralegals and/or associates who will be working on the case.

36. Always get new clients into the office to meet them before giving them any legal advice.

37. Be wary of clients who have lots of complaints about their former lawyers.

38. Always communicate to a new client that what the client tells you is normally covered by attorney-client privilege and that you won't discuss the client's personal affairs with other people.

39. When an interview is over, stand up, walk to the door, and tell the client the interview is completed.

40. After the interview or meeting, walk the client back to the reception area or elevator.

41. When the case is over, send a letter to the client telling him the case is closed and thanking him or her for the opportunity to have been of service. In this manner, the client will understand the case is closed and you are not expected to do more work on the case.

42. When a client offers you a cash fee, saying, "Nobody will know," don't forget that the client knows and may be setting you up for blackmail.

43. When a case is lost, be simple, direct, and honest. Tell the client by phone or in person and follow up with a letter.

44. When quoting settlements, be sure the client understands the difference between gross settlements and net settlements after fees, costs, and liens.

45. When quoting fees, be sure to cover (in writing) the difference between fees and costs and what the fee does and does not cover.

46. When collecting fees, remember that people are more willing to pay for what they desperately need and don't have than for what they used to desperately need and already have. Clients are more eager and willing to pay before the work is done than after the work is done. They will and you will feel better if you get the advance retainer check before you do the work.

47. If, during a meeting with a client, you are interrupted by an emergency long-distance call or secretarial inquiry, be sure to say to the client in the office, "Don't worry, I won't charge you for the time I spent on that matter."

48. Always ask a client whether to send mail to the home or the office, or whether the client wants to pick up the mail (to keep information from getting into the wrong hands).

49. Keep a photo of your children or family on your desk facing you to remind you of unpaid bills and your need to be sure that clients clearly understand from the beginning their financial obligations in the case, and that they can meet them.

50. If you have word processing equipment and computers, be sure you demonstrate them to clients so they are aware you are using modern technology to serve them.

51. Have someone telephone your office for you while you listen

in and determine how the query is handled. See if the receptionist projects a helpful attitude or simply is functioning as a human answering machine. Remember, people can and do hang up and call other lawyers when they're not pleased with the way their calls are handled.

The Importance of Doing It Right

My very first client was the man who installed my telephone. He installed my telephone at the end of March. He looked on the wall and saw my CPA license. He told me that he had prepared his own income tax return and would like me to review it for $5. In those days $35 was a reasonable minimum fee for an income tax return. I told him that I would need about an hour of his time for an interview to ascertain whether the income tax return was correct. He begged me to please look it over for $5 and he wouldn't hold me responsible for any mistakes. I told him that I wouldn't do anything unless I did it right and that $35 was my minimum fee. He said he wouldn't pay that much and we talked about something else until he finished his work. (Multiply these prices by three for the 1991 equivalents.)

Two days later the phone rang and it was the installer. I said hello and told him that the phone was working fine because my wife had already called twice. He said he was calling me for professional help and would I see him that evening in the restaurant of the building. I asked him the nature of the problem. He explained that his wife had a daughter by a prior marriage and that the father was a drunken bum. He had promised the wife that if anything happened to her, he would do his best to keep the child away from the natural father. He had not adopted the child. His wife had just died in an accident and he wanted to keep the child from the natural father.

I discussed the case with a couple of lawyers in the building who told me the case was an absolute loser because the natural father would get the child unless it could be conclusively proven that the father was unfit. They also told me that in those days $2,500 would be a reasonable fee and to be sure to get $2,500 for investigators, deposition costs, child psychiatrists, etc.

I met the client that night in the restaurant and told him that he had a losing case and not to waste his money, and that I needed my fee and costs paid in advance before I would begin work. Truthfully, I was trying to dissuade him from proceeding with the case. He told me he had already been to another lawyer who told him essentially the same thing but who was a little more optimistic and who would charge less. I said nothing. He said he would drop by the next morning.

The next morning he came by with a cashier's check for $2,500 and 14 $100 bills and asked if I could wait a few days for the next $1,100. As a phone company employee he had accumulated a large amount of AT&T stock and was borrowing against it to get money for my fees. I could have waited six months.

I then got cold feet and told him that I had never handled this type of case before and in fact had never handled any kind of case before. He told me that he knew this was my first time but that he had promised his wife that if anything happened to her he would do his best. He said that I had told him when I refused to do his tax return for $5 that I wouldn't do anything unless I did it right. Therefore he was confident that even though the case was a loser and I had no prior experience, I would do whatever could be done and he would have fulfilled his promise to his late wife.

I won the case (by default) after lining up all sorts of witnesses and devoting all of my time day and night to the case. The other lawyer caved in when he and his client saw the huge array of evidence I had prepared.

I got a $2,500 fee on the custody case, and a $3,000 fee on his wife's industrial accident case, all within a short time of opening my practice, because I turned down a low fee and told a prospective client that I wouldn't do something unless I did it right.

Believe me, over the years you'll do better and get more clients and fees if you make it clear that you'll only do things the right way. Always do your best. Even when you underestimate the fee, do your best. When the client is not worthy of your best, give your best anyway.

Checklist for Opening
Your First Law Office

Foreword

This is a checklist for opening a law office. It was initially prepared at the request of the Young Lawyers Division of the American Bar Association through its then President, David Weiner of Cleveland, Ohio, and its then Section of Law Practice Management Representatives, Kenneth Rice, of Everett, Washington, and Karen Feyerherm of Seattle, Washington. Sam Smith of Miami Beach, Florida, then Chairman of the American Bar Association's Section of Law Practice Management, encouraged its preparation and Bob Wilkins of Columbia, South Carolina, gave me valuable suggestions and advice as he has so often done in the past. Bill Blaine of the California Continuing Education of the Bar was most helpful in suggesting its dissemination by CEB. Curt Karplus, Assistant Director of CEB, served as editor.

This list is as comprehensive as I can make it based upon my experiences in doing programs for young lawyers throughout the United States and Canada and as Chairman of the New Lawyers in Practice Committee of the American Bar Association. I welcome your comments, and suggestions for revisions.

Make a Timetable and Priority Checklist

After learning of the approximate lead time you'll need for each step in the checklist, make a priority checklist. Do the things first that will require the longest time. This checklist reflects upon my experiences with the difficulties in decision-making and getting things done. The things requiring the most lead time should be at the top of your list; the things that require less lead time should be toward the bottom. You will have to rearrange many of the items into your own list, depending on your personal situation and local circumstances.

Consider the Area in Which You Wish to Practice

1. Where are your friends and relatives?

2. Pick a growing rather than decaying area. Watch out for blight and decay. Consider possible changes in economic patterns due to escalating energy costs.

3. Do you want an urban, rural or suburban practice? Analyze whether you can really be happy in a rural or small-town atmosphere or in an urban atmosphere. This is a matter of your personality and background.

Consider Quality of Life Factors

1. *Quality of professional life:* What kinds of cases and clients can you expect to get where you will practice?

2. *Quality of social life:* Do you want proximity to museums, symphonies, young intellectual people, etc.?

3. *Quality of atmosphere:* Is there smog and pollution, or clean air and water?

4. *Quality of recreational life:* Do you want proximity to swimming, skiing, boating, hiking, hunting, etc.?

5. *Quality of home life:* Is the area safe for your spouse and children? Will you be afraid to go out at night or to sleep with the windows open?

6. *Quality of economic life:* What kind of money can you earn there?

Consider Miscellaneous Factors

1. Proximity of office to public transportation for staff and clients.

2. Proximity to eating places for client entertainment and meetings.

3. Proximity to law library.

4. Proximity to major anticipated clients.

5. Type of practice you are planning. For personal injury, work-

er's compensation, and criminal law, proximity to courts and administrative hearing locations or jails may be important.

6. Proximity to other lawyers for possible consultation, referral of overflow work or library sharing.

7. Will office and building be accessible for people on crutches or in wheelchairs, or elderly people?

What Size Office Will You Need?

You'll need 400 to 600 square feet of office space per lawyer, as follows: personal office, 150 to 200 square feet (smaller is OK if you have access to a conference room for meetings with clients); secretarial area, 150 to 200 square feet (try to defer this for a few months, if possible); reception area, storage, copy machine, etc., 100 to 200 square feet.

Consider Office Sharing

Office sharing can be very economical. Shared suites are becoming common. You give up some individuality, but you save a lot of agonizing and decision-making. It is obviously cheaper to divide costs for receptionist, library, reception area and furniture, secretary, photocopy equipment, conference rooms, etc. You also have access to experienced lawyers for assistance and possibly some referral work. Ask the lawyers already in the suite how long they have been in the suite and what they like or dislike about the arrangement. Be careful to control your own phone number.

Consider Cheap Space in an Expensive Building

Inside, non-window space is very cheap. With imaginative drapes, lighting and decorating, the client won't realize that the offices are inside offices. Cost savings in rent can be very significant. Indicate that you are willing to accept inside space for price or other considerations.

Make Contacts to Find Space

Helpful sources of information include your local legal newspaper, nonlegal local papers and local bar association journals. A commercial broker may be a good source, if the space you require is not too small. Other lawyers can be of assistance. If there is a particular building in which you want space, try a form letter sent or delivered to every existing tenant and to the building manager. This is a good source of leads on sublet space that becomes available when offices move or firms break up, which often creates opportunities for reduced rent.

Determine the True Rental Cost

Always ask for the *net* square footage figure from the broker or landlord, and put it into the rental agreement. Divide the monthly or annual rent by net total square footage to get cost per *net* square foot, which is the only true way to measure rent cost for comparison shopping. There can be a 20 percent difference between net square footage and gross square footage, due to poles, beams, corridors, window sills, ducts, stairwells, irregularly shaped premises, etc.

What to Negotiate and Include in Your Rental Agreement

1. Parking for yourself, staff and clients at fixed prices. Don't automatically accept the story that parking is controlled by a separate concessionaire. If pushed, buildings often grant parking as a part of the lease.

2. Access to office at night and on weekends. Will air conditioning, heating and lights be available then at no extra cost? Is building security provided after hours?

3. Is there any furniture from the outgoing tenant you might have?

4. Right of first refusal on additional space in the building if you expand.

5. Air conditioning and heating thermostat controls for your part of the suite.

6. Are electric outlets where you need them? If not, get the landlord to install them.

7. Carpet cleaning or replacement.

8. Painting, replacement, or cleaning of wall coverings.

9. If old drapes can't be cleaned, insist on new ones.

10. Janitorial services such as trash removal, vacuuming, etc., and frequency of service.

11. A one-year term, with two one-year renewal options is best for a starting lawyer. You can stay or move after a one- or two-year experiment.

12. Try to delay the effective date for as long as possible to gain time for delivery of furniture, mailing of announcements, etc., before you have to start paying rent.

13. Don't commit malpractice on yourself before you get your first client. Whether you lease space, share space, or enter into any other arrangement, be sure to *get it in writing* before you move in or spend money on furniture or announcements. Don't depend on a handshake deal.

Start on Announcements

1. Prepare mailing lists.

    a. Law school class (get addresses from alumni association).

    b. Undergraduate classmates (get addresses from alumni association).

    c. High school classmates, if appropriate (get addresses from alumni association).

    d. Church members, if appropriate.

    e. Family.

    f. Organizations such as sports clubs, social clubs, philanthropic clubs, etc., you belong to (get addresses from club secretary).

    g. Professional associations you belong to.

2. Get sample announcements from printer.

3. Get time and cost estimate from printer.

4. Decide on style, for example, whether to list your principal areas of practice.

5. Order professional cards, and enclose one with each announcement.

6. Use engraved announcements and cards, on good stock.

7. Get cost and time estimate from professional addressing service for addressing, stuffing and mailing.

8. Start addressing the envelopes while the announcements are being printed.

9. Consider buying old postage stamps from a stamp dealer to attract attention to the announcements.

Order Stationery

1. Allow up to two months delivery time for high-quality stationery.

2. Get catalogs with samples.

3. Order letter-size bond letterhead, and second sheets; blank letter-size bond; letter-size envelopes; professional cards; announcements; paper and covers for wills; billing stationery with window envelopes; and other items suitable to your own practice.

4. Separately buy inexpensive envelopes to use when paying bills.

Get Telephones Ready

1. Estimate number and kind of instruments needed, and number of lines needed by meeting with phone company marketing representative. Don't forget that your secretary, receptionist, and clients will also be using your phones. Consider a second extension in your office for your clients' use.

2. Order equipment, get estimate of waiting time for delivery.

3. Order installation, which may require several days.

4. Reserve telephone number in advance of opening office, so you can give it to printer to put on announcements, cards, and stationery.

5. Consider microwave transmission subscription service if you will have a lot of long-distance calls.

6. Consider yellow page advertising, and listings in directories for other localities.

7. Try to negotiate low cash deposit on telephone equipment.

8. Get an answering service used and recommended by other lawyers or by doctors.

9. Consider getting a cable address (or telex, if you can afford it), if you want to attract international clients.

Order Furnishings

1. By subletting a furnished office you may be able to postpone many of these capital expenses.

2. Determine if major items can be rented instead of being purchased.

3. Determine if used furnishings are available. These cost about 60 percent of the price of new furnishings. Also keep in mind that new furniture often takes from two to six months to deliver.

4. Read ads in local legal newspapers for used furnishings.

5. Minimum furniture for your office:

    a. Picture of family members for desk.

    b. Your desk should be at least 6 feet wide with overhang in front, and treated to protect against scratches and spills.

    c. Your chair. Try it out next to the desk you have selected.

    d. Two to four straight-back chairs.

    e. Wastebasket to match desk.

    f. Clear floor pad for chair if office is carpeted. Don't skimp on pad size, or chair will roll off the edges.

    g. Floor lamp, if additional light is needed.

    h. Potted plant.

    i. Bookshelves.

6. Minimum furnishings for reception room:

    a. Four straight-back chairs.

    b. Magazine rack or table.

    c. Reading light.

    d. Bookshelf.

    e. Coat rack and umbrella stand.

Order Equipment

1. Determine if secretarial service can provide you with dictating equipment as part of its service.

2. Determine if equipment can be rented rather than purchased.

3. Determine if used equipment is available. Should be about 60 percent of new equipment price.

4. Read ads in local newspapers for used equipment and for equipment specials.

5. Minimum equipment:

    a. Secretarial desk, with return for typewriter.

    b. Secretarial chair. If possible, let secretary choose own chair.

    c. Small copy machine, unless one is available nearby.

    d. Dictating equipment including dictating unit, transcription unit and two portable tape recorders, one for your briefcase and one for your car.

e. Typewriter. Get used if possible, and integrate with word processing equipment.

f. Word processing equipment. This requires serious study. Don't depend on vendors to advise you. Consult secretaries, office administrators, and other lawyers. Read the publications listed in this book.

g. Accurate postage scale and postage meter. This will save you considerable money over the years.

Order Office Supplies

1. Get catalogs from several nearby office supply stores.

2. Open charge accounts with these stores. Negotiate for a discount from the list prices in the catalogs.

3. Ask your secretary or another lawyer's secretary to help you make up an initial order list. Consider such items as staplers, paper clips, scissors, two-hole punch, three-hole punch, telephone message pads, rubber stamps with inking pads, scratch pads, legal pads, paper cutter, felt-tip markers, staple removers, Scotch® tape, desk calendars, pens and pencils, manila envelopes, Rolodex® files, coffee maker and cups, check protector, fireproof safe, etc.

Order Insurance

Engage an insurance broker or agent who is likely to refer you business, or buy from several brokers:

1. Malpractice insurance against errors and omissions. Get occurrence rather than claims-made coverage, if possible.

2. General liability insurance.

3. Worker's Compensation insurance.

4. Non-owned automobile insurance.

5. File replacement and valuable papers coverage.

6. Fire and theft insurance, for replacement value.

7. Get "umbrella" coverage, if available.

8. Check with broker or bank for financing of premiums through monthly payments.

9. Check if "office block" policy available.

Start Secretarial and Nonlawyer Hiring

1. Adopt a personnel manual. A checklist of the topics to cover appears in *The Lawyer's Handbook,* available from ICLE, 1020 Greene St., Ann Arbor, MI 48109, or from ABA Order Fulfillment.

2. Check with local high schools, junior colleges, business colleges and universities for trainee secretarial and clerical help who will work without pay or for low pay to get work training credits. Excellent source of capable trainees.

3. Adopt *A Style Manual for the Law Office,* available from ABA Order Fulfillment, 750 N. Lake Shore Drive, Chicago, IL 60611.

4. Find out what monographs or other publications are available from the American Bar Association Section of Law Practice Management. New monographs are continually being published.

5. Allow three weeks for advertising and interviewing of applicants, and an additional two weeks notice which the successful candidate may have to give his or her present employer.

Start a Filing System

1. Get help from a legal secretary or office administrator in setting up a filing system. The file folders are just part of the system.

2. Allow six to eight weeks for delivery of supplies.

3. Install a numerical system rather than an alphabetical system, using vertical rather than horizontal files. Various systems are suggested in the publications listed below.

Start an Accounting System

1. Engage a CPA to be your accountant. Have the accountant install a system for bookkeeping and for timekeeping, and order accounting supplies for you.

2. If you choose not to use a CPA, review the systems suggested in the publications below, and adopt a system appropriate to your practice.

3. Consider contracting with a service bureau for timekeeping and billing.

4. Again, contact the American Bar Association Section of Law Practice Management for appropriate publications.

Prepare Budgets

1. Get help from a CPA in preparing budget statements that can be used in applying for loans for credit from a bank.

2. A practice cash budget should be prepared for the first year, by month, estimating your expenses. Include such items as rent, telephone, insurance, furnishings and equipment, copy equipment charges, stationery, office supplies, bar dues (including lawyer reference service fees), legal newspapers, attorney service, salaries, announcements (including postage and addressing), continuing education seminars and programs, diploma framing, automobile, parking (if not included in rent), estimates of costs to be advanced, and business development (lunches, entertainment, etc.)

3. A personal living expense cash budget should also be prepared by month for your first year. Allow money for some recreation and for medical expenses.

4. To cover these expenses, consider:
   a. Estimated income from fees for services.
   b. Savings accounts.
   c. Working spouse.
   d. Relatives who may offer help.
   e. Bank loan.
   f. SBA guaranteed loan.
   g. Credit union loan.
   h. Bar association credit union loan.

Licenses, Permits, etc.

1. Obtain federal employer identification number.

2. File federal quarterly income tax estimates for personal income taxes.

3. Obtain city or county licenses or permits, as required.

4. Notify state bar of address.

5. Join local bar association.

6. Join Young Lawyers Association or Section of your state bar.

7. Join lawyer reference services.

8. Notify possible sources of court-appointed work of your availability.

Open Bank Accounts

1. Open office account and get checks printed.
2. Open client trust account and get checks printed.
3. Open credit line with banker.
4. Arrange for a safe deposit box for wills and other client valuables.

Buy Only Essential Library Items

A library is a bottomless pit, which should be avoided during the first year of practice to the extent possible. Unannotated codes and some legal journals are probably essential. Use other libraries, at least at the start. Don't try to build your own until you can afford it.

Where to Get More Answers

Every law office should have the publications listed below as its basic reference library for management suggestions. In this basic library you will find the solution to almost any problem you will have to face. This may be the best investment in your practice you can make.

1. *The Thrifty Fifty* (1990), by James E. Brill. A fantastic source of tips for in-house systems and procedures for a law office. Should be read by all nonlawyers in office, as well as lawyers. 31 pages. Available from ABA Order Fulfillment.

2. *The Lawyer's Handbook*, available from ICLE, 1020 Greene Street, Ann Arbor, MI 48109 or from ABA Order Fulfillment. Covers several areas of practice management. 463 pages.

3. *Law Practice Management*, bimonthly publication of ABA Section of Law Practice Management, 750 N. Lake Shore Drive, Chicago, IL 60611. Buy all back issues available and subscribe currently. Almost any problem you have can be found in one issue or another. Section dues include subscription to this publication.

4. Various monographs, including *Model Accounting System, How to Create-A-System for the Law Office, Style Manual, Management Controls, Word Processing Equipment*, etc., available from the ABA Section of Law Practice Management. You need not be a Sec-

tion member to order these materials. Ask for the Section catalog (750 N. Lake Shore Drive, Chicago, IL 60611).

5. Articles by J. Nick De Meo of Santa Rosa, California, in back issues of the *California State Bar Journal*. Mr. De Meo has created whole systems in different areas of practice management.

6. Articles by J. Harris Morgan of Dallas, Texas, in back issues of *Texas Bar Journal*. In my opinion, J. Harris Morgan is the greatest mind and personality in the management of a law office and practice.

7. *The Bottom Line,* bimonthly newsletter of the Law Practice Management Section of the State Bar of California.

Keep Up with New Developments

The least expensive and most comprehensive way to keep current in this field is by belonging to the Section of Law Practice Management of the American Bar Association and of your state bar. For further information, write to: Section of Law Practice Management, American Bar Association, 750 N. Lake Shore Drive, Chicago, IL 60611.

Index

About the Author

Jay G. Foonberg was sworn in as a lawyer in January of 1964 and immediately opened his own practice. Today he is a senior partner of Jay G. Foonberg & Associates, a Beverly Hills law firm with affiliate offices in South America and Europe. His firm specializes in business law, taxation, real property, land use regulation, international law, corporate law, estate and retirement planning, probate, and litigation.

Mr. Foonberg has been awarded the Harrison Tweed Special Merit Award by the American Law Institute—American Bar Association (ALI-ABA) Committee on Continuing Professional Education for his long-term efforts in continuing legal education. He has also received the Gold Key and Highest Honors awards of the American Bar Association Law Student Division and the Award of Merit from the ABA Young Lawyers Section. He has been a member of the Executive Council of the ABA Section of Law Practice Management and was the first chairman of the Law Office Economics Committee of the Inter-American Bar Association. Mr. Foonberg has been decorated by the governments of Brazil and Argentina in honor of his work to stimulate and increase trade between the United States and these countries.

He has lectured for continuing legal education and bar associations in all fifty states and the District of Columbia, as well as in several foreign countries. He is the author of several articles and *How to Get and Keep Good Clients*, published by Lawyers Alert Press.

Selected Books From...

THE SECTION OF LAW PRACTICE MANAGEMENT

ACCESS 1994. An updated guidebook to technology resources. Includes practical hints, practical tips, commonly used terms, and resource information.

Anatomy of a Law Firm Merger. Provides information on every aspect of a merger and will help law firms of all sizes decide whether they should consider a merger.

Beyond the Billable Hour. A collection of articles on the subject of alternative billing methods, including value billing. Contributors include small, medium, and large firm practitioners, consultants, and general counsel.

Breaking Traditions. A guide to progressive, flexible, and sensible work alternatives for lawyers who want to balance the demand of the legal profession with other commitments. Model policy for childbirth and parenting leave is included.

Flying Solo: A Survival Guide for the Solo Lawyer, 2nd Ed. An updated and expanded guide to the problems and issues unique to the solo practitioner.

From Yellow Pads to Computers, 2nd ed. Thirty-five chapters with real-life computer applications that focus on practical solutions. Especially for the lawyer who's been too busy to use a computer.

How to Start and Build a Law Practice, 3rd Ed. Jay Foonberg's classic guide has been updated and expanded. Included are more than 10 new chapters on marketing, financing, automation, practicing from home, ethics and professional responsibility.

Improving Accounts Receivable Collection: A Practical System. Gives you the basics for developing an easy-to-manage, formal billing and collection system that can cut months off the collection process.

Keeping Happier Clients. Your guide to better client relations. It describes a whole approach to building strong relationships with clients. Includes questionnaires and tips for follow-up.

Last Frontier: Women Lawyers as Rainmakers. Explains why rainmaking is different for women than men and focuses on ways to improve these skills. Shares the experiences of four women who have successfully built their own practices.

Law Office Staff Manual, 2nd Ed. This updated version includes new sections on issues, techniques, and practices. Also includes the text of the manual on diskettes in WordPerfect and ASCII formats so that you can create a customized manual for your law firm.

Leveraging with Legal Assistants. Reviews the changes that have led to increased use of legal assistants and the need to enlarge their role further. Learn specific ways in which a legal assistant can handle a substantial portion of traditional lawyer work.

Making Partner: A Guide for Law Firm Associates. Written by a managing partner, this book offers guidelines and recommendations designed to help you increase your chances of making partner.

Managing Partner 101: A Primer on Firm Leadership. Advice from the corner office that will help any new or aspiring manager. Described as an "indispensable handbook."

Planning the Small Law Office Library. A step-by-step guide to planning, building, and managing a small law office library. Includes case studies, floor plans, and questionnaires.

Practical Systems: Tips for Organizing Your Law Office. It will help you get control of your in-box by outlining systems for managing daily work.

Results-Oriented Financial Management: A Guide to Successful Law Firm Financial Performance. How to manage "the numbers," from setting rates and computing billable hours to calculating net income and preparing the budget. Over 30 charts and statements to help you prepare reports.

A Short Course in Personal Computers. Explains the basic components of IBM-compatible computers in terms that are easy to understand. This concise and accessible guide will help you make knowledgeable decisions in the law office.

Survival Skills for the Practicing Lawyer. Includes 29 articles from Law Practice Management magazine for the attorney with little or no management responsibilities.

TQM in Action: One Firm's Journey Toward Quality and Excellence. A guide to implementing the principles of Total Quality Management in your law firm.

When a Professional Divorces. Discusses how to value a professional license and practice when a lawyer or other professional divorces.

Winning with Computers, Part 1. Addresses virtually every aspect of the use of computers in litigation. You'll get an overview of products available and tips on how to put them to good use. For the beginning and advanced computer user.

Winning with Computers, Part 2. Expands on the ways you can use computers to manage the routine and not-so-routine aspects of your trial practice. Learn how to apply general purpose software and even how to have fun with your computer.

Win-Win Billing Strategies. Represents the first comprehensive analysis of what constitutes "value," and how to bill for it. You'll learn how to initiate and implement different billing methods that make sense for you and your client.

WordPerfect® in One Hour for Lawyers. This is a crash course in the most popular word processing software package used by lawyers. In four easy lessons, you'll learn the basic steps for getting a simple job done.

WordPerfect® Shortcuts for Lawyers: Learning Merge and Macros in One Hour. A fast-track guide to two of WordPerfect's more advanced functions: Merge and Macros. Includes four lessons designed to take no more than 15 minutes each.

Your New Lawyer, 2nd Ed. A complete legal employer's guide to recruitment, development, and management of new lawyers. Updated to address the many changes in the practice of law since the 1983 edition.

Order Form

Qty	Title	LPM Price	Regular Price	Total
_____	ACCESS 1994 (511-0327)	$ 29.95	$ 34.95	$_____
_____	Anatomy of a Law Firm Merger (511-0310)	44.95	54.95	$_____
_____	Beyond the Billable Hour (511-0260)	69.95	79.95	$_____
_____	Breaking Traditions (511-0320)	64.95	74.95	$_____
_____	Flying Solo, 2nd Ed. (511-0328)	59.95	69.95	$_____
_____	From Yellow Pads to Computers, 2nd ed. (511-0289)	64.95	69.95	$_____
_____	How to Start & Build a Law Practice, 3rd ed. (511-0293)	32.95	39.95	$_____
_____	Improving Accounts Receivable Collection (511-0273)	39.95	49.95	$_____
_____	Keeping Happier Clients (511-0299)	19.95	29.95	$_____
_____	Last Frontier (511-0314)	9.95	14.95	$_____
_____	Law Office Staff Manual (511-0307)	79.00	89.00	$_____
_____	Leveraging with Legal Assistants (511-0322)	59.95	69.95	$_____
_____	Making Partner (511-0303)	14.95	19.95	$_____
_____	Managing Partner 101 (511-0272)	19.95	29.95	$_____
_____	Planning the Small Law Office Library (511-0325)	29.95	39.95	$_____
_____	Practical Systems (511-0296)	24.95	34.95	$_____
_____	Results-Oriented Financial Management (511-0319)	44.95	54.95	$_____
_____	A Short Course in Personal Computers (511-0302)	14.95	24.95	$_____
_____	Survival Skills for the Practicing Lawyer (511-0324)	39.95	49.95	$_____
_____	TQM in Action (511-0323)	59.95	69.95	$_____
_____	When a Professional Divorces (511-0326)	49.95	59.95	$_____
_____	Winning with Computers, Part 1 (511-0294)	89.95	99.95	$_____
_____	Winning with Computers, Part 2 (511-0315)	59.95	69.95	$_____
_____	Winning with Computers, Parts 1 & 2 (511-0316)	124.90	144.90	$_____
_____	Win-Win Billing Strategies (511-0304)	89.95	99.95	$_____
_____	WordPerfect® in One Hour for Lawyers (511-0308)	9.95	14.95	$_____
_____	WordPerfect® Shortcuts for Lawyers (511-0329)	14.95	19.95	$_____
_____	Your New Lawyer, 2nd ed. (511-0312)	74.95	84.95	$_____

*HANDLING
$ 2.00-$9.99 .... $2.00
10.00-24.99 .... $3.95
25.00-49.99 .... $4.95
50.00 + ... $5.95

**TAX
DC residents add 6%
IL residents add 8.75%
MD residents add 5%

SUBTOTAL: $_____
*HANDLING: $_____
**TAX: $_____

TOTAL: $_____

PAYMENT

☐ Check enclosed (Payable to the ABA)   ☐ Bill Me

☐ Visa   ☐ MasterCard Account Number:_____-_____-_____-_____

Exp. Date: _____ Signature _____

Name_____

Firm_____

Address_____

City_____State_____ZIP_____

Phone number_____

Mail to: ABA, Publication Orders, P.O. Box 10892, Chicago, IL 60610-0892

PHONE: (312) 988-5522
Or FAX: (312) 988-5568   BOOK